FRENCH ROYALIST DOCTRINES
SINCE THE REVOLUTION

FRENCH
ROYALIST DOCTRINES

SINCE THE REVOLUTION

BY

CHARLOTTE TOUZALIN MURET

OCTAGON BOOKS

A DIVISION OF FARRAR, STRAUS AND GIROUX

New York   1972

Reprinted 1972

by special arrangement with Columbia University Press

OCTAGON BOOKS
A DIVISION OF FARRAR, STRAUS & GIROUX, INC.
19 Union Square West
New York, N.Y. 10003

Library of Congress Cataloging in Publication Data

Muret, Charlotte (Touzalin)
    French Royalist doctrines since the Revolution.
    Originally presented as the author's thesis, Columbia, 1933.
    Bibliography: p.
    1. Political Science—History—France.   2. Monarchy.
    3. France—Politics and government.   I. Title.

JA84.F8M8   1972   320.9′44   72-8904
ISBN 0-374-96025-9

Printed in U.S.A. by
NOBLE OFFSET PRINTERS, INC.
New York, N.Y. 10003

TO

CARLTON J. H. HAYES
IN GRATEFUL ADMIRATION

PREFACE

Now that the United States has had one hundred and fifty years of experience of the reality of political democracy, ideas which were as gospel to past generations are being subjected to a new criticism. During these years the doctrines of equalitarian democracy have, on the whole, been in the ascendant in the western world, and political theories based on other conceptions of society have awakened relatively little interest, at least among English and American thinkers. Today it seems worth while to examine the doctrines of a group of men who were the opponents of democracy throughout this period. This book is not a history of the royalist parties in France since the Revolution. Such a work, if it were conscientiously written, would fill many volumes. It is only the political philosophy of the royalists and its evolution during the last hundred years which I have tried to portray. Whether or not events have justified their attitude these men have at least had the merit of consistently maintaining their own point of view, and among their theories some constructive suggestions are to be found.

Without the kindness of friends in France and in America this book could not have been written. I wish first of all to express my gratitude to Mr. Carlton Hayes and to Mr. Lindsay Rogers, whose advice and encouragement made my work possible. I have to thank Mr. Charles-H. Pouthas for the privilege of access to an unpublished work by Guizot, and Mr. Georges Poignant for many helpful suggestions, based on a remarkable knowledge of French political life in the nineteenth century. Mr. Charles Maurras has given me much valuable information as to the Action française, and I am deeply grateful for his constant kindness and courtesy. Mr. Nicholas Kaltchas has helped me to revise the book, and has given me helpful criticism. I also thank my husband, Maurice Muret, kindest of friendly critics, for his unfailing help and encouragement.

CHARLOTTE TOUZALIN MURET

NEW YORK
November 18, 1932

CONTENTS

CHAPTER I

INTRODUCTION

Of all the forms of government which peoples have evolved hereditary monarchy has been the most enduring and, until recently at all events, the most widespread. It is a natural form of social organization, for it originates in the patriarchal family and in the human need for leadership.

At the end of the eighteenth century monarchy seemed strongly entrenched in the civilized world. A majority of the modern nations were ruled by kings or emperors, and even during the nineteenth century, monarchy was the most favored form of government in Europe. A proof of this is that Belgium, and also the countries which broke away from the Turkish Empire during that century, established hereditary monarchies, although, in some cases, no national dynasty and no definite monarchical tradition existed.

Monarchy, perhaps because of its very prevalence, has been frequently attacked and defended by political philosophers, so that a vast body of literature exists on the subject, but monarchical doctrines, too, have today fallen somewhat into neglect or disrepute. The hereditary principle is greatly discredited, and in this age of democracy, Caesarism, or proletarian dictatorship, kings seem to most people to be mere anachronisms. Monarchical doctrines, however, will probably always attract those to whom strength and durability are the prime requisites of government. A noteworthy instance of this fact is to be found in France for, while the Republic now seems to be firmly established, a school of royalist doctrine has developed there, which, though it has almost no political power, has acquired a certain intellectual influence.

Men are not, as a rule, prone to question political forms so long as their results are satisfactory. Political philosophy has usually been the product of times of struggle, and has originated as attack upon or defense of existing conditions. It is, therefore, natural that during the nineteenth century, which brought many changes of régime in France, much should have been written in that country for and against hereditary monarchy. This book proposes to trace the evolution of the doctrines which have been advanced in its support, from the Restoration to the present day.

In order to follow these doctrines it is necessary to consider exactly what is meant by royalism in France.[1] Men who differ as widely in outlook as Joseph de Maistre, Benjamin Constant and Charles Maurras have called themselves royalists, and a common basis for definition must be found in their ideas. Belief in an hereditary monarch as head of the State is the essential point of royalism; it separates the most liberal royalists from the most conservative republicans, but this belief, while it implies a conservative point of view, allows great latitude in doctrine as to the origin and character of monarchy.

Two principal theories have existed as to the source of royal authority; that of divine right and that of popular sovereignty. According to the first theory the sanction of power comes from the will of God; according to the second

[1] I have used the words "monarchy" and "royalty" interchangeably, as they were used by the writers under discussion, but they are not synonymous: monarchy is a more general term. All kings are monarchs, but not all monarchs are kings; they may also be sultans, emperors, or merely princes. This book does not treat of "monarchical" doctrines, for that would include those of the Empire, but only of "royalist" theory.

it comes from the will of the people. In the first case, the king is the source of all authority; in the second, he is merely a power among other powers. Two theories exist also as to the character of monarchy; first, that it is absolute, and second, that it is limited. Four types of monarchy have existed in France, based on various combinations of these theories. The monarchy of the Middle Ages was considered to have its source in a divine sanction, but its power was limited by other equally sacred authorities, such as the Church and the feudal suzerainties. The monarchy of Louis XIV drew its sanction from the will of God, but, both in theory and in fact, it had become absolute. The Empire was based on the theory of popular sovereignty; the Emperor claimed to personify the general will, and his power was absolute. The monarchy of Louis Philippe was also based on the doctrine of popular sovereignty, but its power was limited.[2]

For many centuries the kings of France bent their energies not only to developing their country, but to reducing to impotence every power in the State except their own. Their greatest measure of success was attained in the reign of Louis XIV. The king then possessed both the executive and legislative powers and, though his activity was to some extent modified by the influence of custom, and of various bodies, such as the Parlements and the Provincial Estates, yet he was undoubtedly supreme. Both in fact and in theory his will was law, and the political philosophy of the time reflected this condition.

Louis XIV himself was a devout believer in the doctrine of

[2] The monarchy of the Restoration was theoretically based on divine right. It was limited, however, by a charter, granted nominally by the monarch's free will but actually under compulsion of the changed conditions resulting from the Revolution.

absolutism and the divine right of kings. Tradition has it that he said in the Grand'chambre de Parlement de Paris: "L'État c'est moi!" Whether he actually said it or not, the words undoubtedly express his belief. He wrote to his grandson: "He who gave Kings to men wished them to be respected as his lieutenants, reserving for Himself the right to examine their conduct."[3] In his *Mémoires* he says: "One must agree that nothing establishes so securely the happiness and peace of provinces as the entire union of all authority in the person of the sovereign. The least sharing of it always produces great misfortune."

In Bossuet, who agreed entirely with Louis XIV, the doctrine of divine right found the most eloquent advocate it has ever had. His *Politique tirée de l'histoire sainte* and *Discours sur l'histoire universelle* give a wonderful picture of the beneficent monarch, but they would put unlimited power into his hands. "The language which a man would not dare hold to God, he dare not hold to the King, God's lieutenant on earth."[4] Even the jurists who had formerly opposed the encroachment of absolutism, and were again to be its formidable adversaries, were then of the same opinion. D'Aguesseau says:

The nature of the French government lies in two principal points; the first is that the government is monarchical, and the second is that the kings exercise absolute domination, which is vested in their persons . . . and for which they need only account to God.[5]

The Tiers État at the États Généraux of 1614 proposed the formula: "Kings hold their thrones from God."

There were a few who disagreed. Jurieu and Bayle are examples, but their arguments found little echo at that time.

---

[3] *Oeuvres de Louis XIV* (Paris., 1806), p. 336.
[4] Bossuet, *Politique tirée de l'histoire sainte,* I—III, art. ii, prop. i.
[5] *Oeuvres d'Aguesseau,* XIII, p. 553.

It may be said that the doctrine of royal absolutism based on divine right was almost uncontested in France in the seventeenth century.

The traditional and religious basis of this doctrine was undermined by the philosophers of the eighteenth century. Voltaire, Rousseau, and the Encyclopaedists prepared the way for the Revolution by weakening the hold of faith on men's minds, and they furnished its leaders with the ideas which they strove to realize.

The doctrine of popular sovereignty, and that of the rights of man were the basis of all the revolutionary constitutions. The Revolution, however, was libertarian rather than liberal in spirit and it tended to sacrifice the rights of man to the rule of the people. It did not succeed in founding a free, yet stable, government, and it was Napoleon who inherited the power of the Convention and the Directoire. The Empire, although it claimed to emanate from the will of the people, was preëminently a government of authority.

Exhaustion, and the triumph of its foreign enemies brought about the fall of the Empire. Since 1789 France had tried many forms of government, and had endured more than twenty years of struggle within and without. The Restoration came in 1815 as a much-needed era of peace and reconstruction. The Revolutionary spirit was temporarily in abeyance, for the peasants had obtained possession of much of the land, and industry was only in its beginning. The returning dynasty brought to power the lovers of order; that is to say, the remains of the old aristocracy and the emancipated middle classes. A vast majority of the men who played a part in public affairs at that time, whatever their party, were economically conservative, and politically antidemocratic. Louis XVIII wished to establish a government which would unite all these elements of order, but it was a difficult task to reconcile the conflicting ideas and interests of those to whom the Revolution had brought hope and opportunity, and those to whom it had brought only disaster. There was a great revival of Catholic and reactionary thought in France, but, though the country appeared to acquiesce in the reinstatement of its old rulers, there was no such agreement among the supporters of the returning Bourbons as there had been among the subjects of Louis XIV.

Two currents of thought were to dominate the struggles of the Restoration; on the one hand the traditional authoritarian conception of society, and on the other the liberal doctrines which had found partial expression during the Revolution.

The authoritarian attitude is the result of a pessimistic view of human nature, leading to mistrust of the undisciplined activities of men. Authoritarians seek in abstract reason or in divine revelation some absolute good, from which they deduce rules for regulating human conduct. They then advocate the forceful application of these rules for men's own good. It was natural that the dispossessed nobility, and especially the returned *émigrés* should have feared and hated the doctrines of individualism in whose name their time-honored privileges had been abolished. Because they did not profit by the new freedom, they saw its dangers more clearly than did the *bourgeoisie*. To them the excesses of the Revolution were evidence of the evil nature of humanity, and of the results to be expected from the theories of popular sovereignty and of the rights of man. They looked to the king to restore the past and protect the future. The theory of divine right absolutism was not only associated with the past and consistent with their mistrust of men, but it was the doctrine best calculated to support the royal authority from which they expected so much.

Liberalism springs from a strong sense of the value of human personality. It desires for the individual a maximum of spontaneous activity which can only be obtained by organizing society on a basis of coöperation and consent. It is an optimistic attitude, and it implies tolerance and compromise, with all the risks and difficulties these involve. It is not dogmatic, for, as its values are human, it can admit no absolute good, at least in the political and social domain. Liberalism, however, expects much from human nature and affords it little protection from its own weaknesses.

One of the chief results of the Revolution was the emancipation of the individual; the old restrictions on men's activities, the old distinctions of birth made way for the idea of the rights of capacity. The triumph of the Revolution was the phrase attributed to Napoleon. "La carrière ouverte aux talents." In the overthrow of the old order the peasants had perhaps benefited most, but it was the middle classes which were best prepared to take advantage of the disappearance of barriers. They had confidence in their capacities, and they felt that the future was theirs. They needed freedom and security for economic development in order to enjoy the equality which they had won, and they wished to share in the political power which they felt themselves fitted to wield. The optimistic philosophy of liberalism, with its confidence in reason, its insistence on individual rights, and its opposition to state interference, corresponded admirably to their needs. They too, however, feared democracy, and the revolutionary spirit. They saw in constitutional monarchy a solution which promised at once to protect them from the rule of the masses, and to give them a controlling influence in the State.

During the Restoration the doctrines both of authoritarian and liberal monarchy were formulated by men of great talent, from whom they received clear-cut expression. These theories, and the history of their evolution are the subject of this book. Their history divides itself roughly into three periods: the Restoration, the remainder of the nineteenth century, and the twentieth century. During the first period the two conceptions of monarchy were formulated, and the bases were laid for the development of royalist thought in both directions. During the second period these doctrines were modified by the growing forces of democracy and of industrialism. On the one hand liberalism failed in practice, and the theory of constitutional monarchy tended to merge with that of conservative republicanism. On the other hand the theory of authoritarian monarchy, while on the whole remaining stationary in its political tenets, developed a social doctrine in harmony with its own point of view. Toward the end of the century royalist theory in general had lost much of its vitality, and seemed destined to disappear. During the third period, the men of the Action française have revived the doctrines of authoritarian royalism. By approaching them from a positive point of view, and associating them with nationalism, they have given them new vigor and interest.

In order to understand the evolution of royalist ideas, not only each man's view on monarchy itself must be considered, but also the system of thought on which his views are based. A man's philosophic and religious convictions influence his ideas as to the object of society, and its relation to the individual. These ideas give birth to theories of sovereignty, and of the rôle of Church and State. Theories of sovereignty, in turn, determine conceptions of the monarch and of the institutions which should surround him. For this reason I shall, as far as possible, examine in regard to each man, or group of men, their ideas on the following subjects: (1) the nature and object of society; (2) the relation of the individual to the State; (3) the origin and nature of sovereignty; (4) the purpose and character of monarchy; (5) the organization of the State (constitutions, bodies in the State, etc.); (6) the relations of Church and State. I shall then point out the general significance for royalist theory of each thinker examined.

CHAPTER II

THE THEOCRATS

Today it is easy to see that the Revolution destroyed forever the economic, political and social system of the old régime, but this fact was not so obvious in 1814. The successive governmental forms of the Revolution had failed, and had been succeeded by the authoritarian Empire, democracy was temporarily in abeyance, and it was possible to think of it as a fever of revolt, not apt to recur. A period of twenty years is too short entirely to modify human ways of life and thought, and much of the past remained unchanged, so that the return of the Bourbons seemed to some extent to effect a revival of the old world. But this impression was largely illusory. In the first place the revolutionary ideas had given men new conceptions of life which they were not likely to forget; second, the economic changes of the Revolution and the Empire remained almost untouched. The significance of this latter fact is enormous, for it meant that new modes of thought and action must be found to meet new social realities. Would the traditional monarchy face this necessity, and be able to adapt its character and dogmas to a changed society?

During the Restoration much importance was given to political theory. Not only did writers turn their attention to political problems, but all the public men of the day felt themselves obliged to give their views a philosophical basis. Various reasons can be suggested to account for this fact. To begin with, the influence of the eighteenth century was still strong, and the example of Rousseau seemed to prove the effect of doctrines upon events.[1] In the next place, opposed ideas and interests were seeking to come to terms, and struggling to justify their respective points of view. Then, too, there was a lack of experience among the statesmen of the day. The Empire had created administrators and diplomats, but it had not formed party leaders, and the men of the Restoration had more theories than practical knowledge with which to face the problem of establishing a representative government. Moreover, it was exclusively the upper classes which were, at that time, engaged in public life, so that the level of education among political men was high, and hence the tendency to theorize correspondingly strong. The aims of both parties may have been narrow and selfish, but the men who represented them, were, in general, less conscious of this, and more genuinely interested in principles, than were the politicians of a later age.[2]

Most of the men who played a part in the intellectual and political life of the Restoration were, nominally at least, royalists. Though conservative in outlook, and desirous of order and social reconstruction, they differed greatly as to the means by which they hoped to attain these ends. At the extreme right stood those who hated the Revolution and all its works indiscriminately, and hoped to bring about a complete return to the past. They believed that this was to be accomplished not by any compromise with the hated doctrines, but by an increase of authority, and a religious and moral re-awakening.

[1] An interesting analysis of the extension and influence of political theory in France during the eighteenth century is given by A. de Tocqueville in *L'Ancien Régime et la Révolution*, p. 233-48. These reasons account, in part, for the same phenomenon during the Restoration.

[2] For an interesting discussion of this matter see Denys Cochin, *Louis Philippe*, p. 143.

This group represented the ideas of the returned *émigrés,* many of them violent and selfish men, who were known in the political field as the "ultras." But it comprised also many who were animated by less personal motives, and whom the Revolution had genuinely outraged in their dearest beliefs. The strength of the old régime in its heyday had been due in part to faith in the teachings of the Church, and a consequent respect for the established order. These feelings still existed to a large extent at the Restoration, and they found expression in a great Catholic revival. Everything in the moral and political world had been called in question by the philosophers of the eighteenth century, and many considered that it was from this questioning that the Revolution had sprung. There was a spiritual return toward the past, of which Chateaubriand's *Génie du Christianisme* was the herald. Even those most convinced of the truths of Catholic and monarchical doctrines felt the need of reformulating them, in order to provide weapons with which to combat the teachings of the Revolution; that is, liberalism and democracy. A group of thinkers arose whose writings answered this need. The chief common characteristic of their thought was its religious basis and for this reason they were known as the theocrats. Some of them were philosophers and moralists, like Saint Martin and Ballanche, but the two ablest men of the group, Louis Gabriel de Bonald, and Joseph de Maistre, were chiefly influential as political theorists.

Bonald and Maistre, though the quality of their minds differed greatly, were much alike not only in respect to their doctrines, but in the circumstances which formed them. They represented what had been best in the old régime. Both were from the provinces; Bonald from Rouergue, a region where the old ways of life linger even today; and Maistre from Savoy, which was not then a part of France. Both came from families of moderate position, noble, but of the "noblesse de robe" which had won its way to rank by thrift and a record of services to the State, and both were themselves magistrates. They belonged, that is to say, to a class which, having attained to place and power by its own capacities, could not have much sympathy with the idea of equality, nor feel any great need of liberty, since the existing system gave scope to its ambition and abilities. Both Bonald and Maistre were genuinely devout and had strong family feelings. The Revolution, overtaking them in middle life,[3] destroyed not only their ordered existence and their personal hopes, but the whole social fabric which they had known. It is impossible to overestimate its effect upon their thought, and it would have required almost superhuman detachment for such men to have seen in it anything but sacrilege and destruction. Yet, although they did not understand it, it cannot be said of them that they had "learned nothing and forgotten nothing," for it taught them the lesson on which they based their whole philosophy: an incurable distrust of man. Both began to write while they were in exile, and their common point of departure was a wish to combat the Revolution and the philosophy which had engendered it.

In spite of their resemblances, there was a great difference between Bonald and Maistre, both in their way of thinking and in their style. Bonald was dry, logical and abstract. He established his premises and drew from them a series of arguments with almost mathematical precision of reasoning. He seemed to seek not so much to *win*, as to *force* assent to his conclusions. Émile Faguet called him the last of the schoolmen.[4] Maistre, on the contrary, had a vivid style, full of

---

[3] Both were born in 1754.
[4] Émile Faguet, *Politiques et moralistes du XIXe siècle,* Ière série, p. 70.

witty sallies and sarcastic digressions. Bonald was more systematic, but Maistre had more boldness and originality of
thought. He was severe and even violent where Bonald was
merely solemn and didactic, for there was a burning spirit behind Maistre's trenchant arguments.

The ideas of these two men form a system of admirable
consistency. They are founded, however, on two premises,
which are assumed unquestioningly because they spring from
religious faith. The first of these premises is God's close
relationship to man and to the world. "God," said Bonald in
his *Théorie du pouvoir politique et religieux,* "is a fundamental truth and will be taken for granted in this book."[5]
"The Revolution," he declared elsewhere, "began with a
declaration of the Rights of Man, and it must end with a
declaration of the Rights of God."[6] This is the keynote of
his thought. In the same spirit are the opening words of
Maistre's first book *Considerations sur la France.* "We are
bound to the Supreme Being by a fine chain, which restrains,
without enslaving us."[7] There is a difference, however, in the
manner in which Bonald and Maistre conceived of the relationship between God and the world. To Bonald natural
(and he here includes social) laws were emanations of God's
will. They were "necessary," immutable and fixed for all
time, so that man's part is merely to understand and follow
them. To him society, in so far as it is good, was utterly un-
changing, and he had little idea of progress. Maistre was
far more fully aware of the dynamic nature of life, and of
the relativity of political institutions, but he believed that

[5] Bonald, *Théorie du pouvoir politique et religieux dans la société
civile,* Part I, p. 135.
[6] Bonald, *Legislation primitive—discours préliminaire,* p. 1133.
[7] Maistre, *Considérations sur la France,* p. 1.

God is actively at work in the world, guiding its destiny. He expressly stated that the political world is ruled by Divine Wisdom,[8] and considered, for instances, that the Revolution was sent as a punishment and lesson to the French people for their impiety.

The second premise which was advanced *a priori* by Bonald and Maistre, is that the nature of man is radically evil. He is incapable of accomplishing anything good by his own means, and can only live well and happily under God's direct guidance. From these two premises spring their conceptions as to the origin of society, the situation of the individual, and the source of sovereignty.

The great object of Bonald and Maistre was to refute the doctrines of Jean Jacques Rousseau, and particularly the theory of the social contract which had been made the basis of democracy. This doctrine they rejected absolutely as an explanation of the origin of society. What, they asked, is this famous "state of nature" which preceded society? The "nature" of a being is the ensemble of qualities which make him himself.[9] This can only be determined by the knowledge of his development, and the history of man shows that he was created for society. Society, then, was not deliberately chosen, but arose spontaneously and necessarily from the nature of humanity. No real man existed before society, which is for him the "state of nature." These conclusions, reached by the use of common sense,[10] are much nearer to the modern scientific idea as to primitive man than were the artificial creations of Hobbes and Rousseau.

[8] Maistre, *Considérations sur la France,* p. 67.

[9] Maistre, *Études sur la souveraineté,* p. 321.

[10] Vareilles-Sommières, *Principes fondamentaux du droit constitutionnel,* p. 220.

Bonald gave a more complete analysis of society than did Maistre.[11] He defined it as a union of like beings by necessary laws, whose object is their reproduction and conservation. He divided societies into domestic and public. Any family, owning property, is a society, and public society is a union of families for their mutual advantage. He wished to study man not in the abstract, but as a social being, in terms of his activities, and he saw the need for a science of society, but the didactic bent of his mind made the observational method impossible for him. It is a further symptom of his limited point of view that he took great care to point out that possession of property is an essential feature of society. Families or individuals who possess no property scarcely seemed to him to be part of the social fabric. His conceptions had for their background the agricultural community, and he had little sympathy with commerce, and deplored the growth of industry.[12] Although he did not at all realize the immense transformations it was to work, he did see that its tendencies were not in accord with his ideal of a static and uniform society.

To Bonald and Maistre man was not an end in himself; it was only his right development, and his relationship to God which were important. Consequently they completely subordinated the individual to the State. It is society, they said, which makes man and not man, society. He exists only for it, and without it he is scarcely human. He is not even born fit for life, as animals are, but must learn everything, even language, from society, which alone can teach him,

[11] Bonald, *Théorie du pouvoir*, Book I, chaps. i-iv; Book II, chaps. i-iii.
[12] Bonald, *Théorie du pouvoir*, Part III, p. 315. See also *Oeuvres de Bonald*, II, p. 1281.

and to which he owes all. The great error of the Revolution was that it taught the individual to feel that he was important and so let loose his appetites. The wills of men are disorderly, and apt to be in opposition to the general good; they must, therefore, be curbed, and the national will made to prevail over particular wills, or else there will be anarchy. There can be no liberty to do evil, and the abnegation of self for the public good is absolutely necessary. Man has no rights, only duties, and all his capacities and virtues he must employ for society, to which he owes them. Moreover, they pointed out, it is not the individual who is the real unit of society, but the family. It alone is important, and, like society itself, it is almost immortal. The conception of man as an isolated being, with a merely numerical value, is artificial, and no enduring society can be built upon it.

These anti-individualistic doctrines were carried to remarkable lengths by Bonald and Maistre in somewhat different directions. Bonald in his desire for stability was quite indifferent to any progress which might be due to men of genius. He explicitly declared that a well-constituted society has no need of great men; they are more apt to be a danger than a blessing.[13] The very able usually do rise, but it is better for most people to be fixed in their position in life by early education and the family fortune. Thus they are, in a measure, protected from cupidity and ambition. He expressed the idea that children are apt to have an hereditary taste for their father's trade.[14] If, however, there is to be movement in society, it should be the slow work of several generations, and should elevate the whole family. The acquisition of property is the only possible means of achieving this rise in the

[13] Bonald, *Oeuvres,* II, pp. 670-73.
[14] Bonald, *Théorie du pouvoir,* Part I, p. 187.

world, and he disposed of any objection to this criterion of worth by saying that in a well-conducted State property will be the reward of services to society, and there will be no evil ways of becoming rich. These ideas which the rigidity of Bonald's mind erected into immutable laws, match the actual history of a large part of the French middle classes, both then and today.

Maistre, in his dread of evil passions, pointed out that punishment is the real basis of order. It is the executioner who is the corner stone of society, and he ought to be honored accordingly.[15] It is worse, he said, that the guilty should invariably escape than that the innocent should be unjustly condemned. Besides, he added, who is innocent? Many a man who has been executed for a crime he did not commit, richly deserved his punishment for sins which were never discovered. Maistre was a kind-hearted man, and these savage doctrines were, no doubt, a result of the impressions produced on him by the Revolution. They were mitigated by a lofty religious mysticism, a belief in the necessity of sacrifice, and the reversibility of merits, which can alone make acceptable such unbending sternness toward mankind in this world.

It is in regard to the origin and nature of sovereignty that the ideas of Bonald and Maistre are particularly important. Their arguments against democracy and in favor of authority greatly influenced Auguste Comte, and others through him, and they have been largely adopted by the modern school of French royalists. Here, too, lay the fundamental differences which separated them from the Doctrinaires and Liberals, and it is probably their uncompromising attitude on these subjects that kept them from exercising a wider influ-

[15] Maistre, *Soirées de Saint-Pétersbourg*, pp. 32-35.

ence in their own time, although it has caused a revival of interest in their ideas today. They perceived the essentially authoritarian nature of sovereignty, and it is its coercive power and independence of consent that they value. Maistre defined sovereignty as the power that judges, but cannot be judged, and said that it is by nature infallible in the sense that it cannot be convicted of error.[16] It follows from this authoritarian character of sovereignty that it cannot be the expression of the will of all. Bonald said repeatedly that: "When all men wish to dominate with equal will and unequal forces, it is necessary that one should dominate, or men will destroy each other."[17] Maistre pointed out that sovereignty is always taken, never given. Law must emanate from a higher circle, and the result of an agreement is not law and obliges no one. "Law is so far from being the will of all that, the more it is the will of all, the less it is law, so that it would cease to be law, if it were without exception the will of all who owe it obedience."[18]

Both Bonald and Maistre found the source of sovereignty in God. He alone sanctions laws, and without the dogma of a legislating God, all moral obligation ceases, and only force remains. "All nations," said Maistre, "have regarded sovereignty as divine, and the legends as to the miraculous origin of kings are based on an universal idea which is spiritually true."[19]

But the participation of men in the creation of sovereignty was not totally denied. Though sovereignty comes from God, he does not establish it directly, but uses men as his instru-

[16] Maistre conceives judgment as implying a positive sanction ; a punishment.

[17] Bonald, *Théorie du pouvoir*, Part I, p. 194.

[18] Maistre, *Études sur la souveraineté*, p. 467.   [19] *Ibid.*, pp. 330-31.

ments. In the same way that society arose from the requirements of man's nature, sovereignty arises from the necessities of society. The first man was king of his children, and
men acquired masters because, as common dangers united
families, the need for a leader arose naturally. It was necessity which formed power and enforced obedience, but that
necessity itself is a part of God's will. He made men gre-
garious, and, as he willed society, he also willed the sovereignty which is essential to it. The ideas of Bonald and
Maistre are here alike, but Maistre brings out more clearly
the rôle of man in the creation of sovereignty. It is, he admitted, actually founded on human consent, for if people
agreed not to obey, sovereignty would disappear. Legitimate
authority comes from God, and it rests upon the two factors
of possession and consent. "But," he added, "to say that the
sovereignty does not come from God because men are required to establish it, is to say that He is not the Creator of
man because we all have a father and mother."[20] It is this
doctrine of the origin of sovereignty in natural necessity
which enabled Bonald and Maistre to reject the theory of a
social contract.[21] Since sovereignty is absolutely necessary
to the existence of society, how can men pretend that it was

[20] Maistre, *Étude sur la souveraineté*, p. 313.

[21] C. E. Merriam, *History of the Theory of Sovereignty since Rousseau* (New York, 1900), pp. 55-59. Merriam does not, however, make
clear that it is the doctrine of the natural necessity for a single sovereign
which is used by Bonald and Maistre to refute the idea of the social
contract. Vareilles-Sommières in *Principes fondamentaux du droit constitutionnel* (Paris, 1889), rightly pointed out that the doctrine of the
divine origin of sovereignty does not prevent that sovereignty from
being attributed to the people. Indeed, this was the thesis of Bellarmin,
and other writers of the Middle Ages. The Church, while affirming the
divine origin of sovereignty and its sacred nature, has never admitted it
to be necessarily vested in a monarch, and Leo XIII has twice rejected
this idea. (Encyclicals of 1888: *Immortale Dei* and *Libertas*.)

created merely by a voluntary agreement? This necessity orignates in God's will, and therefore, to resist the sovereign is a crime.[22]

It is evident from these doctrines that for Bonald and Maistre sovereignty was absolute. Both perceived, and Maistre expressly stated, the problem which confronts political liberalism, that is, the difficulty of limiting sovereignty without destroying it. A written constitution such as the "Charte" of 1814 will not do this, for who is to establish and execute such a constitution? If it is the king, who will keep him from violating it or revoking it? But, if it is established by others, they will be the true sovereigns. Bonald and Maistre agreed that the difficulty is insoluble, and political liberty must be sacrificed. There can be no right of resistance to the sovereign power, for who is to determine when that right of resistance may be exercised? Maistre recognized no limit whatsoever to sovereignty within its own sphere, although he pointed out that the sphere of a political sovereign is necessarily limited by that of other sovereigns. It is only the Pope, holder of the supreme spiritual authority, whose sovereignty is universal and perpetual, and Maistre, voicing the traditional ultramontane doctrine, saw in him a superior power

[22] Laski, in his *Authority in the Modern State,* says in criticizing Bonald's doctrines, that the basis of sovereignty is in the opinion of men. This conclusion Bonald and Maistre wished to avoid, yet it was a realization of the necessity for at least a passive consent which led them to insist upon religion as the chief support of government, for religion prepares men's minds to accept authority. It may be questioned, however, whether, in ultimate analysis, unity and coercive power are not essential characteristics of sovereignty. There is much likeness between the doctrine of the theocrats and that of Hobbes. According to him, men were driven to make an agreement for self-preservation, and organized society as a necessity. After the agreement, the resulting sovereignty is absolute.

which may authorize resistance to an unjust sovereign. Bonald was more inclined to admit theoretical limits to sovereignty; to be legitimate, it must act in accordance with the fundamental laws of society, which are emanations of God's will. However, he nowhere gave a list of these laws, nor did he admit of any recourse against tyranny, save in the workings of these laws themselves.[23]

Sovereignty is also one and indivisible. The so-called "division of powers" merely represents a division of the three functions of power; the judicial, administrative, and legislative. The last named, which is the essence of government, can be exercised by the sovereign alone, whereas the other two may be delegated. Will, Bonald said, is always single, but its action, since it may have numerous applications, can be divided.[24] When sovereignty itself appears to be divided among several powers, the struggle between them must be regarded only as the deliberations of a single sovereign, debating with his own reason. Bonald pointed out that in an assembly all is decided by half the members, plus one, and that that one is the real sovereign. In the last analysis, sovereignty is always a single will.

This absolute sovereignty both Bonald and Maistre wished to see in the hands of an hereditary monarch. There is, however, an important difference in their views in this respect. The tendency of Bonald's mind was dogmatic and absolute; he always wanted to simplify, and to reduce everything to fixed and unalterable principles. There can be, he considered, but one "necessary," that is, perfect, relationship between two

[23] Maistre who had a taste for paradox seems to think regicide less criminal than revolt. "Men," he said, "may have the right to assassinate a Nero, but never to judge him." Maistre, *Étude sur la souveraineté,* p. 422.

[24] Bonald, *Principe constitutif de la société,* Part I, p. 59.

things, therefore, "necessary" laws may be found for society, which are the best always and everywhere. He was optimistic, for, since God willed these fundamental laws, they must ultimately triumph, and though men may for a time depart from them, society will always tend to return to the forms they prescribe. Monarchy is the form of government which he considers to be natural and perfect, and therefore, to be truly "constituted" a State must be a Catholic and hereditary monarchy.[25] All other forms are the result of human error and are merely transient.

Maistre, on the contrary, said repeatedly that there is no one form of government which is best for all peoples at all times. Institutions must be modified according to the needs of various peoples at various epochs. The same power which made the social order made modifications of sovereignty, according to the character of different nations. The problem is, given the population, habits, religion, geographical situation, political relations, habits, wealth, good and bad qualities of a nation, to find the laws which suit it. But, like Bonald, he was convinced that hereditary monarchy is by far the most desirable form of government.

Bonald and Maistre were inclined to consider democracy, in the sense of the rule of the masses, as not only undesirable, but practically nonexistent. The people, in Maistre's opinion, never do more than accept what comes. They are like madmen, or children; they must always be represented, and can never act for themselves, and it is always a few who rule. Bonald said that at most the people can name only a few legislators. There are, therefore, in reality, only two forms of

[25] The best criticism of these ideas is in Vareilles-Sommière's *Principes fondamentaux du droit constitutionnel*. He shows the error made by Bonald in considering all societies as identical, and attributing necessary and invariable laws of relationship to variable things.

government; the rule of one, and the rule of several. The former is monarchy, and the latter is an oligarchy which calls itself a republic.

The republican form, which is actually the government of a few, is very inferior to monarchy. It is inherently weak, for it is not based on the general will, but on individual wills, and so contains the elements of disorder. It cannot have fixed and unchangeable laws, which, Bonald said, in a monarchy take the place of virtue, and therefore it demands a spirit of association and sacrifice in the people themselves which is rare, and cannot be permanent. At best, it is only adapted to small states. Republics, Maistre declares, because of their weaknesses, depend on monarchies, and no great nation can become a republic and endure.[26]

Bonald found metaphysical reasons in his general philosophy for advocating monarchy. He had a weakness for the number three (Faguet said that he had a triangle in his brain!),[27] and the three social persons were, for him, power, minister, and subject, which correspond to cause, means, and effect. Where these three persons are most distinct, there society is best organized, and this is the case in a monarchy, where the king is the power, the nobility, the ministers, and the people, the subjects. The first two alone are active, but they act solely for the benefit of the subjects. Maistre, on the other hand, gave more weight to practical considerations. He granted the defects of absolutism, but considered them less than those of other systems, and based his preference for monarchy largely on the belief that experience has proved it to be the best form of government.

Bonald and Maistre insisted that in an hereditary mon-

[26] Maistre, *Considérations sur la France,* p. 43.
[27] Emile Faguet, *Politiques et moralistes,* Ière série, p. 77.

archy the interest of the king is identical with that of the nation. The nation belongs to him, and he to it, so much so that in former ages he was not even allowed to have private property. He cannot, by the nature of his position, wish to harm society. On the contrary, he personifies the general will. This general will is essentially preservative, and it is not the same thing as the sum of the wills of all, for individual wills have no continuity, and no thought of the future. There is no general will where there is no king.

Monarchy is also the form of government where the vices of the sovereign cause the least damage. Even a bad king is but one man; he alone is above the law, which can, therefore, be administered more readily than if a number of partial sovereigns claim exemption or misuse their power. The cases where he is tempted to do ill are rare, his power to destroy is limited, and he is restrained by custom, by those who surround him, and by the fundamental laws of society. For the power of the king, they said, though absolute, is not arbitrary. Absolute power is one that is independent of the men over whom it is exercised, whereas arbitrary power is that which is independent of the laws by virtue of which it is exercised. Maistre maintained that neither kings nor Popes can revoke what they have decreed, acting with parliament or council, and Bonald said that in a monarchy the laws can be invoked against injustice, whereas in a republic there is no recourse against the sovereign people. This distinction, however, remains entirely theoretical, for neither Bonald nor Maistre sanctioned any revolt against the sovereign should he violate the fundamental laws of society.

It is necessary that the sovereign should be perpetual and immortal, like society itself, for an intermittent sovereignty cannot exist. These conditions can only be fulfilled by a family, and therefore monarchy, in order to be perfect, must be hereditary. For the sake of avoiding conflicts over the succession it should be established by order of primogeniture in the male line.[28]

Bonald and Maistre were emphatic in declaring that a written constitution can never form the proper basis for a State. The theoretical creations of man's reason will always be inferior to institutions which grow out of the character and instincts of a people. The fundamental laws of a nation should be the work of nature, having their roots in custom and tradition, and it is the business of the king as lawgiver to interpret, rather than to create these, for no law is really valid unless it appears to be already established and sanctioned by universal custom.

They granted the value of representative bodies in the State, but these must be purely consultative, and have no power to legislate. Their function is to enlighten and advise the king, and to present remonstrances to him. Moreover, they should, like the States General, represent not individuals, but interests or classes. Bonald said that the three orders of the French States General represented the bases of society; enlightenment, possessions, and labor.[29]

An hereditary nobility seemed to Bonald and Maistre essential to a perfect monarchy. Bonald distinguished it from an aristocracy which, he said, is a number of families enjoying the sovereign power by heredity.[30] The nobility is an order

---

[28] Bonald says that primogeniture does away to a large extent with a king's natural jealousy of his heir. It is advisable also for practical reasons, since the eldest son is soonest fit to reign. Women are by nature unfit to wield authority. Moreover, they are bound at marriage to come under the power of a man, and thus the line of sovereignty is interrupted.

[29] Bonald, *Oeuvres,* II, 67.   [30] Bonald, *Oeuvres,* II, 681.

which does not legislate, and so does not participate in the sovereign power. Its reason for existence is service, and its reward must be honor, and not wealth or power. For this reason the nobility must not be allowed to engage in commerce or industry. It is an hereditary caste; its function is to defend the State, and to administer public affairs under the orders of the king. In France it was a body of families devoted to the service of the nation in the two social professions, arms and justice. This destiny of service was actual for the family, potential for the individual; it was less a personal obligation than a general availability of the family,[31] and Bonald points out that whereas republics consider only individuals, the French monarchy saw only families. The nobility in France degenerated, for when paid troops appeared it lost a part of its social functions, and, as it had usurped a portion of the sovereign power, the kings further weakened it, in order to free themselves from its encroachments. Maistre considered it just that the nobles should have suffered from the Revolution, for the nobility as a body had erred, and the individuals who compose such an order are *solidaire,* and share in the common responsibility.

The magistracy in France was also an order of nobility, but the exercise of justice had become a purchasable property, instead of an hereditary function, so that this order was rendered accessible to all. Being a property, its possessor was, in a large degree, independent of the State, which neither directly appointed nor paid the magistrates. This Bonald and Maistre both considered an excellent arrangement, for an independent judiciary is impossible if it is paid by the State. They pointed out that justice is venal, not when the magis-

[31] Bonald, "Observations sur l'ouvrage de Madame de Stael," *Oeuvres,* II, 613.

trate buys his place, but when he sells his opinion. Yet these
judicial bodies, the Parlements, although they were independent, were not dangerous, for they did not possess power, but
only exercised one of its functions.

The basis of the whole social structure, as well as its reason
for existing, lies, for the theocrats, in religion. "It gives,"
in Bonald's words, "a reason for the power to command, and
a motive for the duty of obedience."[32] Church and State both
exist to promote the moral welfare of man, and they must
help each other in securing order and the spirit of social
sacrifice, without which that welfare is impossible. They
must, therefore, be in close alliance. The State must support the Church, and can, in return, expect religion to school
men in political obedience. But the entire independence of the
spiritual power must be assured. The Church must have its
own property, which it administers itself, under the protection of the State, and it must itself choose the ministers of
religion, subject to the king's approval. There can be but one
form of recognized religion in any State, and Bonald went
so far as to say that all others should be proscribed. He and
Maistre felt a horror of Protestantism, for they saw in the
Reformation the birth of that spirit of individual inquiry
and revolt which culminated in the Revolution. The welfare
of society, they believed, demands unanimity of opinion; to
question and to doubt is to destroy. Just as there can be no
right to do evil in the social sphere, so there can be no liberty
to err in the domain of faith. Philosophy teaches men to trust
in their own reason and judgment, rather than in the Word of
God, and so leads them into countless errors. "Men" said
Maistre, "need beliefs, not problems."[33] Tolerance is neither

[32] Bonald, *Essai analytique* (Edition of 1800), p. 23.
[33] Maistre, *Étude sur la souveraineté*, p. 375.

possible nor logical, and authority exists to impress the truth upon the minds of men, as it enforces order on their wills. This applies also in political and intellectual matters. It is criminal to attack existing institutions, or to write against accepted morality. "Government," Maistre wrote, "is a real religion; it has its dogmas, its mysteries, its ministers. To subject it to discussion is to kill it, for it lives by political faith."[34] For this reason they condemned the liberty of the press, and Bonald suggested that the State should itself edit all books, so as to expurgate dangerous passages, even from the classics. He considered, for the same reason, that the State should control education, which should only be given to those who are destined to serve it. This instruction must be in the hands of the Church.

Bonald and Maistre were scornful of the idea of political liberty. Consistently with their doctrines as to the origin of sovereignty they believed that men have no inherent right to political power, and they denied that liberty is, in fact, dependent upon the possession of it. Participation in the sovereign power, Bonald declared, is not liberty; it is only the right to coerce the wills of others. Only unanimous consent could give political liberty in any other sense, and that is impossible. Since all is done in society for the benefit of the governed, they need have nothing to do with public affairs. "What," asked Maistre, "is the vain honor of being represented, to the people?" What men want is civil liberty, that is to say, protection against injustice, and of that there is more under a monarchy than in a republic, for in a monarchy justice is less at the mercy of opinion than in a democracy, and the individual is also protected by custom and tradition from the encroachments of the State. "No nation can give

[34] *Ibid.*, p. 376.

itself liberty," said Maistre. "That has always been the gift of kings."

Equality also seemed to them to be a chimera. It is nature which creates human inequalities, and they are hereditary. Glory and shame belong rather to families than to individuals, for human beings are not isolated, but united by various bonds of solidarity, of which the family is the most important. Political equality is a potentiality; it consists merely in the possibility of occupying a post, and great functions and high places will inevitably fall to an élite. Society, though it does not create inequalities, confers distinctions, for it is necessary that the instruments of government should be greatly elevated above the masses. These distinctions, however, lose their offensive qualities when they are the reward of services rendered to society, and when access to them is open to all. What is important is that merit should be able to rise. This they considered to have been the case under the French monarchy.

Both Bonald and Maistre were, in a measure, precursors of the organismic theories of the State. Bonald repeatedly said that society is a real being, but it is Maistre who developed this conception most clearly. Nations, he said, are born, live, and die, like men. Their origin and growth is mysterious because they are living. They have a general soul and a real moral unity which is their very nature, and to speak of the "genius" of a nation is not a metaphor.

Unlike most of the eighteenth-century philosophers, whose point of view was cosmopolitan, both Bonald and Maistre were nationalists. Bonald considered that France, under the old régime, was by far the most perfectly "constituted" state the world had known. Maistre saw that the ruthless policy of the Jacobins had alone saved France from dismemberment

by the Allies, and he considered this so vital to the future of
the world, that he was ready to look even upon those "blood-
stained" men as the instruments of divine providence. France
to Bonald and Maistre was, and must always be, the leader
of civilization in the world. Their nationalism, however, was
cultural, not racial. Maistre, in fact, was a Savoyard, and
served the King of Sardinia all his life.

Bonald and Maistre have been aptly called the "proph-
ets of the past,"[35] for their ideas are entirely based on the
doctrines and institutions of prerevolutionary France. They
were, however, inspired rather by the spirit and conditions
of the Middle Ages than by those of the eighteenth century.
Bonald's view of the proper functions of the nobility, and
Maistre's dream of the renewed spiritual unity of Christendom are distinctly mediaeval. Their conception that society
is static and agricultural, with the people in tutelage to a
paternalistic government, and their insistence on landed property as the basis of wealth and the standard of social value,
are reminiscent of the thirteenth century. They were only
dimly aware of the forces which were creating the modern
world; that is, the development of commerce and industry,
and the rise of the *bourgeoisie*. It was these changes in the
social structure which liberated the individual, and made
possible the philosophy of the eighteenth century. In attributing the Revolution entirely to that philosophy, Bonald and
Maistre took for a cause what was really a collateral effect.

Their lack of insight was largely due to their passionate
attachment to the past. So strong was their respect for all
that is venerable or traditional that they saw the institutions
of the old régime in far too bright a light. For instance, they
insisted upon the superior administration of justice under the

[35] Barbey d'Aurevilly, *Les Prophètes du passé* (Paris, 1864).

Monarchy, yet Arthur Young says of this same system of justice that it was "partial, venal and infamous . . . The bigotry, ignorance, false principles and tyranny of these bodies, the *parlements*, were generally conspicuous."[36] Even allowing for possible exaggeration, this picture contrasts strangely with the complacent admiration of Bonald and Maistre! Whatever the condition of France in 1789, it is not probable that the Revolution would have occurred if the political constitution of the old régime had ensured for the people the large measure of well-being and justice that Bonald and Maistre claimed for it.

Two factors chiefly determined the mentality of these men. The first was their personal situation. They lived in the provinces, away from the corruption and levity of the Court, but far, also, from the stimulating intellectual life of Paris. As magistrates and *gens de robe* they belonged to a class which had less understanding of the peasantry and its needs than had the old landed nobility. They were patricians, rather than aristocrats, and the sense of personal superiority was strong in them; they never felt themselves to be of the people. Moreover, they were trained in the law, a study which is apt to promote a respect for order, and devotion to the past.

The chief factor in their mentality, however, was their Catholicism. Respect for authority; belief in the necessity of self-sacrifice; mistrust of reason and philosophy as ultimate guides in life; love of unity;—all these features of their thought are in accord with the teachings of the Church. Their religion provided them with an ideal, and they did not need to seek another, as did so many, in liberty and equality.

In summing up the contribution of Bonald and Maistre to political thought it must be said for them that they had a truer

[36] Arthur Young, *Travels in France* (Dublin, 1793).

vision of man than most of the theorists of their day. They saw that he exists chiefly in his social relationships and that he is at least as important as father, land owner, craftsman, etc., as in his purely political function of voter. They saw that society is a continuous whole, and that this complex and living thing is conditioned by its past and cannot be dealt with on a basis of abstract reason. They understood something of the part played by instinct and emotion, as opposed to reason, in the growth of institutions. They had a high ideal of sacrifice and social solidarity, and recognized the responsibility of groups within the State.

They saw, also, that the fundamental problem of society is to secure from the individual the amount of sacrifice necessary to ensure the good of the whole. In this connection they justly pointed out the difference which often exists between the real needs and interests of the people, and their wishes. They stressed the important fact that, as the average man is unable to think or act in terms of the future, some far-sighted control is essential to the common welfare.

The theocrats, however, as sometimes happens with those who have much faith in God, had little faith in man. They believed that individual wills are entirely selfish and unreasonable, and for this reason they put order before liberty. They underestimated the value of consent, of voluntary and active sacrifice, as opposed to forced obedience, and, in stressing the necessity for an absolute and unquestionable authority, they only avoided legitimating pure force by resorting to a superhuman sanction for power. Their answer to the fundamental problem of society lies in the teachings of religion, supported by a strong political authority; The former enjoins the sacrifice of the individual to the State, and gives it a sacred motive; the latter enforces this sacrifice on the unwilling. This answer is satisfactory to those who believe in the teachings of religion, and are led by them to resign themselves to existing conditions. Bonald and Maistre, however, wrote at a time when faith was no longer universal. Men were no longer willing to put all their hopes of happiness in another world, as the Church bade them; they had tasted liberty and power, and for many a belief in humanity and its future had taken the place of faith in religion and authority.

The optimism of the eighteenth century was not yet exhausted (indeed it was still to express itself in a hundred years of liberalism and growing democracy), and doctrines based on fear instead of hope made no appeal to the classes which had been emancipated by the Revolution. For this reason, Bonald and Maistre were out of touch with their age. Their doctrines were too exclusively founded on the economic conditions of the past, they represented too closely the ideas of an interested minority, to furnish a basis for the adjustments required by the new society.

Yet they voiced, as do their successors today, the opinion of a valuable element in the community. There are always men who believe in a government of authority. In some cases their theories seem to be merely the efforts of wealth and power at self-justification but often there is a nobler motive. Those who believe ardently in some ideal way of living, may well prefer that ideal to liberty. This must be conceded to have been the case with the Theocrats.

CHAPTER III

ROMANTIC ROYALISM: CHATEAUBRIAND

The theocrats, since they believed in monarchy by divine right, did not admit the need of a constitution, and were hostile to the Charte. A majority of the "ultra-royalists," however, recognized its necessity and hoped to use it for their own ends. The most brilliant and influential of these men was François René de Chateaubriand. His literary fame and his unsurpassed gift of expression made him a power.

Chateaubriand was neither a philosopher nor a statesman; he was a poet who had wandered into politics. The source of his ideas was emotional rather than intellectual, and he was both royalist and liberal from sentiment more than from philosophic conviction. His nature was compounded of sensibility, imagination, and pride, and he was intensely self-conscious; life to him was always a drama, of which he was apt to see himself as the hero. Pride and self-consciousness produced in him a sense of melancholy detachment from society, and a contempt for human weaknesses. He was, in short, a romantic individualist. At heart he believed, like Godwin, that all government is an evil, and liberty an illusion, except in the state of nature. This was the view expressed in his earliest work, the "Essai sur la Révolution Française,"[1] and even in 1828 he repeated it in the apologetic notes on this book. "All governments are detestable. Perfection would be to live haphazard without any form of government whatever."[2] This attitude did not, how-

---

[1] Chateaubriand, "Essai sur la Révolution française," *Oeuvres,* Vol. V.
[2] *Ibid.,* p. 39, Notes.

ever, lead Chateaubriand to advocate, as Godwin did, a minimum of government in practice. The choice, he considered, lies between society and savagery, and although he preferred savagery, if society must exist, he admitted the need of a strong government.

This sceptical individualism was, however, but one side of Chateaubriand's nature. He lived chiefly in his imagination, and this was formed largely by his early surroundings. He came of an old Breton family, very noble, and very poor. His first youth was spent in the stately Château of Combourg, and austere and narrow as was the life there, he was deeply penetrated with a sense of its beauty and dignity. He saw the Court at Versailles in its last days, and served in the royal army, both then and during the emigration. His brother and sister were guillotined at the time of the Revolution, and his mother died in poverty during his exile. Thus every influence of tradition, *milieu,* and experience combined to make him a royalist. Moreover the *Génie du Christianisme,* a work which brought him an enormous reputation at one stroke, is a panegyric of Catholic Christianity, and a poetic exposition of its beauties. Its very success, which made Chateaubriand known as the "orator of the altar,"[3] rendered a change of attitude difficult.

Yet Chateaubriand had an enthusiasm for liberty, though his conception of it was vague and poetic, rather than practical. Two ideas appealed to his imagination; on the one hand, that of the king as defender of the Faith, and source of glory and honor, and on the other hand, the Red Indian, free in the primeval forest.

Chateaubriand's ideas as to the origin of society are not

[3] Sainte-Beuve, *Chateaubriand et son groupe littéraire sous l'Empire* (Paris, 1848-49), p. 286.

clear; like the royalists of today, he preferred to leave such questions in abeyance. He wisely pointed out, however, that these origins could only be found by the study of primitive man, and he criticized Rousseau's doctrine of the social contract from this point of view.[4] The wandering savage does not, he said, enter suddenly into society and form a compact.

He refused to pronounce as to whether sovereignty originates in divine right or in the will of the people. Neither principle, he said, must be denied, and it is best to shroud the origin of power in silence and mystery.[5] But, though he did not deny the principle of popular sovereignty, he steadily maintained that, in practice, its results are no better than a return to savagery. "If the people," he said, "have the right to choose their government, they will also have the right to change it, and this will mean perpetual restlessness— permanent anarchy."[6] He pointed out that, even if the principle of popular sovereignty is admitted, a republican government is not a necessary corollary. He considered that the sovereignty of the people does not favor freedom. There is great danger in making men's liberty depend on their political rights, for these are always debatable. Sovereignty must, he said, always be limited; in entering into society man brings with him an inalienable right to liberty, and no authority can legitimately invade that sacred domain.

There is, he thought, a form of government natural to each stage of human development; liberty for savages; a royal republic for shepherd peoples; democracy for ages of civic virtue; monarchy for ages of luxury; and despotism for those of decadence and corruption.[7] For France, legitimate

[4] Chateaubriand, "Essai sur la Révolution française," Part I, pp. 23-24.
[5] *Ibid.*, Part I, pp. 234-35.　　[6] *Ibid.*, Part II, p. 17.
[7] Chateaubriand, "Essai sur la Révolution française," Part II, p. 48.

monarchy alone can give the necessary guarantees of peace and liberty.

Chateaubriand's imagination gave him a certain insight, and he early realized that the monarchy must adapt itself to the new world, and that the Charte was the best possible basis for this adjustment. "Legitimacy," as he put it, "returning, claimed the power and offered liberty in exchange."[8] He sincerely wished to reconcile the old monarchy with the new liberties. In the *Mémoires d'outre-tombe,* published after his death, he said that he led the old royalists to the conquest of public liberties, which they hated, and rallied the liberals, in the name of these liberties, to the standard of Bourbons, whom they despised.[9] He was not, however, the man to consummate this union; his passions and prejudices were stronger than his political wisdom. He hated the men of the Revolution and the Empire, and he hoped to establish a liberal government, not by making concessions to the middle class, but by creating a landed aristocracy, which would rule in the king's name by means of the Charte.

In order to understand Chateaubriand's attitude it must be remembered that he was, at the beginning of the Restoration, the spokesman of the ultra-royalists in the Chamber. These men were far more reactionary in their views than was the king. The measures they proposed included, besides reprisals against their adversaries, an indemnity for the lands confiscated at the Revolution, the rights of primogeniture and substitution[10] for the hereditary peerage, the restoration, as far as possible, of the possessions of the Church, and a re-

---

[8] Chateaubriand, *Mélanges politiques,* pp. 510, 511.

[9] Chateaubriand, *Mémoires d'outre-tombe,* II, 152.

[10] The right of substituting some other person as direct heir, in default of heirs male.

newed control by it of the civil registers and public education.

Louis XVIII was opposed to this policy, for he saw how dangerous it would be to the régime. Therefore, the "ultras" who had a large majority in the Chamber of Deputies after the Hundred Days adopted the liberal theory of the responsibility of ministers to the parliamentary majority, in order to force their will upon the king. Chateaubriand was in full agreement with these views. At the death of Louis XVIII, the ultra-royalists had the support of Charles X, and the inconsistency of their attitude became evident, for they were no longer willing to admit the supremacy of the Chamber of Deputies, in which they had lost the majority. Chateaubriand, however, had by that time quarrelled with Villèle and the royalists, and again found himself in opposition to the throne, so that there was no need for him to alter his doctrines as to ministerial responsibility. His pamphlet *La Monarchie selon la Charte* was an exposition of the ultra-royalist ideas at the beginning of the Restoration. It was intended as an attack upon the Decazes' ministry, but it was so clear and forceful a presentation of constitutional monarchy that it became the political Bible of the party.[11]

Chateaubriand admired the old constitution of France, founded on religion and respect for the past, but, he said, it has perished; its elements are dispersed, and cannot be reconstituted. This fact must be faced. "One idea," he declared, "has survived the Revolution; that of a political order which protects the rights of the people without injuring those of the sovereign."[12] Only representative monarchy as embodied in the Charte can furnish this combination.

[11] Charles Benoist, *Chateaubriand* (Paris, 1865), p. 187.
[12] "Réflexions politiques," *Oeuvres de Chateaubriand,* p. 115.

The government, according to the Charte, is composed of four elements: royalty, the Chamber of Peers, the Chamber of Deputies, and the ministry. This, Chateaubriand says, is a mixture of three types of power; monarchy, aristocracy and democracy. It is not new, and has been approved by philosophers.

The essential principle of the government resides in the Crown. The king embodies the idea of legitimate authority and of liberty; he is the national will personified in a family.

Religion, habit, the recollections of the past, all are attached to the name of the king. In him the ideas of ruler, magistrate and father mingle. His paternal power is softened by time and custom. From him alone can stability come.[13]

The king occupies his throne by virtue of inheritance, not by gift, for the monarchy is not elective. In an elective monarchy the principle of order, instead of being perpetual, is transitory in a royal person. Thus it is not stable, and to add some element of heredity such as restriction to one family, is merely to create an amphibious power with the inconveniences of both systems.[14] In heredity by primogeniture, on the contrary, lies the principle of immortality. "Well may the state call itself immortal," he exclaimed, "which has seen power pass with the same blood from Robert the Strong to Charles X."[15] Only a king who reigns by right of

[13] "Bonaparte et les Bourbons," *Oeuvres de Chateaubriand*, pp. 30, 31.

[14] "Opinions et discours," *Oeuvres de Chateaubriand*, p. 487. The first two French dynasties were of the type Chateaubriand describes here. The right to the throne was hereditary in the royal family, but the order of succession was not determined beforehand. The choice of the member of the family who was to succeed might be the result of circumstances, or of the choice of the notables of the realm.

[15] *Congrès de Vérone* (Paris, 1838), p. 174.

birth is free to found, in agreement with his people, the institutions which assure liberty.

The king is infallible, he is an inviolable and sacred being. He must be strong and splendid, endowed with enormous prestige. Chateaubriand affirmed that the king under the Charte is more powerful than his ancestors, and he made an imposing list of his prerogatives. He is responsible only to God; he is head of the Gallican Church; he is father to each family by his control of public instruction; he is sovereign legislator, since he accepts or rejects the laws, and can dissolve the Chambers; he is above the law, since he has the right to pardon; he holds the executive power in his hands, since he is sole administrator, and names the ministers; he alone makes war and peace, and commands the national forces. This last point is important, for in France, Chateaubriand pointed out, the army is so necessary that it has much prestige. For this reason, military nominations and advancements must come solely from the throne.[16]

Yet, by Chateaubriand's own admission, the royal power is limited. The king shares the legislative functions with two chambers, and, although he has the right to dissolve them, he must, in the last analysis, bow to the national opinion which they represent. Since he is above responsibility, he can only act through his ministers. They are accountable for all abuses, the king is never involved, and for that reason they are not mere instruments of his will, but act for themselves. The king in his council judges, but does not force his will on the minister. If he decides as the king wishes, it is well; if not, the king allows him to act, and should he make a mis-

[16] "De la Monarchie selon la Charte," *Oeuvres de Chateaubriand,* p. 170.

take, the ministry falls. Even if the king and his ministers agree on a bad measure, it is only the minister who is considered to be at fault. Chateaubriand undoubtedly wished to give the king, as far as possible, the appearance of power, and he denies that his rôle is that of a passive idol. Nevertheless, his position as defined in *La Monarchie selon la Charte* resembles that of the English king, who reigns, but does not govern.

Associated with the king in the legislative function are two chambers. The first, the Chamber of Peers, is, in principle, hereditary, although the king has the right to name members for life only. It is in regard to this Chamber that Chateaubriand considered that the Charte was incomplete. The peerage represents the aristocratic element in the nation, and it should have greater wealth and prestige than the Chamber of Deputies, otherwise the latter may gain a dangerous preëminence. Aristocracies, Chateaubriand said, spring from political rights, and their principle is liberty; democracy, which springs from natural rights, has only equality for its object. Equality is the passion of small souls; born of envy, it tends to disorder and, though it goes well with despotism, it does not agree with monarchy, which establishes a distinction of powers. All that is strong in France, both old and new, is needed to create the vast "ensemble" of aristocracies, national, provincial, and communal, without which a nation of 30,000,000 inhabitants is an inorganic mass, exposed to all the risks of despotism and anarchy.[17] A nobility is always a stabilising force in the State. In France it could play a great part under the new order, for, by the Charte it regained the possibility of political power, which it had lost under the old régime. As represented in the peerage, its rôle should be

[17] *Journal des débats,* January 11, 1821.

to defend the royal prerogatives. But the aristocracy created by the Charte was a fiction; the nobility of France, though it transmitted its principles to the Chamber of Peers, remained outside it. Two things were lacking to this chamber: landed property, and publicity for its debates.[18] Landed property serves as a foundation for the State; it regulates political rights, it is the basis of all financial laws, and it has dominated the common law of all peoples. Its loss causes more lasting damage than the loss of other property. The landed aristocracy, destroyed in France by the Revolution, could be built up gradually by means of indemnities for their lost lands, and by the rights of substitution and primogeniture. Thus the needed third power could be created.[19]

In a mixed monarchy constitutional bodies form a republican element in the government. The old monarchy did not need such a moderating factor within itself, for it found resistances and powers, such as the clergy, the magistracy, the Provincial Estate beside it, establishing limits to its authority. The new monarchy has no outward limits; it is all-powerful in the state, but it has in public opinion an internal limit. Representative government is based on opinion and it is in the Chamber of Deputies that this opinion finds expression, and the interests of the nation are judged. The idea that this chamber is merely consultative is false; it has the right to approve, amend, or reject the laws, and to accept or refuse the budget. It should also, Chateaubriand thought, share with the Crown the right of initiating the laws. The veto and the initiative should not be in the same hands.

[18] Chateaubriand was himself a member of the Chamber of Peers; therefore the question of publicity for its debates was of vital interest to him.

[19] Benjamin Constant said that *La Monarchie selon la Charte* should have been called *La Charte selon la noblesse.*

Like the Chamber of Deputies, the ministry draws its authority from public opinion, and it must command a majority in the chambers. The majority system, Chateaubriand said, is the mainspring of representative government. The ministry must either lead or follow public opinion; if it is in a minority, it must go. It must account to the chambers for the administration of the laws, and its members must always be ready to appear and to justify their acts. A ministry, though there may be mutations in its composition, must be a unit, and be collectively responsible for its acts.

Religion was for Chateaubriand the sole basis of a good State, for it is eternal justice. He considered that the greatest fault of the Revolution was its attack upon the Church. Thereby it overthrew morality, and despised experience and customs, leaving a society without past or future, founded on that fragile thing, human reason. Christianity gives men a true idea of what is just and unjust; it substitutes affirmation for doubt, and embraces all humanity in its idea of universal brotherhood. Religion emphasizes the idea of duty as a corrective to the democratic instinct; it should therefore be encouraged and supported by the State.[20] The clergy since the Revolution is no longer a political order, but it is still a corporation, and as such it should be allowed to receive donations of land, to hold the civil registers, and to be responsible for public education. The high dignitaries of the Church should, by virtue of their function, be members of the Chamber of Peers.

Devoted as Chateaubriand was to the name of freedom, the only practical form of it which he consistently advocated was the liberty of the press. This is, he declared, the soul of representative government, the chief organ of opinion, and no free institution can exist without it. This was perhaps the

[20] *Mémoires d'outre-tombe,* II, 290.

most sincere and fervent of his convictions, a natural enough trait in so eminently articulate a man, whose pen was the chief source of his power.

Chateaubriand's ideas present a certain anomaly when they are compared with those of his contemporaries. His political doctrine is liberal, for he believed in inalienable rights guaranteed by a constitution, and in a limited monarchy, with an irresponsible king, and a ministry dependent on the parliamentary majority. His social aims, however, like those of the Theocrats, were clerical and aristocratic, unfavorable to the middle classes and to the men of the Revolution and the Empire, whom he hated. For this reason he was often accused of inconsistency. If the political system he advocated is examined in itself, however, it appears to be somewhat like the English constitution of his time; a limited monarchy with parliamentary supremacy, supported by a landed aristocracy, and an established Church. Such a system may be relatively liberal, as it was in England, or it may be extremely reactionary, as it bade fair to be in France under the "Chambre introuvable"; its character will depend on the political forces and temper of the nation.

There was little in Chateaubriand's political doctrine which need have prevented him from rallying to the monarchy of Louis-Philippe, but, like Royer-Collard, he mistrusted the good faith and the durability of that régime. Moreover, imagination, sentiment, and his sense of honor bound him to the cause of legitimacy. It was his misfortune that, although he clung to it, he could not heartily believe in it.[21] Sceptical pessimism was a fundamental part of his nature,[22] and he saw too clearly the faults of the dynasty which he served—the

[21] Chateaubriand, *De la Monarchie selon la Charte,* Préface; "Opinions et discours," *Oeuvres,* V, 497.

[22] Chateaubriand, *Mémoires d'outre-tombe,* II, 147-49.

more so, no doubt, that he was never its prime minister.[23]
He once called himself "a useless Cassandra sitting upon
the ruins of a shipwreck which he had predicted."[24] In fact,
"I told you so!" was his usual attitude, and this was highly
irritating to the men of his own time, and later caused Sainte-
Beuve to say that his policy was a nemesis.[25] His romantic individualism has also laid him open to the criticisms of the
modern royalists, and especially of Charles Maurras, with
whose point of view his esthetic royalism has, nevertheless,
some affinity.[26] It has been said that the *Génie du Christianisme* displays the beauties of the Catholic religion rather
as though the Church were a museum. In the same way, there
is undoubtedly an element of dilettantism in Chateaubriand's
attitude towards monarchy; it was easier for his sceptical,
but poetic nature to admire it, than to take it seriously. He
perceived, however, a thing to which the more whole-hearted
royalists of that day paid little attention, namely, that monarchy, if it is to combat the revolutionary spirit, must appeal
to the imagination and emotions of men. To do so, it should
be heroic; it should have prestige and glory, as well as the
poetry of tradition. This lesson Chateaubriand may have
learned from the Empire,[27] and the idea was perhaps his most
valuable contribution to the cause of royalism. The *Génie
du Christianisme* had served the cause of Catholicism by
stressing anew its emotional and imaginative value,[28] and

[23] Sainte-Beuve, *Chateaubriand et son groupe,* p. 286.

[24] Chateaubriand, "Opinions & discours," *Oeuvres,* V, 480.

[25] Sainte-Beuve, *op. cit.,* p. 385.

[26] Charles Maurras, "Trois Idées politiques," *Romantisme et révolution,* chap. i.

[27] Napoleon exercised an enormous influence upon Chateaubriand, and
inspired him with admiration and hatred in almost equal measure.

[28] See Valdemar Gurian, *Die politischen und sozialen Ideen des*

Chateaubriand undoubtedly hoped to render the same service to the monarchy. He never missed an opportunity of showing the royal family in a picturesque or dramatic light, and his pen was always at their service, to portray their lives and actions. It was to give to legitimacy the prestige of military success that, as Foreign Minister, he promoted the war with Spain.[29]

Chateaubriand stood between the two camps into which France was divided during the Restoration. He was not profoundly logical, and he never accepted either system of thought in its entirety; his ideas were too aristocratic for the liberals, and too individualistic for the authoritarians, and, as a consequence, he has been assailed from both sides. Nevertheless it is to his credit that he remained faithful to a cause in which he could only half believe, and his colorful eloquence gave a pathetic lustre to its fallen fortunes.

---

französischen Katholizismus, for an interesting study of Chateaubriand's attitude.

[29] Chateaubriand, *Mémoires d'outre-tombe,* IV, 57.

CHAPTER IV

THE DOCTRINAIRES: ROYER-COLLARD

Between the "ultras" and "liberals" stood a group of men known as the "doctrinaires."[1] They were not a political party, (they were so few that it was said they could have found room on a sofa,)[2] nor did they aim at the possession of power, yet their ability and the elevation of their ideas gave them influence, in spite of the fact that both of the warring factions disliked them.[3] What the doctrinaires wanted was a reconciliation between the two parties, in which what was most valuable in the ideas of each might be preserved. They saw as clearly as did the liberals that the Monarchy, in order to survive, must adapt itself to the results of the Revolution, but, unlike them, they feared the tyranny of popular sovereignty as much as that of royal absolutism. They considered legitimacy as essential to any durable political system. The king represented authority, tradition, and the unity of the nation, therefore they wished him to govern, but they also wished civil equality, and the new economic status to be protected by

[1] Royer-Collard had been educated by the "Pères de la Doctrine de l'Oratoire" which fact may have given rise to the name "Doctrinaires." Spüller says that it was given them by a royalist after a speech in which doctrine and theory were often mentioned. Spüller, pp. 1-35. According to Woodward (*Three Studies in European Conservatism,* London, 1929) the name first appeared in a newspaper of April, 1816. See also Duvergier de Hauranne, *op. cit.,* III, 534.

[2] Nesmes-Desmarets, *Doctrine politique de Royer-Collard* (Montpellier, 1908), p. 9.

[3] Duvergier de Hauranne said they were "intolerant, negligent, disdainful in form, almost always right at bottom." Duvergier de Hauranne, *Histoire du gouvernement parlementaire* (Paris, 1860-72), V, 118.

constitutional guarantees. The Charte was, to them, the source and sanction of these guarantees, and the only possible basis of the future for a legitimate monarchy. They were, as Faguet has said, "liberal legitimists."

The principal doctrinaires were Royer-Collard, de Serre, de Barante, and Camille Jordan. Certain others more or less closely associated with them were Beugnot, Becquet, François Guizot, Victor de Broglie, and Charles de Rémusat.[4] Some of these men were destined to survive the Monarchy of the Restoration, and to play a part in the following régime. Among them Royer-Collard was undoubtedly the leading spirit and his thought is the source of almost all the ideas of the group.

Bonald, Maistre, and Chateaubriand reflect to a great extent the ideas of the social groups to which they belonged: the magistracy or the country nobility, with their pride, their prejudices, and their belief in privilege. It is more difficult to trace the influence of *milieu* on Royer-Collard. By birth, he belonged to the lower middle class, but his ability early raised him to a higher level. His father, Antoine Royer, was a small farmer, while his mother's family, the Collards, were, for the most part, priests or country lawyers.[5] Civil equality and the disappearance of privilege and caste favored such people by opening to them new vistas of opportunity. This is perhaps why Royer-Collard never wavered in his adherence to the social changes of the Revolution. Spüller points out[6] that before the introduction of machinery the lower middle classes lived in close contact with the people and were not clearly

---

[4] Barante, Prosper Amable de, *Vie politique de Royer-Collard* (Paris, 1857), I, 238.

[5] Spüller, *Vie de Royer-Collard*, pp. 20-22.

[6] Spüller, *op. cit.*, pp. 6, 10.

distinguished from them. In the country they cultivated their land side by side with the peasants, and in the cities household industries brought employers and workmen together under the same roof, so that at the Revolution a like spirit animated them all. It was, no doubt, partly because he had known these conditions in his youth that Royer-Collard never distinguished very clearly between the *bourgeoisie* and the people.

Royer-Collard attended the law courts in Paris before the Revolution. He always professed a great admiration for the magistracy of the old régime,[7] and the study of law had much to do with his intellectual formation. At the outbreak of the Revolution he was elected to the Council of the Commune, but was driven into hiding during the Terror. His dislike of popular sovereignty undoubtedly came from the experience he then had of its abuses. Although, unlike the *émigrés,* he accepted the results of the Revolution and labored to maintain them, he felt a great horror of its cruelties and excesses.[8] It was probably this experience which decided his adherence to the cause of legitimate monarchy. He once said: "Many have been proscribed for opinions which they did not hold, but which persecution gave them."[9]

The Collard family had been influenced by Jansenism, and Royer-Collard's mother was austerely devout.[10] The severity of his early training probably helped to develop his characteristics of scrupulous integrity and high-mindedness, combined with stiffness and pride. His nature presents a curious anomaly, for, unlike most people, although his per-

[7] *Ibid.,* p. 14.
[8] Barante, *op. cit.,* I, 220. He repeatedly speaks with disgust of the revolutionary excesses.
[9] *Ibid.,* p. 45.   [10] Spüller, *op. cit.,* pp. 6-7.

sonal character was rigid and unbending, his mind was supple, and he was able to profit by experience, and to adapt his theories to reality. His career reflects this anomaly, for, although he was not a closet philosopher but an orator, engaged in public life, he never became an active statesman, because he was unable to leave the domain of pure thought, and bend his independence and pride to the management of men.[11]

Emile Faguet considers that the doctrinaires were mere opportunists. There is some truth in this, for Royer-Collard did not so much create a political system as advocate a method. He elevated the idea of compromise to the level of a philosophy, and made moderation (the "golden mean") into a dogma. Societies, he saw, are dynamic, and must perpetually struggle against tyrannies of all sorts, and seek an equilibrium among warring interests and powers. He hated force and coercion, and he believed that, in this struggle, compromise is the only reasonable method of solution. Compromise was, in itself, a virtue to him, for it means a system of mutual concessions whereby consent is substituted for compulsion. He believed that much allowance must be made for circumstances, and he has therefore been accused of inconsistency, but to the belief in moderation and justice as the essence of political wisdom he was always faithful.

Royer-Collard was an individualist. He differed fundamentally from the theocrats in the importance he attached to conscience and judgment. He did not demand unity of thought, for he saw that such unity, if it is not spontaneous, but imposed from without, is the death of moral freedom. Authority is the power to compel obedience, regardless of consent. This power may be used for the noblest ends, but

[11] *Ibid.*, pp. 154, 155.

there is apt to be in the minds of those who use it willingly some taint of cruelty, some readiness to dominate and coerce. This is the character of all fanaticisms, and neither Bonald nor Maistre is free from it. They held that men are essentially evil; all they have of good they owe to society, to which they must be completely subordinated. They then identified society with the State, and so gave the latter unlimited power over the individual. Royer-Collard felt the fundamental weakness of this point of view. "According to these men," he said, speaking of the theocrats, "there was a lack of foresight on the great day of Creation in allowing man to escape, free and intelligent, into the Universe . . . A higher wisdom seeks to restrain this imprudent liberty."[12] And he added: "There is at the bottom of all tyranny a scorn for humanity."[13] He does not enter into the question of the origin of society, but he unhesitatingly declares that it is made for men, and not men for it. The State cannot absorb all of men's legitimate allegiances; they have "rights which they hold from nature and its Author"[14] upon which society must not encroach. Nevertheless, he was deeply aware of the necessity of order. He wished the greatest possible amount of liberty for the individual, and he saw that this could only be secured if there was in the state a combination of the elements of stability and of freedom. He considered that popular sovereignty and personal absolutism are alike tyrannies, and he sought a political system in which both might be avoided.

His theory of sovereignty sprang from his unwillingness to concede legitimacy to any form of absolutism. Sovereignty, as he conceived it, is not power; it is a moral obligation, not a physical capacity. Force resides in each individual, but it is

[12] Barante, *op. cit.*, II, 291.   [13] *Ibid.*, p. 294.
[14] *Archives parlementaires*, XXXVIII, 387.

a purely material thing. There is another element in society, and that is abstract right.[15] Justice and right are given to men by God; they are immortal, and transcend the merely material elements of human life. "Abstract right," he said, "is an immortal image, the noblest possession of humanity, without which there is nothing on earth but a life without dignity and a death without hope."[16] It is justice and abstract right which are truly sovereign. "Force," he said, "cannot exercise sovereignty; it constrains, but it does not obligate.[17] . . . When justice and reason cease to rule, power may continue to exist, but it is not sovereign, that is, it does not command men's allegiance, though it may compel their bodies." And again:

I appeal from the sovereignty of the people to another sovereign, the only one who merits the name; a sovereign superior to people and to kings, immutable and immortal, like its author,—I mean the sovereignty of Reason, the only real legislator of humanity.[18]

Justice must be sovereign, and the only object of society is to dethrone force and put justice in its place. No political necessity can dispense the state from being just; it can have "no rights against the Right":[19] nor can individuals dispense with their conscience and obey evil laws; they are bound, at whatever risk to themselves, to resist injustice.[20]

It appears from this that Royer-Collard, like Bonald and Maistre, believed, in the last analysis, in the transcendent origin and nature of sovereignty. He did not, however, like

[15] Royer-Collard uses the expression "le droit" in a wider sense than is conveyed by the word "law." For him, moral right, or legitimacy is implied by this term, and I have therefore translated it as "abstract right."
[16] Barante, op. cit., II, 30.   [17] Ibid., p. 33.
[18] Archives parlementaires, XLIX, 566.
[19] Barante, op. cit., II, 296.
[20] Ibid., p. 305; Archives parlementaires, L, 24.

them, attribute this divine quality to a human institution, and so create an authority which cannot be questioned.[21] "The idea," he said, "that governments alone have natural rights of superhuman origin and that peoples have only the rights those governments choose to give them, is false."[22] Justice and reason are, in their essence, superhuman and absolute, but men conceive them by means of individual conscience and reason, on which they have a right to rely. The idea of the sovereignty of justice seems abstract, as Royer-Collard presented it, but, as Barante points out,[23] its real meaning is simply that no government, whatever its origin, is legitimate in itself; it can only claim to be so, in the measure in which its acts correspond to reason and justice. The practical criterion of this justice can only be, Royer-Collard said, in the opinions of men.

Justice, then, is the true sovereign, but the problem of what forms of social organization and government are in accord with it remains to be solved. Royer-Collard was so far from being doctrinaire in the usual sense of the word

[21] Barthélemy (*Introduction du régime parlementaire en France,* Paris, 1906) clearly points out that Henri Michel (*L'Idée de l'État,* Paris, 1895, p. 294) is mistaken in saying that Royer-Collard considered the ensemble of the king and the two chambers as sovereign. Barthélemy's statement (*op. cit.,* p. 20) that Royer-Collard considered the Charte as sovereign does not, however, appear to be wholly correct. Barthélemy himself points out on a later page (*op. cit.,* p. 198) that Royer-Collard always refused to attribute sovereignty to any institution whatever, reserving it for abstract right. C. E. Merriam (*The Theory of Sovereignty since Rousseau,* New York, 1900, pp. 74-81) gives an excellent discussion of the theory of the sovereignty of reason. He points out the resemblance between this theory and that of the theocrats. However, Royer-Collard's conception of sovereignty as a moral force or obligation rather than a physical power, he does not make clear.

[22] Barante, *op. cit.,* II, 296.

[23] Barante, *Questions constitutionnelles* (Paris, 1849), pp. 7-9.

that he always refused to follow any theory to its ultimate consequences. Doctrines pushed to their limit almost always result in a tyranny, and he hated all tyrannies. He did not maintain, like Bonald, that there is but one form of government which is best for all peoples at all times; on the contrary, he believed like Maistre, that governments must vary according to circumstances. "There are," he said, "for every people principles and conditions which are essential to their institutions."[24] Absolutism, however, in any form is an evil, for unlimited power is the rule of force and the negation of justice; it demoralizes those who wield it, and leads to the worst abuses. For this reason the doctrine of popular sovereignty is dangerous, for it justifies every violence in the name of the general will. The Empire, as an elective military monarchy, he considered the worst possible form of government,[25] because it was the arbitrary power of one man, sheltering itself behind the doctrine of popular sovereignty.

Since popular sovereignty and personal absolutism alike lead to tyranny, he sought a political system in which both might be avoided. There are, he found, two means of accomplishing this; the first is to divide the sovereign power in such a way that an equilibrium of social forces will be necessary for its exercise; the second is to establish for men certain constitutional rights, inviolable even by the State. Monarchy alone, he considered, could afford this combination of freedom and political equilibrium with the necessary elements of stability.

It was because of this promise of stability, that Royer-Collard considered legitimate monarchy so necessary to France. "The stability of the royal power," he said "is the guaranty of the duration of all other advantages. It adds to

[24] Barante, *op. cit.,* II, 16.   [25] *Ibid.*

them the greatest blessing of all—security."[26] The Monarchy possessed this promise of stability, because it was consecrated by tradition, and by 800 years of service to society.

There is no need to prove that monarchy alone is suitable to France; this is a political and sentimental truth, unshakable fruit of experience. . . Monarchy derives its power from the customs, the recollections, and the instinctive respect and love of the nation. . . The king is not a person, he is an institution, the universal one, on which all others are founded. The moral unity of society breathes in the hereditary monarch.[27]

The principle itself of legitimacy Royer-Collard believed to be valuable; he identified it with legality and called it "the living image of law, order, and peace."[28] Moderation, always his ideal, he believed to be its natural attribute. Moreover, he foresaw, unlike certain of the liberal royalists, what events have proved, that once the principle of a predetermined hereditary succession is abandoned, royalty loses one of its most important titles to respect, and must depend upon the sanction of the general will. It is then at the mercy of every change of popular opinion.[29]

On the other hand, Royer-Collard believed that constitutional monarchy, as established by the Charte, guaranteed to men their essential rights and liberties. "We have rights," he said, "considered as inviolable, and superior to legislation; that is why we recognize equally sacred rights in the dynasty."[30] This combination of freedom and monarchy was not new; it had its origin in French history. "The royal

---

[26] *Ibid.*, I, 220.   [27] *Ibid.*, p. 222.

[28] *Ibid.*, II, 369.

[29] "Quasi-legitimacy," Royer-Collard said, speaking of the government of Louis-Philippe, "has not enough weight; it will exhaust the honest people who trust in it." Barante, *op. cit.*, II, 476.

[30] Barante, *op. cit.*, II, 132.

power," he said, "has afforded to many generations its sacred shelter against both despotism and anarchy."[31] It was her kings who freed France from feudal tyranny, and established the liberties of the people. The Charte was a modern expression of a union which dated back to the days when Louis the Fat enfranchised the communes and Philippe the Fair instituted national assemblies. Under the old régime France had possessed a powerful group of private rights, seigniorial and communal, and provincial orders and corporations. Such bodies, which did not issue directly from the power of the king, were independent, and so imposed limits on the exercise of sovereignty, and protected men against the encroachments of arbitrary power. These long-established liberties were swept away by the Revolution, and their functions were inherited by the State. The Convention and the Empire were less impeded in their absolutism than the Monarchy had ever been. Society "reduced," as he said, "to a mere dust of isolated individuals,"[32] was left face to face with the enormous strength of the central power. Whether this power was in the hands of king, emperor, or assembly, Royer-Collard knew its menace. It was the Charte upon which he counted to replace the former liberties of France, and to safeguard the individual against the government, grown so dangerously strong.

In seeking the combination of liberty and order promised by the Charte Royer-Collard felt himself to be the spokesman of the new France, created by the Revolution. "A new nation," he said, "has arisen in France which, though innocent of the Revolution which gave it birth, can yet accept its results. Superior to the factions in strength, dignity, and

[31] *Ibid.*, p. 369.
[32] Barante, *op. cit.*, I, 18. *Archives parlementaires*, XXX, 748.

good sense, it is a stranger to their quarrels. For it the pre-revolutionary times are relegated to history . . . but it is the natural ally of a government which will protect it. It has faith in the king. What it wants is legitimacy, order, and liberty."[33] He was not mistaken in this idea. The middle classes had issued triumphant from the Revolution and were to dominate France during the greater part of the nineteenth century. What they wanted was a stable political order, combined with freedom for development. To them the legitimate monarchy, as limited by the Charte, did at first appear to be the best means of guarding against a return to absolutism on one hand, and the progress of unmitigated democracy on the other. The political theory of Royer-Collard is the expression of this point of view.

The provisions of the Charte limited the central power by dividing the legislative function between the king and two chambers, one hereditary, and one elective. Thus the exercise of the function of sovereignty (which Royer-Collard carefully distinguished from sovereignty itself) depends upon the coöperation of these three powers. "Sovereignty," he said, "is personified in the King . . . but it can only be exercised with the necessary coöperation of the two chambers, so that these share in the function of sovereignty."[34] The principle of the division of the function of sovereignty Royer-Collard always advocated, but his ideas as to the exact distribution of power between the king and the chambers varied. He undoubtedly attributed the preponderance of power under ordinary circumstances to the king.

It is inevitable [he said] that the first will, which is the principle of action, should reside somewhere, and give the government its own character . . . In France this regulating power, which pre-

[33] Barante, *op. cit.*, I, 212.   [34] *Ibid.*, II, 82.

cedes all others, is the royal power . . . The king keeps a striking
primacy; he alone acts, commands, and is author of the laws, whose
initiative is exclusively reserved to him. The other powers are,
properly speaking, limits.[35]

He definitely repudiated the English conception of a king
who reigns, but does not govern. Such a system, he said,
might be appropriate to England, where an old aristocracy
had the habit and tradition of power, but it was not suited
to France.[36] The king of France governs; the entire executive
power is in his hands, and the sole initiative of legislation
also.

During the early years of the Restoration, while the reasonable policy of Louis XVIII was a moderating influence,
Royer-Collard seems to have considered the Chamber of
Deputies as little more than a consultative body, whose actual
power was restricted to the vote of the budget. He attributed
to the king not only the right of dissolving the chambers, but
that of choosing his ministers without regard to the parliamentary majority.

It is not necessary that the ministers should have a majority in
the Chambers . . . The king governs independently . . . The day
it is established that the Chambers can reject the king's ministers
and impose others on him, our royalty is lost.[37]

He appears, however, gradually to have been driven to admit
the doctrine of ministerial responsibility. In 1826 he said:
"the Chamber can withdraw its support from a minister when
he violates the Charte,"[38] and he declared that Ministers
must not abuse their authority or encroach on other powers,
and the Chamber is to judge of which this is the case. In
1830 he was, as President of the Chamber, the spokesman

[35] *Ibid.*, p. 217.   [36] *Ibid.*, p. 232.   [37] *Ibid.*, I, 217.
[38] *Archives parlementaires*, XLVII, 227.

of the famous majority of 221 which announced to the king their non-coöperation with his policy. The speech itself, which Royer-Collard inspired, is moderate in tone, and speaks of the intervention of the chambers as "indirect, measured, circumscribed within wise limits."[39] It amounts, nevertheless, to a demand, though a respectful one, for coöperation, and it precipitated, indirectly, the July Revolution. It is obvious that the ideas of Royer-Collard with regard to the relative powers of King and chamber altered, since in 1830 he refused to the Crown the independence which he had claimed for it in 1816. The fact is that the position of the doctrinaires was illogical. They wished to avoid acknowledging the supremacy of the parliamentary majority, for that implied the sovereignty of the people. On the other hand, as they were determined to resist reaction, they could not submit to the authority of a king who supported it. The theory of the sovereignty of justice was an attempt to escape from this dilemma by refusing to acknowledge any sovereignty whatever. This position was tenable so long as no conflict arose between the king and the chambers which would determine the question of where authority actually lay. Royer-Collard had always maintained that the coöperation of the three powers which shared in the legislative function was essential to the monarchy of the Charte, and he had tried to persuade both parties of the necessity of this coöperation. He refused to consider who would, in theory, be sovereign if the king's will and that of the Nation as represented in the chambers, should clash. Such a conflict seemed to him contrary to reason, for he held that "the interest of the monarch is always in agreement with the public interest."[40] It was evident in 1830 that Charles X had resolved to ignore the

[39] *Ibid.*, LXI, 556.   [40] Barante, *op. cit.*, II, 432.

opinion of the Chambers, and, if necessary, abrogate the
Charte and rule by ordinances. This was a complete abandon-
ment of the union between legitimacy and constitutional government, and Royer-Collard's whole political system rested
on this union, as formulated by the Charte. "My life," he
had said, "belongs entirely to the cause of legitimacy and the
defense of the rights and liberties of our country. *I will
never separate these two things.*"[41] When the conflict came
he placed himself on the side of the Nation, but he considered
that his rôle was ended with the fall of the legitimate monarchy.[42]

The Charte defined and guaranteed to men certain rights
which were destined to be checks on the central authority.
The most important of these was national representation
in an elective chamber, which shared in the responsibility for
legislation. This elective chamber was not, in Royal-Collard's
opinion, to represent the wills of individuals, for that would
imply the principle of popular sovereignty. "Society," he
said, "is not a mere numerical aggregate; it must not be
analyzed into persons and wills, but into interests and
rights."[43] Experience had led him to mistrust the rule of the
masses. "If the people are given the right to command," he
said, "it will be the worst element which will dominate, for
it is the most daring, since it has all to gain and nothing to
lose . . . Democracy is incapable of prudence."[44] He believed
in civil equality, but he denied that political equality is its
necessary consequence. Political power is not a natural right,
like freedom of conscience, but a function, and as such can
be attributed only to capacity. The function of the electorate
requires enlightenment and independence for its exercise,

[41] *Ibid.*, p. 115.   [42] *Ibid.*, p. 446.
[43] *Ibid.*, pp. 463-65.   [44] *Ibid.*, p. 291.

and it must only be extended to those who can be presumed to have these qualifications. A true expression of the will of the people could, in any case, only be obtained either by their direct participation in every measure, or by giving to deputies elected by a majority of the total population a purely mandatory power in regard to every question. Such a system, though logically in accordance with the sovereignty of the people, would not be *representative*. It is only the interests and rights of society which can be represented.

Representation, as Royer-Collard conceives it, is based on the idea that when a group has common interests, each individual of the group will have his share of them. He can, therefore, genuinely represent the interests of the group, since they are united in his person, and he cannot act against them without acting against himself. This conception, though not new, is valuable, for it affords a basis for representation other than the will of a majority. It is the theory on which governments act when they appoint men to represent groups or interests. Its weakness is that it takes for granted the homogeneity of the group, whereas today the economic and social interests of men in political groups are varied. The Chamber of Deputies of 1830 in no sense represented the will of the people, but Royer-Collard maintained that it did represent their interests. It is obvious, however, that, even in the early nineteenth century, a chamber elected by a narrow suffrage based on property did not adequately represent all the interests of France.

In accordance with his theory of representation Royer-Collard advocated the existence of an hereditary chamber. He disliked and mistrusted privileges. "Classes possessing power and privilege," he said, "can only be created by con-

quest or revolution."[45] He denied, however, that justice requires social and economic, as well as civil, equality. Social
superiorities, such as learning, wealth, and glory, will, he
believed, always exist and they should be used for the benefit
of the state. It is their interests which the Chamber of Peers
must represent. It should be a "citadel of superiorities,"
standing between the king and the people.[46] Without such
an hereditary chamber, the government would tend to become a mere "Royal democracy," and that, Royer-Collard
considered, would be inferior even to a republic with an
hereditary senate, for it would have less elements of stability.

The other rights which the Charte guaranteed to men were
liberty of conscience, the irremovability of judges, and the
freedom of the press. All these Royer-Collard defended.
With regard to the liberty of conscience, he advocated complete religious tolerance, and he wished the State to be neutral
in matters of faith. "Religion," he said, "is not of this world,
nor law of the next. Absolute truth is a domain into which
the state cannot enter."[47] Were the law to affirm a religious
belief it would be logical to punish heresy, and this would be
"mediaeval and barbarous."[48] The separation of Church and
State was not in question in France during the Restoration;
on the contrary, the alliance of the religious power with the
temporal was close. Royer-Collard was a Catholic;[49] his first
great speech, pronounced in the Council of Five Hundred,
was in defense of the Church, but he considered the theocratic spirit a menace both to religion and society. He felt

[45] *Ibid.*, p. 466.   [46] *Ibid.*, pp. 468-69.
[47] *Ibid.*, p. 246.   [48] *Ibid.*, p. 245.
[49] The education which he gave his daughter (see Spüller, *op. cit.*,
p. 7), as well as what Barante says of his later life (Barante, *op. cit.*, II,
537-39), are conclusive as to his genuine religious conviction.

that it was not even sincere, for its motives were political rather than religious. He saw, however, that the State must always have a great interest in religion, which is, he said, the sole basis of morality. There may be an alliance between the religious and the temporal powers, the State "making of the divine mission of the priest a social magistracy, on condition that the priest remains in the temple, and does not trouble the government."[50] Royer-Collard pointed out, however, that what the priest gains in security by this protection, he loses in independence. The political influence of the clergy depends on faith, and the moral authority of the Church is lessened when it relies on the temporal power. On the whole, his ideal has some resemblance to Cavour's "free Church in a free State."

Royer-Collard considered permanence of tenure for judges one of the most important guarantees of justice. He points out that the action of all the other social powers is dependent on the judicial power. "Society as a whole," he said, "faces the power that makes the laws, but it is on the power which applies them that the individual must rely." Therefore, the judges must be independent; in the exercise of their tremendous function they must be elevated beyond hope or fear, and protected against the State itself, so that they may be prepared to resist even the authority which appoints them. The magistracy of the old régime possessed this independence, because it was one of the forms of money property. Today, the same result can only be obtained if the judges are appointed for life.

The freedom of the press Royer-Collard also defended. Publicity he considered to be one of the established rights which have replaced the former liberties of France. "It is," he

[50] Barante, *op. cit.*, II, 100.

said, "a form of resistance to the established powers, over which it keeps watch to enlighten and to warn them,"[51] for in order that errors and injustices may not accumulate in the social body, the government must be aware of society.

Royer-Collard was opposed to the theory that ignorance is good for the masses and makes them submissive. "Order," he said, "is in peril when it is a mystery, and enlightenment teaches as much to obey as to command."[52] He rejoiced in the intellectual and economic emancipation of an increasingly large number of men.

Royer-Collard was primarily a liberal; it was always a wish for freedom which animated him. He was, however, essentially moderate, and this wish was not with him as with the revolutionary spirits, a passion for liberty in itself, but rather a hatred of what is arbitrary and unjust. He never defined liberty, nor used the word in the singular. Liberties were, for him, resistances and limits to power.

He saw one of the principal defects of modern society, that is to say, the omnipotence of the centralized State, which tends to destroy all other forms of social organization and leave the individual isolated and helpless, and he saw that the mere possession of a vote does not suffice to safeguard men against this power. He recognized the obvious dangers of royal absolutism, but he saw, too, that popular sovereignty usually means the arbitrary and unreasonable power of a few, and that even a genuine majority may tyrannize over a minority, without regard for right or justice. In order to destroy the theoretical bases of tyranny he made justice the sole title to legitimacy. In order to avoid tyranny in practice he wished the exercise of sovereignty to be divided, and to depend upon an equilibrium of political forces. He saw in

[51] *Ibid.*, p. 132.   [52] *Ibid.*, I, 426.

legitimate monarchy the only means of accomplishing this in France.

Royer-Collard has been called the philosopher of the Charte, and this is true in an even deeper sense than that implied by his constant references to that document. It was, in fact, the practical expression of his philosophy. The Charte and its provisions were not, as they appeared to many, wholly accidental, though their formulation undoubtedly was. They represented the essential demands of moderate people in France after the fall of the Empire; demands which could not be ignored. This is proved by the fact that the Charte was written by men who had no great sympathy with these demands, and granted by a king who would have preferred to reign, like his ancestors, solely by the grace of God, un-hampered by a constitution. The Charte established the liberties, civil and economic, won by the Revolution, with a division of power sufficient to guarantee them and at the same time it created a government strong enough to prevent disorder and revolution. Royer-Collard saw that in it lay the only hope of life for a monarchy not based on popular consent.

It cannot be said that Royer-Collard did not foresee the future, for the régime which he dreaded, namely, a popular assembly, holding in its hands unlimited power unchecked by any constitutional safeguards, is exactly like that of France today. It was against such unlimited power that he sought a barrier in legitimate monarchy, tempered by the Charte. The theocrats dreamed of using the spiritual power of the Church to discipline and teach the masses, as it had civilized the barbarians at the fall of the Roman Empire. Royer-Collard dreamed of using the royal power to safeguard the liberties of France, as it had defended them in the Middle Ages. Both dreams were swept away by the rapid growth of democracy. Commerce, industry, and the increase of free capital had displaced the economic basis of society, and revolutionized men's life, while science and a new philosophy were reshaping their ideas. They were no longer willing to be kept in tutelage or to confide their interest to an authority which they had not themselves created. Nor were the ancient institutions able to adapt themselves to new conditions. Charles X and his followers never sincerely admitted the limitation of royal authority. They did not possess the spirit of compromise which might, as Royer-Collard saw, by avoiding an open conflict, have long kept the legitimate monarchy as arbiter of the State. When the struggle came, authority was found to depend on force, and that force was with the people.

The conceptions of sovereignty of the theocrats and the revolutionists are nearer to reality than the theory of Royer-Collard. To say that justice is sovereign is merely to indicate the manner in which sovereignty must be exercised, not to determine its nature, or location. In the abstract sovereignty may be a moral principle, but in practice it must have at least an element of material power. Its exercise may normally be limited and divided, and its action modified, but in times of crisis there will be found to be in the state some will which is actually sovereign, that is, which has the power to coerce all other wills. Nevertheless, Royer-Collard's theory of the sovereignty of justice survived, and was developed by Guizot under the new régime.

The combination of legitimate monarchy and constitutional government in which Royer-Collard believed disappeared before a monarchy based on popular sovereignty, but he had pointed out the means by which it might have endured, and the only spirit in which the conflict between liberty and authority can be solved: that of reason and compromise.

CHAPTER V

THE LIBERALS: BENJAMIN CONSTANT

We have now examined the theories of the ultra-royalists, and the doctrinaires, who formed respectively the right and centre parties in the Chamber of Deputies. The left wing of the chamber was composed of the liberals. This party, weak at the beginning of the Restoration, grew in strength, both in the country and in the chamber during the latter part of that period. Its composition was mixed; the majority of its members were royalists, though some of these like Laffitte and Thiers were inclined to favor the Orléans branch of the royal family, while others like Manuel and La Fayette were avowedly republicans or Bonapartists. These men were all strongly opposed to reaction, but they were not, as the ultra-royalists pretended, revolutionary in spirit. Their ideas were those of the upper middle class, with its growing financial and industrial interests, and while their sympathies were not legitimist, their aims were certainly not democratic. They wished to establish in France a parliamentary government on the English model, which would assure them of a minimum of state intervention in the economic field, and in which they could hope to play a leading part. They were more individualistic in their views than were the doctrinaires, and they had less respect for tradition, and therefore for the dynasty.

The foremost philosopher and theorist of this party was Benjamin Constant. His position was peculiar; able and popular as he was, he never won the whole-hearted esteem of

his colleagues, and so failed to become a party leader.[1] This
was due to the faults of his personal character, which his
education and life had served to foster. He was born in 1767,
in Lausanne. His family on both sides was of old Huguenot
stock, and belonged to the country gentry of the Canton de
Vaud. His mother died at his birth, and his father was a
professional soldier in the service of Holland; therefore his
youth was spent in wanderings, and in the life of garrison
towns, and his education was directed by a series of worth-
less and unscrupulous tutors.[2] He was naturally passionate,
emotional, and weak-willed, and he never received any steady
discipline, or knew a settled home life. As a result he acquired
a love of independence and solitude, but he never learned self-
control. He was always at the mercy of women, and some
of his most serious mistakes were due to their influence.[8]
Moreover, he was an inveterate gambler, forever indebted,
and sometimes driven to expedients of doubtful delicacy.[4]
He was, in short, a discredited and somewhat disreputable
character, almost a Bohemian; the type of man most deeply
distrusted by the prudent and respectable French *bourgeoisie*.
His ideas, although they were also those of this class,
sprang from somewhat different sources. The liberalism of
men like Guizot, Thiers and Laffitte was, perhaps uncon-

[1] Dumont-Wilden, *Vie de Benjamin Constant* (Paris, 1930), p. 192.
See also Maurice Barrès, *Un Homme libre* (Paris, 1889), and Thureau
Dangin, Guizot, Sainte-Beuve, etc., *Mémoires*.

[2] Dumont-Wilden, *op. cit.,* pp. 14-17.

[8] Notably the article containing the phrase "I will never drag myself
as a miserable apostate from one power to another, covering infamy
with sophism . . ." which he published in the *Journal des débats* on
March 19, 1815, immediately before his reconciliation with Napoleon,
appears to have been due to the influence of Madame de Récamier. See
Dumont-Wilden, *op. cit.,* pp. 158-160.

[4] Dumont-Wilden, *op. cit., pp.* 175, 190, 204.

sciously, an expression of the needs of a class; it involved large aims, and the will to power. The liberalism of Benjamin Constant was the expression of a personal need of independence; it was a system of defense, not of conquest.

Constant had a mind of exceptional power and lucidity. His intellectual vision was seldom obscured by the emotional storms of his life. Moreover, he had courage, sincerity, and a moderation and generosity which are rare in political men.[5] He gave the doctrines of his party their most complete and forceful expression, and although his colleagues might distrust him, they could not dispense with his voice and pen. Though not their leader, he was their teacher and spokesman.

His adversaries reproached him with being unscrupulous because he served each régime in turn. This, however, was perfectly consistent with his ideas; he was first of all a liberal, and the form of government was not, to him, of vital importance. "I will," he wrote, "always avoid overthrowing an existing institution which is compatible with liberty."[6] He judged each succeeding régime solely with respect to the support it might afford to his liberal program, and this program never varied. In his youth he was a republican, but there is no reason to doubt that his conversion to constitutional monarchy was sincere.[7] He had witnessed the failure of sovereign assemblies, and their impotence and tyranny. "All the constitutions which have been given to France," he wrote in his *Cours de politique constitutionnelle*, published in 1818,

[5] *Ibid.*, p. 189.
[6] *Cours de politique constitutionnelle*, III, 60.
[7] De Lauris considers that Constant was always a republican at heart. The quotations which he advances to prove this, however, are without exception taken from speeches or writings of the early part of Benjamin Constant's career, before his avowed conversion to the principle of constitutional monarchy.

guaranteed individual liberty, and under these constitutions individual liberty was constantly violated. This was because a declaration, however sincere, is not sufficient. There must be active safeguards; there must be bodies strong enough to use in favor of the oppressed the means of defense which the written law affords. Our present constitution (the Charte) is the only one which has created these safeguards, and invested the intermediate bodies with sufficient power.[8]

He wrote to Béranger in 1829:

I firmly believe that France can only be free by consolidating the liberty she has on the present bases. I may be wrong, but I am convinced that we must cling to constitutional monarchy. I know, or believe I know, that old governments are more favorable to liberty than new ones.

It is evident from this that his belief in constitutional monarchy was genuine.

The chief characteristic of Benjamin Constant's thought is its intense individualism.[9] He was always ready to defend the rights of the individual, not only against the government, but against society itself. "There is," he said, "a part of human existence which is wholly beyond social control. . . . Men have rights which even the totality of the citizens cannot legitimately invade."[10] The people has no right to strike a single innocent person, and a minority may demand reparation from a majority which has injured it. "The liberty of each is necessary to all, and while there is injustice for one there is no safety for any one in the community";[11] for, he pointed out, the community consists of individuals, and

[8] *Principes de politique,* chap. xviii.

[9] Dumont-Wilden compares him to Barrès, but says that the whole experience of the nineteenth century and of parliamentary government in France lies between them. Dumont-Wilden, *op. cit.,* p. 16.

[10] *Cours de politique constitutionnelle,* pp. 178, 312.

[11] *Ibid.,* pp. 116, 225.

a nation does not exist apart from the fractions which compose it. He emphasized the need of voluntary coöperation as the basis of society. In associations each consents to sacrifice a part of his own independence in order to ensure the enjoyment of the rest, but submission must be founded on consent, not on fear, and the sacrifice must not be greater than the gain. Authority should persuade, not command. Obedience to law is a duty, but it is only relative, and the doctrine of passive submission has caused more evil than error itself. Each man is responsible for his own acts, and reflection is not only a right, but an obligation, from which no one can escape. "It is," he said, "a universal principle, that no one is bound by laws which he has not helped to make, or to which he has not agreed."[12] Political individualism can scarcely be carried further than this![13]

Benjamin Constant believed in human perfectibility, that is, in the unlimited possibilities of human development. "Liberty," he said, "rests on the principle of an indefinite evolution towards justice better understood and better applied . . . This is the only system which explains the enigma of individual existence, and gives an object to life."[14] He had great faith in the power of thought. "Ideas alone," he said, "are active; they rule the world . . . Thought creates everything."[15] He believed in the power of "enlightenment," that is, the spread of knowledge and education, to ameliorate human behaviour. In accordance with these ideas, he considered that

[12] *Ibid.,* II, 96.

[13] This idea is that of Rousseau and Proudhon. It is a principle of anarchy rather than of liberalism and most liberal thinkers reject it.

[14] *De la religion* (Paris, 1824).

[15] *Mélanges politiques,* p. 400; *Esprit de conquête,* p. 145. "Men," he said, "must not be despised for supporting errors; false or true, man's thought is his most sacred belonging." *Cours de politique,* IV, 133.

the object of society is to guarantee to men the utmost possible amount of unhampered activity.

The liberty of the individual is the object of all human association; on it rest public and private morality; on it are based the calculations of industry and commerce, and without it there is neither peace, dignity, nor happiness for men.[16]

Benjamin Constant was not content, like Chateaubriand, to advocate a vague and undefined liberty; he explained exactly what he meant by the term. The ancients, he said, confused liberty with sovereignty. What they called freedom was a direct participation in the conduct of public affairs. This conception of liberty belongs to primitive types of life, and is no longer adapted to our modern needs. By carrying over into our times an extent of social power and collective sovereignty which belonged to other centuries, Rousseau and Mably gave a pretext for many sorts of tyranny.[17] In the modern world the individual is independent in his private life, but, even in the most absolute democracies, he is sovereign only in appearance. His sovereignty is always limited, and usually "suspended"; it is only at rare intervals that he exercises it, and then only to abdicate it at once. What we understand by liberty today is "the peaceful enjoyment of private independence; the right to pursue our own ends unimpeded, so long as they do not interfere with the equal legitimate activities of others."[18] The whole object of society and of the State is to secure this freedom, and political organization is only a means of obtaining the order necessary to it. Governments must, therefore, interfere as little as possible in the affairs of men. "The interference of the state," Constant said, "is almost always bad in its re-

[16] *Cours de politique constitutionnelle,* I, 317.
[17] *Ibid.,* IV, 253.   [18] *Ibid.,* IV, 252.

sults."[19] He did not, however, wish to destroy all authority. Government is created by the needs of society, to prevent its members from injuring each other. It has its own sphere, and as long as it remains therein it can do no harm. Its function is to protect individuals against mutual offenses, and against foreign injury or aggression. In order to do this a government must possess public approval; to regard it, as Godwin does, as a necessary evil, is to discourage it in any attempts at improvement. The government must be strong, but an alert public opinion should keep watch over the State. The authoritarians, he said, are wrong in seeing in human intelligence only a cause of troublesome resistance; opinion alone is the bond between men and the basis of morality; in it both liberty and order find their source. "A people without opinion, is only a chaotic assembly of strangers or enemies."[20]

All Benjamin Constant's political theory springs from this idea that the object of the State is the protection of the individual. It gives rise, in particular, to his conception of sovereignty. He admitted that the source of authority is the general will. "The principle of the supremacy of the general will over particular wills is," he said, "incontestable."[21] It is not, however, the origin of sovereignty which seems to him important, but the fact that its nature must be limited. He pointed out that the doctrine of popular sovereignty is not in itself a principle of liberty, but only a means of preventing individuals from usurping the authority which belongs to the people as a whole. "The whole association of citizens," he said, "is sovereign in that no individual may arrogate a power which is not delegated to him, but not even the universality of citizens may dispose sovereignly of the

<hr>

[19] *Ibid.*, III, 249, 358.   [20] *Ibid.*, I, 178.   [21] *Mélanges*, p. 1.

existence of individuals.''[22] The consent of a majority does not suffice to legitimate all acts; there are some which nothing can sanction. Even the forms of law do not make injustice and immorality legitimate. "God Himself," Constant exclaimed, "should He interfere, could only sanction justice!"[23] If the sovereignty of the people is unlimited it will be a great evil, for it is the degree of power, and not its location which makes a tyranny. It is not against the holders of power, whether these be king, aristocracy, or people, but against an unlimited amount of power that men must react. Absolutism, even in the hands of society itself, is a curse; it must not merely be displaced, but destroyed. It should be recognized openly that sovereignty is always limited, for this fact will then be guaranteed by the force which supports all truth recognized by opinion.

The doctrinaires held that sovereignty must be limited by justice, and Royer-Collard often spoke of the inalienable rights of man, but he never defined them. Benjamin Constant was more precise. He pointed out that sovereignty must be limited in two ways: First in the manner of its exercise, which must be in accordance with justice. In order to ensure this, all the agencies of authority, from the highest to the lowest, must be held responsible for their acts. No superior power can impose arbitrary action upon them, nor can they justify such action by any plea of social interest. If you give the depositaries of authority the right to attack individual liberty under pretext of danger to the State, or of orders from above, you annihilate all guarantees of justice. Observa-

[22] *Ibid., Cours de politique,* I, 176.

[23] *Ibid.,* p. 188. This principle, Constant believed, is becoming more and more widely recognized. No civilized State, he says, now claims the right to execute its citizens without trial or judgment. This was probably truer in 1818 than it is in 1932.

tion of legal forms is a great protection against the tyrannical exercise of power. Both order and justice depend on rules, and cannot endure arbitrariness.

In the second place, sovereignty must be limited in the extent of its competence; individual liberties are a domain upon which it must never encroach. Constant enumerates the rights of the individual which he regards as inviolable. They are: (1) personal liberty; (2) trial by jury; (3) religious liberty; (4) industrial liberty; (5) inviolability of property; (6) liberty of the press.[24] These rights limit the authority of the State, and every government must secure them to the individual, or forfeit its claim to legitimacy.

The theoretical limitation of sovereignty, as, for instance, by declarations of the rights of man, is not sufficient. Sovereignty must, in practice, be divided, and its limitation assured by a balance and distribution of power. Unity of power, though much admired by theorists, is not desirable. "It is," he said, "a bizarre doctrine, which pretends that, because men in general are corrupt, a few must be given much power! They must, on the contrary, be given little, and wise institutions must counter-balance their weakness and vices."[25] A political organization must be found which so combines the interests of the various holders of power that their obvious advantage lies in remaining each within its respective attribution. In constitutional monarchy Constant saw the system which could best realize this ideal. "Three political powers," he said, "have hitherto been known; the executive, the legislative, and the judicial."[26] The legislative power resides in the representative assemblies; the executive in the ministry, and the judicial in the tribunals. These powers make the laws, see to their general execution and apply them in especial cases.

[24] *Ibid.,* p. 140.   [25] *Lettres sur Julie* (Published with *Adolphe*).
[26] *Cours de politique,* I, 14.

These are the three mainsprings which must coöperate in the general movement, but there should be a force to coördinate them. Constitutional monarchy creates this neutral power in the person of the king.

The doctrine of Divine Right as the origin of royal power has, Constant says, been abandoned, but a king may safely base his claim to power on his utility. Hereditary monarchy is not a preference given to one person, but an inherited supremacy, consecrated beforehand. It is not enough to declare oneself an hereditary monarch—one must inherit the throne, and hereditary monarchy only exists in the second generation. Such a monarch is a being apart, an abstract person at the summit of the social edifice. He is supported by tradition, and by the memories and affections which give it political force, and he lives in a superior sphere of security and impartiality. He has a special and permanent attribution belonging to his whole race, which separates him from all the individuals of his realm. His title is a family patrimony, not to be compromised by his ministers, or involved in the details of his administration. He stands among the other powers as a regulating authority to maintain their equilibrium, for his interest demands that no one of them should destroy the others, but that all should act together in harmony. Thus, in respect to the other powers the royal authority is, as it were, judicial; it establishes their limits. If the ministers make a mistake, the king dismisses them; if the representative bodies act to the disadvantage of the State, the king dissolves them, and he uses his right to pardon in order to temper the action of the judicial power. There has always been, Benjamin Constant pointed out, a feeling among the people that the royal power has a neutral and regulating character; the old saying "Si le Roi le savait" is an expression of this idea.

The chief difference between absolutism and constitutional

monarchy lies in the fact that in the latter the royal power does not act in place of the other powers. The executive authority emanates from the king, just as the legislative authority emanates from the people, but neither of them exercises these powers in person. If the king himself wields the executive power he ceases to be inviolable, and the question of responsibility then arises, and is insoluble. The dismissal of the responsible executive power is a difficulty in a republic, and in an absolute monarchy it can only be accomplished by a revolution. The great advantage of constitutional monarchy is that it provides a neutral power which can dismiss the executive (the ministry) without violence. The enormous advantage of a neutral position is lost, however, if the executive authority is attributed to the Crown. It is most important that these two powers should not be identified. The king's prerogative is quite distinct from the executive functions of his ministers. He proposes nothing except through them, but they are not his instruments. He appoints and dismisses them, but they act upon their own judgment and responsibility. They propose the laws in their own names, and themselves countersign all executive acts.

The king, however, has many functions.[27] The essence of the royal prerogative lies in the appointment and dismissal of ministers, but equally important is the king's power to adjourn or dissolve the legislative bodies. Liberty exists only where there are representative bodies endowed with wide powers; but these assemblies are more dangerous than the people itself, and the king must have the right to dissolve them, and refer to the opinion of the Nation.

The king decides on peace and war without prejudice to

[27] Benjamin Constant considered that Chateaubriand exaggerates the passivity of the king in a constitutional government.

the rights of his subjects, for legislative assemblies are ill-fitted to judge of the requirements of the foreign situation. In Constant's opinion only the Crown can bear the weight of such a responsibility.

The king has the right to pardon. It is sometimes said that, if a law is just, no one should be able to modify the results, but laws are general in their bearings, and the king must be able, if necessary, to soften their application in special cases.

The royal sanction is necessary for the resolutions of the respresentative bodies to become law. When the executive and legislative functions are separated, there is danger that the legislating power may not realize the inexpediency of measures which it will not itself have to apply. The authority which executes them needs some means of averting inapplicable laws. The king has this power in the right of veto, which should not be merely suspensive, but absolute.

Benjamin Constant considered that the royal power is essentially preservative. "The king," he said, "has the right to keep, as far as possible, what exists. In maintaining existing laws the royal power never exceeds its limits."[28]

Constant believed in the necessity of a constitution. It is a contract which establishes the form of government, determines the limits of the various powers, and defines the rights of individuals. It can not be suspended by any of the powers in the State, or even by all these powers united, since they themselves are created by it. It should, however, be short, and deal only with the general principles of which it is the guarantee. Constant was favorable to the Charte, which was to a large extent an expression of his ideas. "It is," he said, "our right and our safety."[29] He had not, however, the ven-

[28] *Cours de politique constitutionnelle*, I, 212.
[29] *Ibid.*, Part II, p. 10.

eration for it which was professed by the doctrinaires. To
them it was the means of retaining a connection with the
past, while to Constant it was a basis for further develop-
ments.

The legislative function should reside in two chambers. A
single chamber is dangerous, for its self-imposed checks are
easily swept away. The first chamber should be hereditary.
Constant disliked privileges; in France they had, he believed,
been the result of conquest, and so had left evil memories.
The ideas of caste, of slavery, and of feudalism are allied.
There have been four great revolutions: the first destroyed
theocratic slavery; the second, civil slavery; the third, feudalism; and the fourth, privileged nobility. These are all steps
towards natural equality, and perfectibility itself is the tendency toward such genuine equality. Nevertheless privileges,
though they are abuses, may be means of social improvement. "Gentle customs and manners," he said, "produce
delicacy of soul. These advantages are indispensable elements
of social happiness, and they must be saved and put to use."[30]
He perceived that an hereditary class was necessary to monarchy. If the principle of heredity is everywhere else rejected,
it will not long survive in the head of the state. Even in an
elective monarchy, an aristocracy is needed to support the
king. "When you elevate a man so high, unless he is to be
always sword in hand, you must surround him with men
who are impelled by self-interest to defend him." Moreover, heredity gives the force of independence to its pos-
sessors, so that, although they support the king, they will not
be merely his satellites. For these reasons, Constant admitted
the need for an hereditary peerage. This was the greatest
concession of principle which his conversion to monarchy
required.

[30] *Ibid.*, p. 151.

The second Chamber is chosen by direct election, which alone can constitute a real representative body. This, how-ever, does not imply universal suffrage. Constant considered political rights to be the guarantee of individual liberty, but, like Royer-Collard, he looked upon their exercise rather as a function than an inalienable right, such as freedom of con-science. No country, he pointed out, has ever considered as members of the State all who inhabit its territory; even in the most absolute democracies aliens and minors are not given the rights of citizens. There is, then, some principle accord-ing to which individuals living on a given territory are, or are not, admitted to active citizenship. This principle obviously consists in the possession of a certain degree of enlighten-ment, and a share in the common interest. Minors have not the enlightenment, and aliens have not the common interest. This principle must be extended; those who have no more enlightenment than children, and those whom poverty makes dependent, and who, therefore, have no more share in the common interest than foreigners, must be excluded from the conduct of public affairs. The possession of a certain amount of property, enough to ensure enlightenment and independ-ence, seemed to Constant, as to Royer-Collard, the best criterion of political capacity. "The laboring class," he says, "is often patriotic, but it does not understand the public interest."[31] All assemblies should be composed of the repre-sentatives of property owners. It is not true that the interests of all are alike; the first interest of those who own nothing is to acquire property, and they would use political rights solely to that end, to the detriment of society. Benjamin Constant's attitude is not generous. He declared, like Royer-Collard, that political rights are the guaranty of individual liberty, and he also realized, what Royer-Collard did not see,

[31] *Ibid.*, I, 139.

that the interests of property holders are not the same as those of the laboring classes. Yet he was willing to deny to the latter the means of assuring the individual rights in which he so strongly believed. Both men were, in fact, afraid of the revolutionary tendencies of the people. They preferred to entrust political power to the middle classes.[32] "The greatest benefit of the Revolution," Constant says, "was to admit the middle classes to the administration of public affairs."[33] He foresaw that they would dominate the representative assemblies.

Benjamin Constant was vague as to the exact meaning of the responsibility of ministers, on which he so often insisted. Like the Doctrinaires, he was loath to admit the parliamentary system as we know it today. The king has the right of dissolution and veto, and he also names and dismisses the ministers. "The essence of the royal prerogative," Constant said, "lies in the independent right to the nomination of ministers."[34] Nevertheless, he held that the legislative function belongs to the representative bodies; they share in the initiation of the laws, and have the right to amend or reject them, and to refuse the budget. He admitted also that, if the ministers are in disagreement with the king, public opinion is to judge between them. But he did not follow this admission to its ultimate implication in actual practice, namely, the responsibility of ministers to the majority of the chamber.

With regard to the relations of Church and State, Constant's ideas were largely conditioned by his Protestantism

[32] Dumont-Wilden says that in regard to the suffrage, the liberals were caught between their principles and their conservative instincts.

[33] *Mélanges politiques,* p. 416.

[34] *Cours de politique constitutionnelle,* II, 93.

and liberalism. Religious liberty he considered as an inviolable right. A majority has no rights whatever over a minority in matters of conscience, and there must be complete tolerance for all cults. It is false to allege that religion is useful only to the people; it has its source in the hearts of men, and all alike need both its consolations and its restraints. To consider it merely as a useful instrument for authority is to injure it, for such ideas detach the masses from their faith. The people will not long believe what their leaders do not accept. Theocracy is dangerous, for, if there is union between the priesthood and the civil power, religion becomes a tool of government, and political doctrines are inscribed among religious dogmas. Nevertheless, the State should actively support religion. Constant carried these ideas to conclusions which are unusual even for a Protestant living in a Catholic country. He declared that the State should endow equally every cult both old and new, and should leave them all entirely independent, seeking neither to direct them, nor to protect them from examination. Religions are like public highways; the State must keep them up, but each man must be free to choose his own path.

Much of Benjamin Constant's thought can be traced to his early environment. It must be remembered that he was Protestant and Swiss. Protestantism in its pristine purity was an expression of individualism, and despite its subsequent evolution along authoritarian lines, it remains true that it engenders an individualistic temper. The value thus attributed to the personal attitude in the spiritual domain tends to develop a sense of the value of independent thought and opinion in general. Protestantism, like liberalism, is well adapted to the needs of people who wish to better themselves, morally or materially, by their own efforts. Benjamin Constant's desire that men should be free to work out their own destinies without interference or regulation is the counterpart in the political and economic field of Protestantism in the spiritual field.

The Swiss society to which Constant belonged, was an aristocratic *bourgeoisie*. Both Berne and Geneva were ruled by a few families, whose remarkable energy and ability had created their power and wealth, and the independence of their State. Benjamin Constant's birthplace, the Canton de Vaud, was long under the domination of Berne, but, though its patrician families hated this tyranny, they shared the austerely aristocratic point of view of the Bernese oligarchy. Constant early emancipated himself from the puritanism of Swiss society, but he retained a certain Swiss simplicity, and something of the independent pride of that middle-class aristocracy, which had always owed its own position to itself, and never to the favors of a king.

Sainte-Beuve declares that Constant was more French than any other Swiss. It is true that he had an amiable cynicism and an intellectual lucidity, which are often found in Frenchmen, but it was to the France of the eighteenth century, not to that of earlier or later periods, that his spirit was akin. Like the men of the eighteenth century, he believed in "perfectibility"[35] and enlightenment, and, like them, he was cosmopolitan in outlook, and tolerant of all ideas. These qualities are not characteristically French.

Constant was a great liberal. All that is best and most interesting in that philosophy (its deep respect for personality; its belief that society exists for the development and happiness of the individual; its generous faith in human possibili-

---

[35] Compare Turgot *Les Progrès successifs du genre humain;* also the writings of Talleyrand and Godwin.

ties; and its love alike of order and of liberty) are to be found in his writings. He possessed to a high degree the moderation and respect for the opinions of others which are part of a truly liberal spirit. He formulated and defended all the rights on which individual liberty depends. The only one which he has been accused of omitting is that of association, and it is doubtful whether this right is really conducive to liberty, although it has certainly served to promote the welfare of the laboring classes. It may be that Constant attached too much importance to intelligence. Men are apt to use as social criteria the qualities in which they are themselves superior. Intellect, however, though not the best, is perhaps the only precise standard of human value that can be found.

His belief in perfectibility savors of the eighteenth century, but it is naïve in expression rather than in content. A belief in unlimited possibilities of social and moral improvement has saved Western thought from falling into the slough of Oriental fatalism. It is a doctrine too useful to be abandoned, and modern psychology may throw new lights upon the subject.

The reproach which can most justly be made against Constant as a defender of liberty is that, although he saw the growing importance of industry and looked on it with approval, he did not at all foresee the evil results of liberalism in the economic field; results which have necessitated an increasing intervention of the State on the behalf of the weak against the strong.

Constant's political ideas are interesting and original. He saw that liberalism and constitutional monarchy are a natural combination. Liberalism is the creed of those who have faith in their own powers, and want freedom to develop them. It is essentially aristocratic, and its emphasis is on values.

Disorder and the rule of the masses are as unfavorable to it as is a rigid hierarchy. Constitutional monarchy is a system of compromise and equilibrium, and hence the form of government which most favors liberalism.

Constant's conception of the position of the king is important. His great originality lies in distinguishing between the executive and the royal power. The French king, according to his theory, had much the same prerogatives that belong to the king of England, but Constant conceived of him as using them much more actively than does the latter today. He did not foresee the increase of power which was to fall to the parliamentary majority. It is interesting to note the gap left by the empty place of the king in the French constitutional laws of 1875. The president of the Republic was given a large part of the regulating powers which Constant attributed to the Crown, but he has not succeeded in using them all, and it is possibly due, in part, to this lack of a neutral authority, strong enough to survive a crisis, that the French Chamber of Deputies has acquired so large a share of power; Benjamin foresaw the danger of such a situation, and this was one of his reasons for defending the monarchy. Constitutional monarchy, as he described it, became the ideal of the French liberal royalists during the nineteenth century.

CHAPTER VI

THEORY OF THE JULY MONARCHY: GUIZOT

During the Restoration the idea of absolutism and that of constitutional monarchy were opposed to each other, and their differences were therefore very evident. As we have seen, the fundamental point on which the "ultras" and the liberals disagreed was the nature of sovereignty. The former wished to preserve the unity and absolutism of royal power, while the latter demanded that sovereignty should be limited and divided. Apart from this great difference in doctrine questions of interest and sympathy separated the two parties, but in spite of their divergencies, they had many ideas in common. The theorists of both parties based their system upon religion. Even Benjamin Constant, whose personal creed was entirely unorthodox, believed that religion is the sole basis of morality and order. Authoritarians and liberals alike were opposed to democracy and equality, and preferred civil to political liberty. Both were devoted to the principle of order. In spite of these resemblances, however, and of a common dread of revolution, the royalists did not succeed, during the course of the nineteenth century, in burying their differences and forming a united conservative party. Dynastic rivalry and the personal hatreds which resulted from the events of 1830 were probably as largely responsible for this as were differences in doctrine.

The Revolution of 1830 was not a great popular movement; it was the answer of the *bourgeoisie* to the decision of Charles X to do away with the Charte, and rule by ordinances. The Liberals were determined to resist such a return to absolutism, and moderate men had been discouraged by the reactionary policy of the King. The parliamentary leaders did not, for the most part, actually intend the overthrow of the dynasty; they rather allowed events to take their course than actually promoted them, and the sight of revolution in the streets of Paris soon alarmed even those who had provoked it. In order to secure a stable government, the Liberals hastened to install Louis-Philippe, first as lieutenant-general of the realm, and then as king. Some of them later regretted that, on the abdication of Charles X, they had not proclaimed the Duc de Bordeaux king, under the regency of Louis-Philippe.[1] This might have averted the separation of the royalists into Legitimists and Orleanists, a division which was fatal to their cause in later years. It was, however, only with difficulty that the proclamation of a republic had been averted, and a regency would probably have been too weak to resist the revolutionary impulse.

With Louis-Philippe the Liberals came to power and the rule of the middle classes began. The new king himself perfectly understood the needs of the *bourgeoisie*. He wrote in his youth:

I believe that absolute democracy drives away wealth, because of the jealousy which it inspires, and the lack of effective protection. Democracy tends to the leveling of fortunes, and this tendency is both a check upon the industry which procures wealth, and a cause of disquiet to those who, having already acquired it, wish to keep it. Only a blind respect for law can attract wealth and allow it to show itself and grow without fear. I doubt whether this blind respect can endure in a democracy.[2]

The practical and utilitarian conception of society here ex-

[1] Guizot, *Histoire de trois générations* (Paris, 1863), pp. XCVIII-CX. See also Denys Cochin, *op. cit.,* on the refusal of Charles X and the Duchess de Berry to allow the Duc de Bordeaux to remain in France.

[2] Denys Cochin, *op. cit.,* p. 103.

pressed, is the keynote of the régime. Nevertheless, the principle of popular sovereignty was recognized, and the liberals amended the Charte in order to conform to it. The constitution was no longer bestowed *(octroyée)*, but was recognized as a pact between the king and the nation. The king's right to make the ordinances was limited to purely administrative measures in accordance with the law.[3]

Of this new régime one of the most typical and influential leaders was François Guizot, and his political theory, which was drawn in large part from the ideas of Royer-Collard, furnished it with a philosophic basis. He was a man of remarkable intellectual and physical vigor. He was born in 1787 of a modest *bourgeois* family, and he owed his great career entirely to his own energy and talent. He was a Protestant, and received his early education in Geneva. The influence of that austere *milieu* is evident in his character and his thought. Although his father was guillotined, he always felt that he owed much to the Revolution. "I am of those," he said in his *Mémoires,* "whom the movement of 1789 elevated, and who will not consent to sink."[4] He was proud, extremely ambitious, and well aware of his own powers. Entirely indifferent to popularity, he appeared cold and arrogant, except to his intimates.[5] He believed heartily in religion and morality, yet under an appearance of stern rectitude, his intense ambition and self-confidence sometimes made him unscrupulous.[6] He was a statesman as well as a writer, and

[3] See Dugit & Monnier, *Les Constitutions et les principales lois politiques de la France* (Evreux, 1925), for the changes in the Charte.

[4] *Mémoires pour servir à l'histoire de mon temps* (Paris, 1858), I, 27.

[5] Barante, *Souvenirs,* II, 375. See also Charles Pouthas, *Guizot sous le Restauration* (Paris, 1923), pp. 26-28, 162-66.

[6] Ernest L. Woodward, *Three Studies on European Conservatism* (London, 1929), pp. 198-99. Royer-Collard is said to have called him an "austere intriguer."

he admitted that he preferred action to thought.[7] His political theory was largely composed in the early part of his career, and after his retirement from political life he turned his attention to history rather than to philosophy.

Soon after his arrival in Paris, he joined the small group of doctrinaires who gathered around Royer-Collard, and during the "hundred days" he was delegated by them to bear their advice and warnings to Louis XVIII at Ghent.[8] He held office under Pasquier and Decazes, but when de Serres broke with the doctrinaires in 1819 he went into the opposition and there remained until the fall of Charles X.[9] At the advent of Louis-Philippe, he did not, like Royer-Collard, hold aloof from the new régime, but accepted office, and became one of its chief political leaders. From 1840 to 1848 he was virtually the head of the government.

Guizot was proud of his *bourgeois* origin, and he was devoted to the aims and interests of the middle classes. "I believe with all my heart," he said in 1837, "in the preponderance of the middle classes."[10] Even in an article published in 1855, he repeated that "although alone they do not suffice for government, the middle classes are right to claim a definitely predominant influence in the government of France."[11] His political doctrines are a justification of this point of view. Like Royer-Collard, he wished to avoid both absolutism and popular sovereignty, and to create a philosophical basis for the policy of the *juste milieu,* which was his political creed.

The point of departure of his beliefs is not unlike that of the theocrats. Men, he believed, are subject to the laws of

[7] Woodward, *op. cit.,* p. 165.

[8] Charles Pouthas, *op. cit.,* chap. iii.

[9] *Ibid.,* chap. viii. Barante, *op. cit.*

[10] Speech of May 3, 1837.

[11] "Nos mécomptes et nos espérances," *Revue contemporaine* (Paris, 1855), p. 12.

God which are absolute truth, reason and justice. The object of human life is not happiness, but the recognition and fulfil-ment of these divine laws. Guizot, however, unlike Bonald and Maistre, was an individualist. He believed that no au-thority, not even that of the Church, can give men knowledge of these laws. They must be discovered by means of reason. Reason is not a good in itself to Guizot, as it was to Kant; it is merely the instrument by which men can attain, at least in part, to truth and justice.

Although he did not, like Constant, share the ready belief in perfectibility of the eighteenth century, Guizot was not wholly pessimistic as to human nature. He considered that there is both good and evil in man. The world is ruled by moral laws, but, as men are imperfect, and can never attain the absolute, to find and follow these laws requires ceaseless effort. The slow process of time tends to ameliorate society, but there can be no immutable rules, only a constant develop-ment, an unending search for greater justice and greater truth. This idea, which had already been suggested by Ben-jamin Constant, is perhaps the truest and most valuable part of Guizot's philosophy. Unfortunately, he did not always apply this principle of development to the facts with which he had to deal.

Society, for Guizot, is a moral, not a material fact; it be-gins at the moment when men feel and recognize a bond of union among them which is not force.[12] Force may bring people together in various relationships, such as that of mas-ter and slave, but society no more exists in such cases than it does between a man and the animal he hunts. Society, since it is the recognition of a common rule, implies the existence

---

[12] *Philosophie politique,* chap. ii. *Histoire des origines du gouverne-ment représentatif et des institutions politiques de l'Europe* (Paris, 1855), p. 87, 136-39.

of a power to enforce that rule. This power is government, and it and society are born together, and cannot legitimately be separated, even in thought, for their object is the same, that is, to satisfy men's need to discover the true law which must govern their relationships.[13]

In primitive times force ruled; men were near each other, rather than united, and the weak were outside of society. Sovereignty was then nowhere, or rather, each man possessed it in his own sphere. It is this absence of concentrated sovereignty which has made Rousseau and others think that primitive life was free and happy. As a matter of fact, Guizot said, that condition is the negation of reason and justice. When there is no acting sovereign, that is to say, no government, brute force will triumph. This gradually brings about the government of the strong.[14]

Government and sovereignty are not identical. Like Royer-Collard, Guizot conceived sovereignty as the right to power, not power itself. He defined it as "the absolute and inherent right to make the law"[15]—its characteristics are unity and infallibility. The great object of his political theory was to withhold this right both from the king and from the people. It is the divine and immutable laws of reason, truth and justice which are sovereign. They alone are infallible, and by their mere existence compel obedience. "We do not admit reason," he said, "we recognize it."[16] There can, therefore, be no true sovereignty in the world; earthly authority merely represents the laws of God, which are alone legitimately sovereign.

[13] This idea resembles that of Bonald who said that no society exists which is not "constituted," i.e., which has no government.

[14] *Philosophie politique,* chap. i.

[15] *Origines du gouvernement représentatif,* p. 88.

[16] *Ibid.,* pp. 91, 142.

This important truth has not always been recognized. Men are forever seeking God and so they are prone to idolatry. They tend to identify their rulers with the divine law which they represent, and so to invest them with its inalienable rights. Little by little, however, experience has led men to doubt the infallibility of rulers, and so has taught them to distinguish between sovereignty and government.

Guizot was well aware of the advantages of a strong government. "It is absolutely necessary," he says, "that there shall always be a power which judges and is obeyed . . . Resistance and the search for Truth must somewhere have a limit in the will of a master."[17] Governments, he says, should not be classified according to their outward forms, such as monarchy, the government of one, and democracy, the government of all; this is superficial. The true division, according to the fundamental natures of governments, lies between those which claim to possess an inalienable sovereignty that does not exist on earth, thus setting up a tyranny, and those which admit the constant need of proving their legitimacy. Moral legitimacy is conformity to reason and justice, and political legitimacy is the presumption of this. Such a presumption cannot be for ever mobile; it must have some stability, and it establishes itself in favor of institutions, if they correspond to the needs of the nation, and if time has sanctioned them. A good government is one which, although possessing the

[17] *De la démocratie,* p. 23. Guizot devoted chap. xiv of his "Philosophie politique" (unpublished manuscript, Val-Richer No. 11) to the question of the right of resistance. On this subject, his mind was evidently divided between a sense of the need of authority and the logic of his ideas. He admitted the existence of such a right, based on the fact that governments may cease to act in accord with justice, and so become illegitimate, but he insists that it must only be exercised with precaution. Revolutions usually set up tyrannies worse than those they overthrow.

presumption of legitimacy, does not claim an inalienable sovereignty, but is always ready to prove its conformity to reason and justice.

In order to secure these conditions, the exercise of power must be divided. Whenever one element in the State, either king, aristocracy, or people, has in fact possessed the supreme power, not only has it abused that power, but it has claimed to hold it by inalienable right. The exercise of sovereignty must, therefore, be compound, and the powers which share it must feel their mutual dependency. These powers may have various origins; their number and character differ in various countries. In France they are four: the king, the two chambers, and the electoral body. No one of these possesses the sovereignty, but their decisions, reached by mutual agreement after careful search, are presumably in accord with the laws of truth and justice, and therefore society owes them obedience.

These powers are mobile, and if they do not agree, sovereignty will not exist. But society requires a law which obliges individual wills, and a power continuously present to enforce respect for this law. Here, then, is a dilemma. Society has needs which appear to be contradictory; on the one hand it requires that power should be permanent, and on the other that, in its search for the true law, it should be liable to changes and suspensions of its authority. If the existence and the activities of power are united in the same person or body, this problem is insoluble; either the acts of power will be independent and so tyrannical, or its existence will share the risks of its activity, and so be uncertain. The existence and the activity of power must be separated, and constitutional monarchy alone could accomplish this. Heredity assures the permanent and continual existence of authority, and the representative system allows it all liberty to submit its action to whatever trials and conditions will best guarantee conformity to reason and justice.

The part played by the moral nature of man in the formation of monarchy is much greater, Guizot said, than is usually supposed. Monarchy springs from the natural human impulse to personify the Supreme Being in an earthly ruler. The king's power, like that of God, is unique, absolute, permanent, and sublime. The monarch himself is like the images offered by religion to worshipers, a present and visible object of love and reverence. If sovereignty existed on earth, Guizot says, it would belong to the monarch, for unity and permanence are its characteristics,[18] but there is no true sovereignty on earth, therefore the king cannot possess it, and royal power is only legitimately sovereign if it accords with reason and justice, otherwise it is a mere usurpation and tyranny.

Democracy springs from the equally natural human impulse to resist tyranny and the oppression of an alien will. It is based on two principles: first that of personal sovereignty, that is to say, the right of each individual to determine his own actions; and second that of the sovereignty of the people, that is to say, the domination of a numerical majority. The first principle is in itself false, for men are not their own masters, free to make each his own law; all are subject to the superior laws of reason, truth and justice, which are not man-made. The logical conclusion of this principle of personal sovereignty would be that no man need obey laws to which he has not consented. This is absurd, for in regard to every law there will be a minority which must either be coerced or expelled from society. Since the persons who constitute this minority change with every measure.

[18] "Philosophie politique," chap. ix.

there·would in the latter case soon be no society left. As to the second principle, a numerical majority could only pretend to possess sovereignty as an absolute right if its measures were invariably in accordance with truth and justice. This is very far from being the case; democratic majorities are at least as liable to error as kings or aristocracies. They can, therefore, have no claim to an inalienable sovereignty.

It might be supposed that the constitutional monarch, according to Guizot's theory, would be purely passive. Such however is not the case. Guizot did not, like Benjamin Constant, wish to dissociate the royal from the executive power. "The Crown," he said, "is the executive power, the power that is always in being."[19] In a speech of 1846 he declared that the throne is not merely an empty chair; it is occupied by an active being with will and ideas of his own. It is the duty of the king to govern in accordance with the other great powers in the State. It is the duty of the ministers to win his support for the policy which is approved by the chambers. This is the essence of parliamentary government.[20]

The object of monarchy is a strong government. Society always needs this, and so much so, at times, that all other needs must be subordinated to this one. Permanence and unity are the features of monarchy which give it such strength. Of these, permanence is the more necessary, for men will only devote themselves to what appears lasting. Permanence, too, gives an especial legitimacy, for to have endured for several centuries is a genuine proof of value for political institutions, since it shows that they have been tested and approved by time.

The heredity of the throne is the special form which le-

[19] *Histoire parlementaire,* III, 683.
[20] *Ibid.,* V, 227; and his *Mémoires,* VIII, 84.

gitimacy takes as a rule under monarchy. There is then a double legitimacy implied: first that of monarchy as an institution, and second that of the family which occupies the throne. The first expresses the fitness of a system of government, the second gives a special legitimacy to a series of passing creatures, and decrees not only what is, but what will be. This detracts from the very principle of legitimacy, which is to belong only to what has been tried, and proved just. Thus the second legitimacy, that of a family, is more fragile than the first. The monarchical system may remain legitimate when the royal family has ceased to be so. Such has been the case in Scotland, in Portugal, in England. Heredity, too, as a principle, has usually been approved, even when its beneficiaries were not, for it introduces a further guaranty of stability for monarchy. It is easy to see that Guizot is here trying to justify the exclusion of the elder branch of the Bourbons, and to keep for Louis-Philippe the fullest possible title to legitimacy.

Like Royer-Collard and Benjamin Constant, Guizot believed in civil, but not in political, or economic, equality. He thought that to speak of equality in connection with political rights was to confuse individual and social existence, the civil and the political orders. According to his theory those men should govern who are best fitted to discover the laws of truth and justice. There is, he admitted, some recognition of this principle in the idea of aristocracy. In practice, however, aristocracies have been the result of conquest, and have meant the hereditary rule of a few, who claimed sovereignty by right of birth. This is not in accord with the sovereignty of reason and justice. Guizot was not, however, unfavorable to the idea of an hereditary peerage, which fitted in with his conception of a state composed of various powers, working together to exercise authority. There should be a "political class," devoted by birth and education to public affairs, but open to ability, and constantly recruited from the whole body of the nation. Since heredity is one of the fundamental principles of life, recognized in the inheritance of property, it may justly find expression in a chamber of peers.

Capacity is the power to act acording to reason. There is in every nation a certain amount of this capacity distributed among individuals, and all combinations of the political machine must tend to extract it, and to apply it to the business of government. The object of the suffrage is to select such capacity and make use of it in the search for truth and justice. Capacity, Guizot said, is the sole principle of the franchise, and it alone confers the right to vote. "Election is a trial imposed on those who aspire to political power, and a sovereign, but limited right for those who confer political power on this or that aspirant."[21]

Men have rights of two kinds. The first are permanent and common to all; they may be summed up in the right to obey only just laws. The second are variable and belong only to capacity; they consist in the right to judge of the justice of the laws. The franchise is the expression of the latter type of rights and it must be restricted to the sphere where capacity exists. This sphere may be wide or narrow, it varies ceaselessly, and the franchise must not be arbitrarily fixed, but must vary with it.

It is interesting to note that, in spite of this declaration, Guizot, as minister, obstinately refused to widen the suffrage. He believed that capacity was limited in France to the middle classes, and therefore he was satisfied with a high property qualification for the franchise. This was perhaps his most

[21] *Origines du gouvernement représentatif,* p. 96.

serious mistake as a statesman. It was the result of his economic and social ideas, which were both superficial and rigid. He divided society into three classes: those who live on income, and who have leisure to acquire knowledge; those who exploit capital by their labor, and whose work obliges them to have general ideas; and those who live solely by their own labor, and whose work prevents them from having other than personal interests. Only those in the first two categories, he considered, can have political capacity. This would exclude all intellectuals, professional men, and functionaries, from political rights! Yet, narrow as this arbitrary classification is, it must be remembered that there is probably no country in the world where the ownership of property comes so near to being a gage of capacity and social value as it does in France, for the first object of every Frenchman, whatever his position, is to acquire property of some kind, and so join the great class of *rentiers* (those who possess an income).

Guizot saw in the growing demand for political democracy only the restless spirit of revolution, which he knew to be unfavorable to liberty, as well as to government. The promises of socialism seemed to him vain delusions. The time will never come, he said, when all men will share in social well-being and in political power.

As a Protestant in a Catholic country Guizot naturally believed in tolerance for all creeds, but he saw that religion is the ally of government, since it teaches love of order and respect for authority. Governments should, therefore, support it. At the accession of Louis-Philippe, Catholicism had ceased to be the official religion, but the Concordat was maintained, and Guizot demanded the financial aid of the State for the education of the clergy.

Guizot was not primarily a philosopher; he did not so much

believe in a political system because it corresponded to his theories, as seek a theory to justify the conditions in which he believed. The July monarchy was nominally based on the theory of popular sovereignty, which was recognized by the amended Charte, but it was, in reality, the government of a few. Guizot's philosophy was an attempt to modify the doctrine of popular sovereignty in such a way as to reconcile it with this fact, and so to justify the triumph of the middle classes.

His political doctrine is a summary of the principal ideas of liberalism: the abolition of absolute sovereignty; the balance of power among the various organs of the State; the rights of capacity. The weakness of his position, and of French liberalism in the nineteenth century, is indifference to social and economic problems. The essence of liberalism lies in the doctrine of the rights of capacity, and Guizot sought by his theory of the sovereignty of reason as interpreter of the moral law, to furnish this doctrine with a metaphysical basis. It is true that the rule of a numerical majority gives no guaranty whatever of wisdom in the conduct of affairs. Superiority, understood in a sense broad enough to include moral and social values, may conceivably have a claim to govern. The error of Guizot's doctrine lies in the fact that the capacity to reason is not identical with the sense of social responsibility. Royer-Collard had urged the representation of *interests,* and on that basis labor might eventually have been given a share in the direction of the State. According to Guizot's more rigid theory, poverty and labor can never be represented, the defense of their interests is necessarily entrusted to their superiors in the social and economic scale, and, in an individualistic society, there is no certainty that these superiors will consider any interests but their own.

This was, in fact, the fatal defect of the July monarchy. The men who governed France during the eighteen years of Louis-Philippe's reign were able, and, in many cases, high-minded, but they were blind to the economic and social evils caused by the industrial revolution. They thought, as did Guizot, that the spread of education and the maintenance of business prosperity were all that could be expected of the government. The régime they instituted was the supremacy of a class. It was too materialistic and too ungenerous in its aims to find wide support.[22] Guizot was undoubtedly a royalist, but the emphasis in his system is on the powers which represent the reason of the nation, and in his system the place of the king is small. Sovereignty as a right has disappeared, and its exercise belongs to those who are constantly ready to justify their claim. To say that the king retains a permanent authority is inconsistent. What is the source of that authority? It is neither divine right, nor the will of the people. The king, whatever his actual part in the functioning of government, has, in fact, become a mere convenience.

This conception of monarchy is reasonable, but, as Chateaubriand saw, the king, in France, must appeal to the imagination and feelings of his subjects. Guizot, both as statesman and theorist, had an excessive faith in reason. He forgot that opinions and actions have sources deeper and more compelling that thought. He was not willing to enlarge the franchise, and so endeavour to make the July monarchy a true expression of the will of the people, and utility was too narrow a basis for a throne which had neither tradition nor glory to support it. It could not survive the mistakes of its founders.

[22] Guizot's answer to the demands for a wider suffrage is said to have been: "Enrichissez-vous."

CHAPTER VII

LIBERAL MONARCHISTS AFTER GUIZOT

There was a marked decline of interest in political theory after 1830. Among the royalists of that period no men can be found who embodied in their writings, as did those of the Restoration, the entire philosophy of a group. The overthrow of the legitimate monarchy brought a change in the political atmosphere of France. The elements of the old prerevolutionary society, which had still played a part during the Restoration, were pushed into the background, and men of a new type took their place. These men were more practical both in their point of view and their aims than their predecessors had been, and, in consequence, they were more interested in political life itself than in its underlying philosophy. The chief reason, however, for this decline of political theory was probably that the development of the industrial revolution during the July monarchy and Second Empire brought economic and social problems into the foreground, and the deepest and most original thinkers of the day were occupied with these matters, rather than with questions of government.

A poverty of political theory is particularly evident among the liberal royalists. This was, no doubt, in part because their doctrines had been very fully developed by the men of the earlier period. After Benjamin Constant and Guizot little remained to be said either as to the philosophic basis or the political forms of liberal monarchy. Nevertheless, it is a significant fact that the liberal royalists did not, like the authoritarians, find a new point of departure for the development of their ideas.

The three principal currents of political thought of the nineteenth century—the beginnings of socialism, the expansion of democracy, and the growth of nationalism—were all unfavorable to the doctrine of the liberal monarchy. For this doctrine, as it was understood in France during that period, postulates the inherent claims of social superiority to political leadership and the acceptance of private property. Now the Revolution had already denied all claims of the *élite* to govern unless sanctioned by a popular mandate, and demanded political and civil equality; while the new schools of thought, such as the utopian socialism of Saint-Simon and Fourrier and the philosophical anarchism of Proudhon, taking their cue from Rousseau and carrying the civil and political equalitarianism of the Revolution into the economic field, denied the legitimacy of private property. Furthermore, liberalism is, by definition, inimical to the State, and tends to be cosmopolitan and pacifist; while nationalism exalts the State and is self-righteously exclusive and militant. Thus it was republicanism, socialism, democracy, and nationalism, doctrines more or less implicit in the great Revolution, whose nineteenth-century reincarnations the liberal monarchists undertook to combat, using the experience afforded by recent events to reinforce their arguments.

The liberal monarchists as a party were strong, for they represented the interests of a powerful and influential class. Their position was a compromise between reaction and revolution, and therefore it appealed to those who feared both extremes; that is, to many of the most reasonable people in France. Their doctrines, however, suffered from the very compromise which made their position as a party so strong; they were too subtle for the average man. Moreover, they had no emotional appeal. The legitimists could call on tradition and religious enthusiasm to touch men's hearts; the republicans could invoke the rights of man to arouse the self-interest of the masses; but the doctrines of the sovereignty of reason, and the rights of superiorities, however well founded, left men cold.

French political life tends to create small groups; "chapels" as they are familiarly called, which cherish particular shades of opinion. The influence of such groups may be considerable, for it must be remembered that in France no two great parties have ever divided the political field. The theory of liberal monarchy always tended to be the creed of such a coterie. It was developed during the Restoration by the Doctrinaires—Royer-Collard, Barante, Guizot, Broglie, Rémusat. During the July Monarchy it was to some extent the official doctrine of the governing class, but after the fall of Louis-Philippe it became once more the philosophy of a few. The effort of the liberal monarchists was to discredit the idea of a republic, using the experience afforded by events to point their arguments. Those whose writings were most important in this respect at various periods were: Barante, the two Broglies, d'Haussonville, and Denys Cochin.

Among the liberal monarchists must also be included Alexis de Tocqueville, although his ideas differed in several respects from those of the other royalists, and he therefore stands rather apart. He was a grandson of Malesherbes, and his father was a prefect of the Restoration. He himself was successively a magistrate, a deputy, and minister during the second Republic. He was a man of originality, and the ten volumes of his published works contain a genuine contribution to political thought. It is, however, as the critic of democracy that he is best known, and although he was undoubtedly a royalist, he paid little attention to the theory of monarchy.

Prosper Amable de Barante was one of the group of the Doctrinaires. He is better known as an historian than as a political theorist, but he published in 1849 an able little book called *Questions constitutionnelles,* in which he exposed the philosophy of the Doctrinaires, and which also dealt with some of the points chiefly insisted on by the later Liberals. The book was written under the influence of the events of 1848, and the shadow of the coming Empire.

The Broglies are a great aristocratic liberal family of a type frequent in England, but rare in France. The Dukes Victor de Broglie (1785-1870) and his son Albert (1821-1901) both played a prominent part in the history of liberal monarchy in France. Claude-Victor de Broglie, their ancestor, was among the representatives of the nobility at the States General of 1789, and was guillotined by the Jacobins. When dying he charged his son to be faithful to the republic, ungrateful and unjust as it was. Victor de Broglie served the Empire, and, like Barante, was a doctrinaire during the Restoration. He was a close friend of Guizot, and he cemented his alliance with liberalism by marrying Albertine, the beautiful and accomplished daughter of Madame de Staël.[1] He was Prime Minister for a brief period under Louis-Philippe. His chief contribution to political theory is a book, remarkable for its penetration and clarity, called *Vues sur le gouvernement de la France.* It was published privately in 1861, and was seized by the censor, but it was republished in 1871. The Duke Albert de Broglie, his son, was more active as a statesman, but his purely theoretical writings are inconsiderable and are scattered through a series of books and articles on politics, history and religion.

[1] With regard to Albertine de Staël see Dumont-Wilden, *Vie de Benjamin Constant.*

The Haussonville family are allied by marriage to the Broglies. During the Second Empire the Count Joseph Bernard d'Haussonville (1809-1884) collaborated in a series of anonymous pamphlets (published in book form to avoid the censorship of periodicals) called *Varia* which expounded the doctrines of liberalism, but which did not have a definite monarchical impress. His son, Count Gabriel Paul Othenin (1843-1924) was for many years the representative of the Comte de Paris in France. He revived the name of *Varia* as the title of one of his principal works (1902).

The Cochins were, like the Broglies, an old family with a long tradition of liberalism, and of service to the State. Denys Cochin was deputy for Paris for many years, and he was noted for his eloquence. He was a faithful defender of liberal royalism in France, and was in close touch with the Orléans princes, whose ideas and interests he represented in the Chamber.

The liberal royalists acknowledged, in general, the sovereignty of the people; they resisted, however, the republican and equalitarian conclusions which may be drawn from this doctrine. Three principal ideas, all tending to modify the application of popular sovereignty, can be traced in their writings. The first is decentralization, the second is the creation of an upper chamber, different in its origin and character from that issuing from universal suffrage, and the third is the superiority of a king over a president as head of the State.

Decentralization has always been a part of the program of the French royalists, both liberal and authoritarian, although it must be admitted that no party, when in power, has made a serious effort to carry it into effect. Decentralization was demanded by the "ultras" during the Restoration because they believed that the local influence still exercised by the country nobility would act in their favor,[2] and the idea has been further developed by later legitimist writers. Theoretically, however, decentralization is allied in several respects to liberalism. In the first place, the political activity of small local groups is usually believed to favor the *élite* and to give freer play to personal superiority than it can have in a wider field. In the next place, the independence of local authorities lessens the power of the central administration, and tends to temper the omnipotence of the unitary State without resorting to federalism. Royer-Collard and Benjamin Constant advocated it, because of their dread of the administrative machine which the monarchy had inherited from the Empire.[3] The later liberals also strongly insisted on it, for they saw that in France the excessive power of the unitary State made democracy peculiarly dangerous.

De Barante pointed out that it was the alliance of the king with the communes which had broken the power of feudalism in France, and suggested that this alliance might profitably be renewed.[4] Experience showed, he said, that the elections which gave the best results were those of local magistrates.[5] "It is through their local interest, the 'esprit de clocher,' that men feel both patriotism and responsibility most keenly."[6] In these feelings are to be found the best barriers against despotism. In order to develop the sense of responsibility in the communes, the central power should subject its minor agents to the control of the local authorities.[7]

According to Victor de Broglie, the history of France for

[2] See A. Rousseau *L'Idée de décentralisation et les partis politiques sous la Restauration* (Vannes, n.d.).

[3] Above, p. 57.

[4] Barante, *Questions constitutionnelles,* pp. 77-80.

[5] *Ibid.,* p. 30.

[6] *Ibid.,* p. 31.

[7] Barante, *Des communes et de l'aristocratie* (Paris, 1821).

centuries has been the gradual suppression of all local independence. He recognized that the communes need support when they are poor and backward. No great nation, in his opinion, could be composed merely of a union of small groups under a federal régime. Only neutral countries, like Switzerland, can subsist under such a form of government.[8] But France tends to be the slave of her capital, and in order to avoid this the communes should be given a greater share in the responsibility of government. Only the exercise of authority teaches men to respect it, and it is participation in public affairs both great and small which trains public men. Therefore, though the execution of general laws must be left to the agents of the central power, local affairs should, as far as possible, be self-directed. He suggested also that, in order to revive the old feeling of local pride, the army should be organized on a territorial basis. The names of the old French provinces could be given to military units which should each be recruited in the lands which once formed these provinces. The same plan could be followed with regard to the universities, which might thus benefit by a revival of local pride and vigor.[9]

Albert de Broglie saw that the lack of civic education in liberty and responsibility is a great evil in France. "Public employment," he acutely noted, "not local responsibility, has formed the political spirit of France. Political men still seem to be 'les gens du roi.' "[10] The communes once possessed liberties, but the kings took advantage of certain abuses to revoke them. The enormous machine created by the Monarchy and

[8] Victor de Broglie, op. cit., p. xxiii. He included the United States among the powers whose neutral position, as well as their insignificance, permits a republican form of government.

[9] Victor de Broglie, op. cit., pp. 200-5.

[10] Albert de Broglie, Études morales et littéraires (Paris), p. 106.

the Empire has continued to exist, merely passing from hand
to hand. France has had no real local powers for centuries,
and no traces of independent corporations are left. The result is that the individual is weak and the State is strong.
This is most unfavorable to liberty. Broglie concluded that
decentralization is a necessity.

The ablest and most ardent advocate of decentralization
was Tocqueville. Unlike most of the men of his party he considered that the advent of total democracy was inevitable.
He felt that the great error of the liberals was in refusing
to accept this inevitable fact. Tocqueville had studied democracy in America, and it seemed to him that its worst evils
were mitigated in a country where local powers and spirit
were strong. The object of all his efforts, therefore, was to
save democracy from centralization.[11] In writing to a friend
of the centralizing tendency of democracy in Europe he said:

To show men how to escape from this tyranny and abasement, even
though remaining democratic, is the general idea of my book (*La
Démocratie en Amérique*) and will appear on every page of the
one I am now writing. (*L'Ancien Régime et la Révolution*). To work
for this is, in my eyes, a holy task.[12]

In his second work: *L'Ancien Régime at la Révolution,*
Tocqueville showed that the centralization of France was
largely the work of the Monarchy, and not, as the royalists
were fond of saying, that of the Revolution and the Empire.
The latter, in destroying the feeble remains of the old liberties and privileges, had merely completed the task of the
French kings. By undermining all local powers and interests,
by depriving the nobles of their functions as administrators,

[11] Émile Faguet, "Tocqueville" in *Politiques et moralistes du 19ème
siècle,* 3ème série, p. 100.
[12] "Correspondance," *Oeuvres,* VI, 340.

the kings had brought about the deep division between the classes which made the Revolution inevitable, and gave it so much bitterness. Equality and excessive centralization were the result of these errors. The State has taken all functions upon itself, and suffers no intermediaries. The industrial classes absolutely require legislative protection, and this contributes to enlarge the power of the State. The electorate is no remedy for this impotence of the individual before the State, for the citizen elector merely comes out of his dependence for a moment to name a new master.[13]

Tocqueville did not believe in the possibility of creating a new aristocracy;[14] it was by decentralization alone, he considered, that the government could remain liberal in France.

Instead of living from day to day on the centralized machinery of the Empire, the Bourbons should have hastened to modify it, to initiate the people in the management of their own affairs, and to create local interests, and, above all, the legal habits and ideas which are . . . the only possible counterpoise to democracy.[15]

Although the liberal monarchists agreed as to the need of decentralization, they were not, in general, prepared, like Tocqueville, wholly to renounce the aristocratic principle. Both for practical and theoretical reasons they were anti-equalitarian, and one of the questions most important to them was the organization of a second chamber which, though compatible with the growing demands of democracy, would represent the interests of the upper classes, and balance to some extent the power of the popular assembly. Both the Broglies pointed out the evils which result from recognizing only the power of elected bodies, which are totally subservient to

---

[13] Tocqueville, *La Démocratie en Amérique,* III, 497, 506, 522.

[14] *Ibid., Oeuvres,* VII, 172.

[15] *Ibid.,* V, 315-16.

opinion, and cannot understand the value of experience, or safeguard the enduring interests of successive generations.

In his book on the government of France Victor de Broglie elaborated a scheme for a senate. This body was to have financial privileges equal to those of the other chamber, and was also to be closely associated in the administration of the laws. He wished that all measures regarding tariffs and public works should be initiated first in the senate. This would, he believed, mitigate the excessive influence which local interests exercise on the deputies in regard to these questions. The senate, too, was to have a right of supervision over the ordinances and administrative measures of the executive power. Broglie proposed that this senate should be elected, but not by universal suffrage. In order to form an electoral college, lists were to be made out for each department, in three columns. In the first column were to be inscribed the heads and all the members in the direct male line of the families whose names had appeared on the rolls of the Chamber of Peers of the two constitutional monarchies, and of the Senate of the Second Empire. In the second column were to be inscribed all the land owners resident in the department who paid over 10,000 francs in yearly taxes. In the third column were to be inscribed the cardinals, archbishops, marshals, generals, admirals, presidents of higher tribunals, and ministers or former ministers of State residing in the district. The list would thus represent all the illustrious names, landed fortunes, and assured positions of France and it would always be open to newly-acquired fortunes or dignities. The general council of the department, together with those inscribed on the list, would choose the senators from the members of the list. The senate was to be renewed by thirds simultaneously with the election of the lower chamber.

The law proposed by the Duc Albert de Broglie in 1877 for the formation of a senate somewhat resembled this plan, but it was much more complicated. There were to be three categories of senators, some elected, some members of the conservative party and some named by the executive power. Those of the first category were to be chosen by an electoral college composed of deputies, ex-deputies and ministers, the chief legal dignitaries of the department, officers of the higher grades, the upper clergy, and a few of the most highly-taxed residents. The second category was to be composed of the cardinals, marshals, admirals, and presidents of the highest courts. The members of the third category, who were to form one-half of the whole number, and to be nominated by the President of the Republic, were to be chosen from lists much the same as those who elected the Senators of the first category, but with some additions, including members of the Institute, Governors[16] of the Banque de France, and ambassadors. Ten members might be nominated by the President outside of these lists as a reward for distinguished services.

Both these schemes were efforts to organize the existing social superiorities into a public power, without resorting to the hereditary principle, which had become inacceptable. Such a Senate would have been highly aristocratic; Gambetta is said to have declared that, if it was accepted, democracy would be put off for fifty years. Yet it would have come into being, if the legitimists in the National Assembly had not joined with the Republicans in voting against it.

It was from the point of view of experience that the liberal monarchists insisted upon the need of a king. According to Victor de Broglie, the natural tendency of a popular assembly

[16] "Régents."

will always be towards change and progress, while the executive is always given to resistance; "I will maintain" is its motto.[17] There must be constant compromise between these two, and a moderator is needed to prevent conflicts. A magistrate, such as the president of the republic, whose power dates from yesterday, who is without prestige, and depends on the suffrage either of the nation or of the chambers, cannot fill this rôle; he will not have sufficient independence. His authority will easily be swept aside, and the legislative power will then reign supreme. Constitutional monarchy supplies the needed moderator; it consecrates the work of time, that is to say, the free development of natural superiorities, of which royalty is the highest expression.

Albert de Broglie pointed out that the modern administration of France is only the further development of that of the old régime; the responsibility of the president, and his right of veto and of dissolution, are monarchical ideas. But the basis of this system, the royal power, is lacking; no old and respected authority exists to support it, and therefore the whole structure has feet of clay. Although in a constitutional monarchy the king leaves questions of policy to his ministers, whom he must choose among the leaders of the parliamentary majority, his power is not merely nominal, and his influence is always great. Royalty is an hereditary political *milieu,* and a king is an expert, for he is familiar from childhood with the political and military arts, and with foreign policy. Broglie cited Queen Victoria, Leopold of Belgium, and Victor Emmanuel as examples of the power and utility of modern sovereigns.[18] The king, who will have to face the future,

[17] Duc de Broglie, *Vues sur le gouvernement de la France.*

[18] He quoted Madame Roland on the impression produced upon her by the knowledge and political tact of Louis XVI.

will naturally have greater elevation of ideas and longer views than a president. "The excellence of the monarchical principle is that it gives the holder of power some of the wise prudence of paternal feeling. A king will have the same desire as father and as sovereign to assure the future."[19] A president will be apt to be an insignificant and harmless person, for no man of first rate ability will accept the passivity and silence which this rôle requires.[20] He will inevitably be the creature of a party, whose interest he will consult first, for, should it go out of power, he would be at the mercy of the opposing faction. A king is above these questions of party, thanks to his special character, which forbids his being attacked and despoiled. When a nation has traditions, and an organization formed by liberal monarchy and bearing its mark, it cannot prosper without a fixed and durable power. Albert de Broglie concluded that the constitution of 1875 would lead to the unlimited power of the Chamber of Deputies.[21]

In a work called *La Diplomatie et le droit nouveau* Broglie pointed out the advantages of a monarchy in regard to foreign relations. The king, who is, in a measure, the proprietor of his country, will always labor to make it powerful and prosperous. The word of the king was formerly the basis of treaties, and this word was kept. Universal suffrage now demands consultation at all times on all questions. This means that foreign relations will be deprived of secrecy, and of the far-reaching wisdom and consistency which characterized the

[19] Albert de Broglie, *Questions de religion et d'histoire* (Paris, 1860), p. 373.

[20] Broglie points out that Thiers refused the presidency for this reason.

[21] The same note was sounded in a speech of the Duc d'Audiffret-Pasquier of 1888. The president, he said, has no authority, and the ministry is dominated by party passions. The monarchical principle would bar the road to the illegitimate ambitions of party men.

foreign policy of kings. Morever, how can treaties be relied on which depend on the faith of a power which is always liable to change?

Denys Cochin noted that a king, since he naturally commands respect and confidence, will not feel the need of perpetually legislating on all subjects, in order to strengthen his position, as does an elected body. His rule will, therefore, be less apt to stifle private enterprise. Cochin remarked also that democratic republics are always exposed to the danger of a "savior" who promises to rescue them from their difficulties. He mentioned the Boulangist episode as a case in point.

The practical nature of these men's thought is evident. They did not try to establish the philosophic or metaphysical necessity of monarchy, but only to prove that it would be useful. In this they were like the royalists of today. But in spite of their efforts to resist republican democracy, the theory of constitutional monarchy lost ground. One cause of this is the nature of the doctrine itself. Liberalism is essentially pragmatic; it submits its beliefs to the test of experience. "Fundamental laws," Barante wrote in 1849, "are not immutable, they must be subject to experience,"[22] and Broglie said in 1831: "There are no dogmas or principles prior to reason and the social interest."[23] The monarchy of Louis-Philippe was an expedient, whose reason for being was utility, but when revolution broke out, the king did not, after all, prove to be a source of strength and authority. This practical failure discredited the idea of liberal monarchy more than if it had been based upon some dogma, such as divine right, or the national will.

The difference in doctrine between the legitimists and the

[22] Barante, *Questions constitutionnelles,* p. 165.
[23] Speech of Albert de Broglie, *Moniteur,* October 15, 1831.

Orléanists tended also to discourage the idea of monarchy among the liberals. These practical men were well aware of the unpopularity of the traditional legitimist doctrines. Even if they had themselves been willing to accept the unlimited authority of a king, they felt that France would not do so. "There can be no return to the past," wrote Victor de Broglie. "If constitutional monarchy is to be reinstated the royal family must give up all hopes of a second 'Restoration'. . . . The only monarchy possible today is one which will be new in the general character of the government, new in the name and formation of the constitutional bodies, new as to the extension of political rights and local institutions. . . . Only a republic much like a monarchy, or a monarchy much like a republic is acceptable to the friends of liberty."[24]

The journalist Edouard Hervé,[25] one of the most faithful upholders of the cause of liberal monarchy, declared that France has a weakness; she fears all that savors of the Old Régime. "When one dates from before 1789 one can overcome the general suspicion only by giving undeniable pledges to the new order of things."

Thus, although in general they were prepared to acknowledge that the Comte de Chambord was the true representative of the principle of hereditary monarchy, the liberals were reluctant to join with the legitimists in supporting him. After 1848 they hoped for a time that the second Republic might become socially conservative and politically liberal, and they preferred to work for this end, rather than to abet a legitimist restoration.[26] Their attitude was much the same

[24] Victor de Broglie, *Vues sur le gouvernement de la France*, p. LXX.
[25] He was for many years editor of the *Soleil*, the official organ of the Comte de Paris.
[26] Thureau-Dangin, *op. cit.;* Charles de Lacombe, *Vie de Berryer;*

after the fall of the Second Empire. The men who then held power—Thiers, de Broglie, Audiffret-Pasquier, Decazes—desired a restoration,[27] but a king who would reign independent of constitution and assembly seemed to them both undesirable and impossible. Since the Comte de Chambord would not accept their conditions, they tried to consolidate the Republic on a basis which would allow of an Orléanist restoration on his death. In the meantime they hoped to keep the direction of affairs in their own hands. In this they miscalculated, for the Republic once established, its supporters quickly grew in numbers, and the royalists soon fell from power.[28] They might well claim, however, that this rapid development of republicanism proved that an unlimited monarchy could not have lasted.

The most fundamental reason, however, for the disappearance of the theory of constitutional monarchy is the fact that, since the liberals accepted a large part of what the legitimists called "the doctrines of the Revolution," that is to say, the rights of the individual, and its corollary of popular sovereignty, their consequent respect for public opinion made it difficult for them to resist a Republic which was apparently the expression of the popular will. Freedom was their first object, order their second, and to compromise both these aims by any violent opposition to a government which maintained the public peace, and had general support was not only contrary to their inclinations, but also to their principles of tolerance and respect for opinion.

For monarchy to be restored, Victor de Broglie wrote, it is

Falloux, *Mémoires d'un royaliste;* Albert de Broglie, "Mémoires," *Revue des deux mondes,* Jan. 1 and Jan. 15, 1932.

[27] It is doubtful whether this was really the wish of Thiers.

[28] In 1877.

not enough that it should be preferred to all other govern-ments; a man must appear, of the stuff of which kings are made. "If there are several pretenders," he added, "the part of wisdom is to prefer a Republic to civil war."[29]

Denys Cochin expressed much the same opinion. "We re-pudiate the 'politique du pire,' " he said, in one of his speeches, "and we will never vote with or help those who wish to over-throw society. We are persuaded that . . . the sole refuge of the friends of order and liberty will be constitutional mon-archy, but our mission is to combat the immediate danger of violence."[30]

The point of view of the liberal royalists at the end of the century is illustrated by the writings of Eugène Dufeuille. He was for some years secretary to the Comte de Paris, and the head of his political bureau. On his retirement he published several books in which he presented what were, according to the title of the most important of them, the *Reflections of a royalist*. Royalists, he said, hold that a republic is one of the two forms of free government, but they prefer a constitu-tional monarchy. He pointed out the advantages usually at-tributed to monarchy by the royalists, such as the king's con-ciliating influence upon the political parties, his facilities in dealing with foreign potentates, his value as head of the army, where he will not awaken the fears which a military chief rouses in a republic.[31] Theoretically, then, a monarchy is better than a republic, and in practice it is better suited to France, but, Dufeuille says, in 1874 the monarchists missed the opportunity of a restoration, and this opportunity has not

[29] Victor de Broglie, *Vues sur le gouvernement,* p. 227.

[30] Denys Cochin, *L'Esprit nouveau,* p. 156.

[31] Eugène Dufeuille, *Réflexions d'un monarchiste* (Paris, 1901), pp. 2 0-50; *Du souverain dans notre République* (Paris, 1907), p. 24.

yet recurred.[32] To think of restoring constitutional monarchy by force or by surprise, is worse than useless. In the first place liberty is the object of political institutions, and therefore the use of force should always be avoided. Moreover, if the republic should disappear, royalty would probably not be its heir. "If those who believe in absolutism ruin the love of liberty in the heart of the nation, the result will be the appearance of a dictator."[33] There are only two methods of seizing power by force; one is to offer material satisfaction to the lower classes at the expense of the upper, and the other is to excite patriotic feelings against some foreign power. The result in either case would be fatal to liberty, and therefore those who put freedom above monarchy must be moderate in their opposition to the republic. Dufeuille concluded that constitutional monarchy could only be reëstablished if the republic should perish by its own fault. Royalty must be considered as an eventual resource, a precious reserve for liberty in case of the failure of the present régime.[34]

The gradual decline of the monarchical idea may be traced in the writings of all the liberals whose works we have examined. Royer-Collard saw that if the king is to be a source of genuine authority, he must, in last analysis, possess the sovereignty. He therefore tried to avoid recognizing the responsibility of ministers to the elected chamber, for this implies the sovereignty of the people. Although Benjamin Constant also avoided the question of ministerial responsibility, and made the king the pivot of his composite State, he deprived the monarch of the exercise of the executive, as well as of the legislative power. Guizot accepted the dominance

---

[32] Eugène Dufeuille, *Réflexions d'un monarchiste*, p. VIII.
[33] *Ibid.*, p. 266.
[34] Eugène Dufeuille, *Réflexions d'un monarchiste*, pp. X, XI.

of the parliamentary majority, and, as we have noted, according to his theory the king is scarcely more than an hereditary functionary, whose existence and power depends not on a genuine right, but on his usefulness to the general system. In the writings of the two Broglies, this point of view is even more evident: a king is a useful national possession, much can be said in his favor, but he is not considered as essential to good government, much less as the sole source of legitimate power. Although they saw the advantages of monarchy, neither the Broglies, the d'Haussonvilles, nor Dufeuille felt that they could justify active resistance to the established government. From this attitude, to complete acceptance of the Republic, there was only a step. Albert de Broglie wrote in 1884 that, although he had voted against the Republic, and had no illusions as to its character, he had ceased to oppose it. He doubted whether equality under some sort of despotism were not the natural government of France.[35] Thiers may be said prophetically to have expressed the resignation of liberal monarchy in the words: "The Republic is the government which divides us least."[36] Thus, at the beginning of the new century the idea of constitutional monarchy remained only as a preference, or a matter of tradition and personal attachment among a few individuals.

The liberal royalists had broken the old alliance between the throne and the people, and made the king an instrument of the middle-class oligarchy which they set up. Consequently democracy, when it triumphed over their system, felt only mistrust for the constitutional monarch.

Tocqueville, alone among the liberal monarchists, had seen that this was a mistake. "The Bourbons," he wrote to a legiti-

[35] *Questions de religion et de politique*, pp. 49-50.
[36] Speech of February 13, 1850.

mist friend, "instead of seeking apparently to reinforce the aristocratic principle, which is dying in France, should have labored to give the democracy an interest in order and stability."[37] He saw, too, the weakness of the liberal position. In an article of October 1847,[38] he pointed out the growing indifference of the public to the parliament, and its activities. In a speech of January 27, 1848, which caused much anger among the liberals, he predicted the fall of the July Monarchy. "The Constitution,"[39] he later wrote, "had a fearful defect—its limited number of electors. Thus a little oligarchy was created, remote from the people, and indifferent to their fate. The result was that the class in power was hated both by the masses, and by the dispossessed upper classes."[40]

Liberalism, as it had developed in France, was, in fact, unable to cope with the most important problems of modern times. The urgent necessity for industrial legislation had, perforce, modified the policy of economic *laissez faire,* and the liberals were aware of the need for social action. Haussonville and others studied economic and social problems and tried to find remedies, but the theories of individualism and free competition furnished no constructive basis for resistance to State socialism. The royalist reaction against democracy and the parliamentary régime was to be made in the name of the doctrines of authority, not of liberalism.

[37] "Correspondance," *Oeuvres,* VI, 315-16.
[38] *Ibid.,* "De la classe moyenne et du peuple," *Oeuvres,* VI, 5-14.
[39] The revised charter.
[40] "Letter to W. R. Greg," *Oeuvres,* VI, 214.

CHAPTER VIII

PARLIAMENTARY LEGITIMISTS: BERRYER, LA ROCHEJAQUELEIN, FALLOUX

The men who remained faithful to the elder branch of the Bourbons after the revolution of 1830, were known as the "legitimists." They were characterized by their devotion to the principle of hereditary monarchy in the order of primogeniture, and they rejected the theory of popular sovereignty and the supremacy of parliament. To them the monarchy of Louis-Philippe, which owed its authority to the popular voice, and was therefore "elective" seemed a usurpation. While all legitimists agreed on these points, two divergent tendencies are to be distinguished among them. On the one hand were those who, though they did not agree with monarchists of the type of Guizot or Broglie, and were indeed their bitterest enemies, were yet so little reactionary in their point of view as to merit the name of "liberal legitimists" given by Faguet to Royer-Collard. Their leader, like Royer-Collard, declared that he had "dedicated his life to defending the alliance of liberty and royalty."[1] These men accepted the formula of the Monarchy as it had existed during the Restoration. Although they wished the authority of the king to be supreme, they favored some form of representative or parliamentary government. They opposed the middle-class régime of Louis-Philippe, but were not hostile to all the results of the Revolution, for they accepted civil equality, liberty of the press and of conscience, and the settlement of the relations of Church and State as effected by the Concordat. It

---

[1] Berryer, Letter in *Gazette de France,* April 23, 1832.

was for the most part men of this type who formed the royal-ist opposition in the Parliament during the July Monarchy and the second Republic, and their point of view was the official doctrine of the legitimist party, at all events until after the election of Louis-Napoléon to the presidency in 1852.

The greatest of these men, and one so identified with the legitimist cause that Odilon Barrot called him "legitimacy personified,"[2] was the lawyer Berryer. Born in 1790, An-toine Pierre Berryer was of middle-class origin. His father was a lawyer of distinction, and he became himself one of the most eloquent barristers, and certainly the greatest orator of his generation in France. He was elected to the Chamber of Deputies just before the Revolution of 1830, and he there defended the cause of the fallen dynasty during the greater part of his life. As long as he lived he was the acknowledged leader of the Legitimist party in the Parliament and in the country.

Berryer was not a man of letters; his political philosophy, like that of Royer-Collard, is to be found entirely in his pub-lic speeches and his pleadings before the law courts. Berryer's thought was based on the classic ideas of monarchy, as ex-pounded by Bossuet, by Bonald and by Maistre; but in the interpretation of these ideas he showed a tolerance and adapt-ability which the theocrats lacked. This was no doubt due in part to his long years of close contact with the realities of political life, but also to the generosity and breadth of his intelligence.

Like the theocrats he held that society is not made by indi-viduals, but is ordained for men by God, to permit their moral development. With Bonald, Maistre, Comte, Le Play, Guizot, and also Blanc de Saint-Bonnet and La Tour du Pin, he be-

[2] Odilon Barrot, *Mémoires,* IV, 178.

lieved in immutable social laws, given by a divine legislator. These natural rights, created by God, on which society is founded may be summed up as religion, family and property. Authority is necessary to their maintenance, and therefore it has a divine sanction. "There is," he said, "one divine right for men, and only one: the eternal law of their creation, which calls on them to live in society."[3] It is false to distinguish between society and the government which is its very framework, the cord which binds the social group together. Power exists solely for the benefit of society, and therefore, authority is sacred, and must be regulated by the divine law.

Although Berryer admitted that God has not said to one or another "Thou shalt be King!" it follows from the above that authority does not proceed from the will of the people, and cannot legitimately be held by one man, acting arbitrarily in their name. Popular sovereignty, the most despotic of all powers, recognizes no obligation to law, tradition, or duty, and respects neither God nor man. "Woe," Berryer exclaimed, "to the nations whose existence and governments have their basis in popular passions! They lead to shame, or to the dreadful annihilation of society by the power and genius of one man."[4] As to the sovereignty of reason, Berryer pointed out that every party claims to act in accordance with its dictates, but only the laws of God can claim such absolute sanction.

So far the ideas of Berryer are in perfect agreement with those of the theocrats, and, like them, he believed that hereditary monarchy was the form of government decreed for France by natural law; he did not, however, maintain, as they did, that the Bourbon monarchy was directly sanctioned by divine right. Its claims derived, in his opinion, on the one

<hr />

[3] *Plaidoyers,* I, 301.   [4] Speech of July 17, 1851.

hand from tradition, and on the other from national necessity.

Natural rights find expression in principles which, developed in accordance with the needs of a people, and consecrated by time and tradition, become its fundamental laws.[5]
Of these principles, heredity is one of the most important, for
in it resides the conservative force of society, and the guaranty of order and stability. Sovereignty, to be legitimate,
must follow rules and forms; it must be "regulated in an un-
changing order, known and understood by all."[6] The fundamental law of France has always been the heredity of the
throne by primogeniture.

So long as the elder branch of the Bourbons was on the throne
sovereignty resided in the person of the king, and was transmitted
by an inviolable order. Thus, consecrated by time, by the law, by
religion, the sovereign right was the title of all other rights, the
royal heredity was the guaranty of civil successions . . . it was
the patrimony of the past, promised as heritage to the future.[7]

But it was not only upon traditional law that the French
kings could base their claim; experience also proved, Berryer
held, that monarchy is necessary to France. Berryer himself
was first of all a patriot; his greatest preoccupation, he
admitted, was always the position of France in regard to
other countries. No rights, no doctrines could, he felt, be superior to the interests of the nation. "One is never unjust
in defending against anyone whatever the interests of
France."[8] Thus he was opposed to the abolition of slavery,
because he felt that, at the time, it was contrary to French
colonial interests, and he disapproved of the help given by

[5] Letter to the *Gazette de France,* April 23, 1832.
[6] *Moniteur,* October 6, 1831.   [7] *Plaidoyers,* II, 207.
[8] Speeches, *Moniteur,* July 3, 1839; August 20, 1842.

France to Greek independence, though he called it a "glorious mistake."[9]

It was, he said, his patriotism which led him to become a "national royalist." "I am," he declared, "attached to the principle of the irrevocable and legitimate transmission of sovereignty in the interests of the country. I believe it to be necessary to the development of France . . . and to her situation in Europe."[10] Great sovereigns are rare, he added, but the principle which lives in all kings, and assures the stability of power, is a great one.

Like all authoritarians, Berryer believed that power has a right to demand respect for its principle, for when authority is shaken, society ceases to exist. A government is lost, he said, if its principle is subject to constant discussion. Nevertheless, during the July Monarchy he claimed for his party the full benefit of the rights of free speech and political agitation guaranteed by the Charte. To the contention of the liberals that the constant use of these rights by the opposition make government difficult if not impossible, he retorted that the responsibility was theirs, these subversive weapons were concomitant to the dangerous principle of popular sovereignty on which they had founded their precarious régime.

Berryer was also opposed to the idea of political equality. An aristocracy always exists in a great nation. Formed by the history of that nation, it acts as the preserver of its traditions and culture. His ideas as to an hereditary peerage were much the same as those of Benjamin Constant. Human beings have two vital interests: acquisition, which is that of the majority; and conservation, which is that of the minority. Since these interests are not alike, two bodies must exist to represent them. That which represents the permanent interests of

[9] *Ibid.*   [10] Speech, *Moniteur,* January 15, 1844.

acquired situation should be hereditary. The force of all aristocracies is heredity, which only preserves natural inequalities. If prudence is honorable, if it is good to keep what one has acquired, whether glory or wealth, it is honorable also to transmit it.

In accordance with royalist tradition, Berryer always defended property and the family. He was actively opposed to divorce, and he considered that property, and the right to transmit it, are the bond of society. He was particularly favorable to agricultural interests—indeed the word "property" was for him almost synonymous with land. "It is," he said, "with agriculture, with the extension of territorial property that my convictions are bound up."[11]

Like all the royalists, Berryer was strongly in favor of decentralization. In addition to their usual arguments, he pointed out the excessive growth of the bureaucracy. Under the old régime, no more than 25,000 individuals, at the most, had depended on the caprice of ministers; now at least 500,000 did so. This produced servility, intrigue, and uneasy ambitions.

In spite of this fundamental agreement in point of view, Berryer's ideas differed from those of the theocrats in several important respects. In the first place, he was not, like Bonald and Maistre, a royalist by tradition. His attitude in political matters, like that of the present day royalists, was pragmatic and "positive," and his belief in hereditary monarchy was the result of a reasoned conviction. He was first of all a patriot. In his early days he was attracted by the glory of the Empire, but events, as well as a study of the Cahiers of the Constituent Assembly opened his eyes to its despotism, and its fall convinced him of the inherent weakness of the

[11] Speech of May 15, 1843.

arbitrary rule of one man. As a Catholic, he also favored a social order in accordance with the teachings of the Church. He was convinced that experience proved legitimate monarchy to be the political system most propitious both to such an ordering of society and to the glory and strength of France. It was for this reason that he devoted his life to its support.

In the second place, although, like the theocrats, Berryer attributed sovereignty to the King, he held that the royal claim sprang, not from an abstract right, but from the traditional constitution of France, and therefore he insisted, as Bonald and Maistre did not, on the limits which this constitution imposed on the power of the monarch. The king, he repeatedly declared, is not absolute, he is subject to the national will.[12] His conception of the monarchy was not unlike that of Benjamin Constant; in early periods, he said, royalty leads and enlightens the people. It later becomes the supreme arbiter, and the power which holds the force to execute the laws. The royal power, as it was constituted in France on a century-old basis, was fully compatible with all modern liberties. The traditional law of France asserted, besides the royal prerogative, and the order of succession, the rights of the people to meet in public assemblies, and to deliberate on the taxes. Like Royer-Collard, Berryer seems to have felt that the two chambers, created by the Charte, were the necessary modern embodiment of these rights. "I know of no other recourse for the country than parliamentary government," he said, on January 15th, 1851, apropos of the revision of the constitution.

He was, however, strongly opposed to the narrow electoral laws of the July Monarchy. He called the property qualifica-

[12] *Plaidoyers,* I, 302, 404.

tion of the franchise a "monstrous injustice."[13] "I have never understood the enormous gulf which separates the man who pays 200 francs in taxes from the one who pays 199 francs 95 centimes!" He saw that this system brought about the exclusive supremacy of the middle classes. Was it to establish this domination, he asked, that the action and influence of the upper classes were to be sacrificed? In 1830 the liberals had invoked the principle of popular sovereignty to overthrow the legitimate dynasty, but they were unwilling to accept its consequences. This roused Berryer's indignation. The policy of the *juste milieu,* he said, satisfies nobody—it is neither justice nor wisdom. The history of society is a gradual ascent, the summits fall, and the lower classes reach the top. But the middle classes in France, once entrenched in power, refuse to extend their rights to the masses. "Do not hold the barrier closed!" he warned the *bourgeoisie* in 1847.

Berryer, however, was not in favor of universal suffrage as it is usually practiced. The electoral system should not rest, he said, on individuals, but on those "aggregations of political families," the communes. He wished an election in two degrees; all Frenchmen inscribed on the rolls should be called on to vote for primary communal assemblies, which would, in turn, name the deputies to a national chamber.

In regard to the relations of Church and State, Berryer differed entirely from the theocrats. He greatly disliked Protestantism, and saw in it, as did so many of the royalists, the spirit of revolution. "The Protestants," he said, "see man in everything, while the Catholics see God. . . . The thought of Protestant Geneva, between Guizot and Broglie, oppresses me!"[14] Nevertheless, he believed in liberty of conscience, and

---

[13] Speech of February 27, 1831.
[14] Lecanuet, *Vie de Berryer* (Paris, 1895), p. 204.

tolerance for all forms of worship. He was hostile to the idea of a State-supported Church, and wished the entire separation of the spiritual and temporal powers. He was not averse to the Concordat, but he considered that the liberty of the common law would suffice for the freedom of the Church.[15]

Berryer did not, like Royer-Collard, confuse the people with the middle classes, or believe, with the liberals, that the latter were the best protectors of popular interests. He boasted that he was himself a plebeian, and he had a real perception of the needs of the working classes. The Revolution had destroyed the old guilds—(*jurandes and corps de métiers*) —which had been the framework of industrial life under the old régime. These had, no doubt, grown oppressive, but the new order had put nothing in their place, and the working classes had not even the franchise as a substitute for such liberties and privileges as these organized bodies had enjoyed. This was at a time too when the expansion of capital and industry was revolutionizing the conditions of labor!

The right of association may well be defended on individualistic grounds. To agree, and to coöperate voluntarily would appear to be a natural human need, with which the law can have no right to interfere. Obviously, however, organized bodies, formed with a view to concerted action, will, if their objects are anti-social, become a great danger to society. As a matter of fact the liberals were, for the most part, strongly opposed to the right of association. It was contrary to the interests of the class to which they belonged that workers should be allowed to form associations with the object of offering a collective resistance to their employers. Liberal theory, however, rationalized the fears of the middle classes and combated the right of association as contrary to liberal

[15] *Plaidoyers*, I, 236; Speech of February 24, 1832.

doctrine, which required the complete independence of the individual, and the free play of unlimited competition.

The legitimists were, for the most part, landowners, and so their interests did not clash so directly with those of the workers. Their doctrines led them also to conceive of society as organized into groups and hierarchies, with collective rights and responsibilities. Berryers' speeches on the right of association reflect these ideas. The spirit of association is the engenderer, he said, of social order, and all political men rely on it. To agree by legitimate means for proper ends is a duty, and union is the most legitimate right of those who have common interests. Associations will always exist, but they should be open and legal, sanctioned and regulated, not suppressed by authority. The middle classes, he pointed out, do coöperate to exploit their capital; why, then, should workmen be reduced to a unicellular existence, and punished for combining in order to escape from this narrow circle? The entire freedom demanded by the liberals has proved oppressive to those most in need of protection.

Berryer's love of justice transcended his political sympathies. Early in his career he defended both Ney and Cambronne against the government of the Restoration, and he later represented the interests of the Orléans family, whom he considered as usurpers, when their property in France was confiscated. Legitimate monarchy was to him synonymous with legality, and, as one of its chief representatives, he believed that in defending those who were persecuted, he was serving its cause.

Throughout his career he was a defender of law and order and opposed the use of violence against established authority. "Force," he said, in taking the oath of obedience to the new régime, in 1830, "does not destroy a right . . . but when force dominates in a State, individuals must submit to it, in order to avoid worse evils."[16] This oath he considered as a promise to make no illegal attempts against the new government. "The greatest misfortune for any party," he declared in 1844, "would be to become the cause of disorder." When in 1832 the Duchess de Berry landed in Vendée, to attempt to place her son on the throne by force, Berryer hurried to meet her, at the risk of his life, in order to try to dissuade her from causing civil war. He always advised the Comte de Chambord not only against a *coup d'état*, but against the appearance of violence. Nothing, he said, must be undertaken in France save through the national will. It was the duty of public men to develop their principles, and labor to convert the nation to them, but always within the bounds of legality. This attitude is in conformity with that expounded by the Catholic Church, and it is a logical one for a believer in authority. A large part of the authoritarian royalists, however, both during the Restoration and in later days, showed themselves unwilling to obey any authority, whether that of king, pope, or people, which did not fully agree with their own views.

Berryer was, in a measure, the successor of Chateaubriand and Royer-Collard.[17] It is perhaps to the latter that his point of view is most closely related. Although he was much less individualistic than the "great doctrinaire," his ideas present somewhat the same mixture of respect for tradition and authority with a liberal spirit. Berryer's conceptions of the divine origin of society, of its immutable laws, and of the purpose and necessity of government were those of

[16] Speech of August 11, 1830.
[17] It must be remembered that both these men considered their careers to be bound up with the cause of legitimacy.

the theocrats, but his idea of the limitation of power by an old, though unwritten constitution, and by organized bodies in the State, his desire for a free Church and tolerance for all cults, were liberal.

The royalists of a later period reproached Berryer for his faith in parliamentary government, but he undoubtedly looked on the Parliament as it then existed rather as a field of action for propaganda and influence than as a satisfactory organ of government. The assembly which he asked for, based on the representation of the communes, would have been in the nature of a renewed Estates General.[18] He had a faith which Guizot lacked, but which experience has to some extent justified, in the fundamentally conservative instincts of the French peasants, who would have formed the vast majority of the electors under any form of universal suffrage.

In declaring that the organization of labor is a great political problem, and in defending workmen's associations both at the Bar and in the Chamber, Berryer was the forerunner of an important modern movement, and also anticipated some of the most constructive ideas of the later royalists.[19]

Berryer was also the precursor, in many respects, of the men of the Action française. Like them he was intensely nationalistic, and was converted to royalism because he thought that legitimate monarchy was the form of government most favorable to the greatness of France. As with them, too, it was a study of the past which brought him to this conclusion, and he claimed that experience verified his belief.[20] Like

[18] Marchand, *Les Idées de Berryer.*
[19] Notably Chambord, Veuillot, de Mun, La Tour du Pin. See also Paul Nourisson, *Trois précurseurs* (Bar-le-Duc, 1922).
[20] Speech of May 15, 1843.

Murras he disliked Protestantism, and was distrustful of foreign influences.

The monarchy, Berryer saw, could only be reëstablished by the union of all lovers of order, and therefore his political tactics always had a double aim: to prepare opinion for the return of the king, and to prevent civil war. These ideas were those of the majority of the Legitimists during the twenty years which followed the revolution of 1830. During that time Berryer was the acknowledged leader of the party, and had the confidence of the Comte de Chambord, who left to him the entire direction of the Legitimist party, even on the vital matter of the revision of the constitution in 1851 After the *coup d'état* of 1852, however, the Comte de Chambord, greatly to the regret of Berryer, gave definite instructions to his followers to take no part in the political life of the Second Empire. Berryer allowed himself to be elected to the Corps Legislatif in 1863, at a time when the defense of the Church seemed a vital question to all Catholics, but he was the only legitimist in that body. He died in 1868, too soon to see the fall of the Empire, which he hated, or to contribute his wisdom and moderation to the guidance of his party in the crisis of its fate.

Berryer advocated a broad franchise. He believed that monarchy exists for the benefit of the country, and that a king is subject to the national will. Certain legitimists carried these ideas much further, and proposed to appeal to the nation by means of a plebiscite, or referendum. The leader of this movement was the Marquis de La Rochejaquelein. He was a member of an old and distinguished family, which had played a chivalrous part in the revolutionary wars in Vendée. He had ability, and was extremely ambitious. He was supported by the Abbé de Genoude, editor of one of the most influential legitimist papers, the *Gazette de France*. Genoude had been ennobled by Charles X. He wrote a number of books on religious questions. Like La Rochejaquelein, he was ambitious, anxious to play a part in political life, and jealous of the ascendency of Berryer in the legitimist party. Both these men believed that the best hope of restoring the legitimate monarchy lay in a direct appeal to the people, and they urged this policy in the meetings of the royalist party, in the chamber, and in the *Gazette de France*. A number of royalist papers in the provinces followed their lead.

La Rochejaquelein declared that hereditary monarchy draws its authority from national sovereignty. "We no longer believe in divine right," he said. "The principle of French society has always been the national sovereignty. This is the source of legitimate monarchy."[21] Nations take a chief, and so alienate their sovereignty in their own interest, but this cession of the national sovereignty is only partial.[22]

Our forefathers, believing that the nation would be the better for the hereditary transmission . . . of power, established and maintained this conservative principle for nine centuries. But it was by the consent of the nation that monarchy thus endured during many generations, and for this reason the King belongs to France, and may call himself genuinely national.[23]

A changed form of government resulting from revolution is defensible only if it is sanctioned by the nation. But France, he said, had never been consulted on the various constitutions since the Revolution all of which claimed to have originated in national sovereignty. In 1830 two hundred and nineteen deputies deposed the King, and illegally disposed of the throne. Louis Philippe was an usurper, who pro-

[21] *A mon pays* (Paris, 1850).
[22] Letter to Lamennais (Paris, 1849).   [23] *Ibid.*

claimed without justification that he was chosen by the national will. The constitution of 1848 declared that sovereignty resides in the totality of citizens, but the Chamber of Deputies of the July Monarchy was not a national representation, it was a mere "chamber of notables."

How is it possible, La Rochejaquelein asked, to return to legitimate monarchy without civil or foreign war? Only by consulting the people. To close the era of revolutions, an agreement between the king and the nation must be made the basis of monarchy. This is how kings were made of old. Charlemagne wrote that "Lex fit consensū populi et constitutione regis," and the Comte de Chambord himself said: "Tout pour la France et par la France." Universal suffrage *is* France, said La Rochejaquelein, and the legitimists should demand its reëstablishment. "We must give back to France the voice of her citizens, who are the life and honor of the Nation."[24] Hereditary royalty would not suffer by such an appeal; the nation, using its full sovereignty, would recognize the monarchical principle, which is of natural origin, and, without altering its nature, or giving it an elective character, would invest it with a new sanction. "We would not *make* a King," he said, "we would only claim the royalty which exists by traditional and historic right."[25]

For the execution of these ideas La Rochejaquelein placed before the chambers a proposal whereby the people would have been called on to choose, by a general vote, between a monarchy and a republic. "I believe," he said, "in the wisdom of the nation." The project of an appeal to the people was definitely rejected by the Comte de Chambord in a circular letter written at Wiesbaden in 1850. La Rochejaquelein's

[24] *La Révision de la Constitution* (Paris, 1851), p. 14.
[25] *Ibid.*, p. 11.

theory of monarchy was inacceptable to the "pure" legitimists who held that the Comte de Chambord, as head of
the royal family, possessed an absolute right to the throne,
independent of any form of popular assent. If a contract
between king and people is admitted as the origin of royal
power, that contract may easily be held to be revocable.
Bonald and Maistre emphatically denied that monarchy had
such a source; it arose, they said, not from contract, but
from natural necessity. Berryer considered that it owed its
right to the fundamental laws of the land, as evidenced by
tradition and history, and to its preëminent utility. No confirmation by popular acclaim could strengthen such a right,
nor could rejection by the people diminish its validity.

The attitude of La Rochejaquelein and Genoude resulted
from a pragmatic view of royalty; that is to say from the
belief that monarchy is desirable principally because it is the
government most favorable to the national interest. From
this point of view it was natural that they should have asked
for an appeal to the people, for the idea of a "national"
monarchy appears to imply at least the consent of the nation.
It was true in 1851, that, since the plebiscites of the Consulate
and the first Empire, no government had made any attempt,
even apparent, to consult the masses, and the royalists themselves believed that the outcome of such a consultation would
not be hostile to the legitimate monarchy.

The political situation in France in 1851 appeared also
to justify La Rochejaquelein from a practical point of view.
In 1848 the lower classes had shown themselves to be violently hostile to the *bourgeois* régime of Louis-Philippe;
yet France, as a whole, was anxious for order and authority. La Rochejaquelein hoped that the legitimists, by an appeal to the people, might profit by this situation. It was,

however, Louis Napoléon who reaped the benefit of popular discontent, and the alarm of the upper classes. He promised peace and security to everyone, but once the *coup d'état* had established him in power, he took care to secure the sanction of popular approval by a general plebiscite. The Second Empire was, as a matter of fact, founded on exactly the theory of monarchy exposed by La Rochejaquelein, and the latter was quite consistent when he rallied to it, and in 1856 accepted a seat as senator.

The coup d'état of Napoléon III was a terrible blow to royalist hopes. It meant that the policy of the parliamentary legitimists, who were both the most active and the most moderate members of that party, had failed. The legitimists had never been united, and after this failure more reactionary views prevailed with their chief, the Comte de Chambord. He forbade his supporters to present themselves for election, or to take any part in public life, so that the legitimist opposition during the Second Empire, in so far as it existed, was entirely passive. Certain royalists were at first inclined to accept the new régime with resignation, especially during its early authoritarian and conservative phase. But the war in Italy and the quarrels of Napoléon III with the Vatican awakened the resistance of the Catholic royalists, and the fall of the Empire in 1870 gave them new hopes. Royalists of all shades of opinion presented themselves for election to the National Assembly, and legitimists and Orléanists together won a majority of the seats. The ideas of liberal legitimacy had never entirely disappeared, and they were revived and strengthened by the reconciliation of the two branches of the Bourbon family in 1873.

One of the men most representative of this point of view was the Comte de Falloux. He appears to continue the traditions of Chateaubriand, Royer-Collard, and particularly of Berryer, with whom he was long closely associated. He was, however, more definitely liberal in his ideas, than they were, and less faithful to any principle except that of the defense of the Church. This was his chief concern, and seems to have motivated his various changes of policy. Falloux was an active member of the legitimist opposition during the July Monarchy, but he rallied unreservedly to the Republic in 1848.[26] Louis Napoléon, as president, named him Minister of Public Instruction, in order to win the support of the Church, but he left the post in 1849, and took up a position of discreet opposition to the Empire. After 1870 he was active in trying to bring about the "fusion" of the Bourbon princes and the combination of the royalist parties. Although by belief and tradition he belonged to their party, the legitimists did not consider him as one of themselves, and prevented his election to the National Assembly.

The point of departure of Falloux's ideas, like those of Berryer, is the national interest. To pretend that all forms of government have the same advantages is absurd; the Republic in France has always been criminal, whereas the Bourbon monarchy brought peace and prosperity to the country. Peoples identify themselves with a dynasty for their own advantage and glory, and no royal family has ever paid its debt to a people better than did the Capetiens. It was by intelligent fidelity to its monarch that France won its place as one of the first nations of the world. Like Berryer, whom he quoted, Falloux refused to "separate the cause of the old royalty from that of the new liberties."[27]

---

[26] By demanding the immediate dissolution of the National workshops he helped to precipitate the terrible results of the "June Days."

[27] *Mémoires d'un royaliste* (Paris, 1888), I, 225.

The difference between absolutism and freedom is resumed in the position of the minority: all governments are absolute in which minorities have no regular organs for making themselves heard; those governments are free under which a constitution guards the interests of minorities and permits the legal expression of their ideas and wishes. Democracy, he said, was not a conquest of the Revolution; it developed naturally during the course of centuries, and was favored and protected by the throne. It was despotism which the Revolution created, by destroying the *cortège* of traditional rights, organized bodies, and independent magistracies of the old régime. "For me," Falloux said, "the career of the Revolution is closed, and that of liberty begins!"[28] Nevertheless, he added, it is a mistake to suppose, as do extremists, that the Revolution is bankrupt, and to condemn it in its entirety. Both Chateaubriand and Maistre realized that it was an epoch, rather than an event. Certain parts of its results, such as civil equality, liberty of conscience, and freely elected assemblies, will endure.

The Revolution, however, diminished the position of France in Europe, and for this Falloux saw no remedy save in the restoration of the legitimate prince.[29] The principal question, to him, was how this was to be accomplished. There was, he said, no irremediable disagreement between the ideas of the two branches of the Bourbon family. The Orléanists wished a representative government, but the legitimists did not intend a return to absolutism; the Orléanists wanted the free development of modern society, but the legitimists did not seek to restore the old régime. There was therefore no fundamental reason why all monarchists should not agree. The only tribunal fit to pronounce

[28] *Ibid.*, I, 60.   [29] *Ibid.*, p. 323.

on their difference, and to decide on a restoration was the nation itself. It was no innovation for the Monarchy to consult the country; the kings of France always listened to the voice of their people in the Champs de Mai, the States General, or the parliaments. In 1872, Falloux concluded, the nation was best represented by the National Assembly, its supreme resource. The Comte de Chambord, although in 1851 he had rejected the idea of a direct appeal to the people,[30] had often proved his confidence in universal suffrage; why, then, should he not accept the verdict of its representatives? To do so might be qualified as a compromise, a transaction, but "all political attitudes which exclude moderate men and ideas are, by that very fact, reduced to nothing."[31] The reign of Henry IV was itself a result of compromise.

It is evident, even from so brief an analysis of his theories, that Falloux, although he professed himself a legitimist, and had no personal connections with the liberal monarchists, or the Orléans princes, was closely allied to them in ideas. The refusal of the Comte de Chambord to abandon the white flag, and the consequent failure of the attempted restoration gave the death-blow to this conception of legitimist monarchy. It was a modification of authoritarian doctrine peculiarly adapted to circumstances, and in other conditions it ceased to have a reason for being. The element of compromise which might have made it useful if the Comte de Chambord had reigned, prevented it from surviving the failure of the Restoration.

[30] Wiesbaden circular.
[31] Quoted by Falloux from Dupanloup.

CHAPTER IX

AUTHORITARIAN LEGITIMISTS

The conception of society on which authoritarian monarchy is based is essentially opposed to the revolutionary ideas of individualism and democracy. The parliamentary legitimists tried to compromise with the conditions created by these ideas, and therefore they were condemned by those royalists who clung to the "pure" monarchical tradition.

For authoritarians, the individual exists for society, and the group is more important than its members. Among the royalists who held this point of view, a place belongs to the great novelist, Honoré de Balzac. He was not a philosopher, and in the vast field of his writings only a few political ideas are to be gleaned, but these are remarkably clear-cut and uncompromising.[1] As a novelist he belonged to the romantic school; he had an extraordinary understanding of humanity in its most excessive manifestation of individualism and eccentricity. The master criminal, the adventurer, the prostitute, the miser, and other anti-social types, play a great part in the "human comedy" as he saw it. For this reason some moralists disapprove of him. Yet, though Balzac described the society of his day, it is not certain that he approved of it, and the whole *Comédie humaine* may well be taken as an indictment of the modern world. There is reason to believe that he attributed much of the evil he portrayed

[1] Balzac's political ideas are to be found chiefly in the introduction to the study on Catherine de Médici, in a pamphlet on the *Droit d'ainesse* (Paris, 1824), and in one called *Enquête sur la politique des deux ministres* (Paris, 1831).

to the excessive individualism, and consequent social disorganization of the age.[2] He called individualism "the hor-
rible product of division, which suppresses the family, and
devours everything," and he spoke of Protestantism as "the
spirit of negation, based on those terrible words: tolerance,
progress, and philosophy."[3] Our century, he said, has tried to
establish political liberty on the doubtful theory of free will,
and the liberty of conscience.[4] France today, without authority or patriotism, is solely interested in material welfare, and nothing great or noble can ever be expected from
interests; they are too changeable.

The Catholic Church proclaims the one doctrine which is
salutary for modern societies: "una fides, unus Dominus."[5]
For all who wish a well-ordered State, social man is a subject, and he must not profess a right to liberty of judgment.
The words "subject" and "liberty" are contradictory.

The elective principle is based on discussion. But power
is action, and where there is permanent discussion there
can be no authority, no settled policy. As soon as human
thought, instead of remaining "divinely axiomatic,"[6] takes
a multitude of forms, ideas, as well as men, must be resisted by authority. It was in this struggle that the royal
power in France succumbed. No society can exist without
some guaranty for the subject against the sovereign, but this
must consist not in unlimited freedom, but in defined and
restricted liberties. All great statesmen have granted such
rights to their subjects, but none have ever admitted the entire liberty of anti-social thought and action. All power,
whether legitimate or not, must defend itself when it is at-

[2] "Catherine de Médicis," *Oeuvres* (Edition Calmann-Levy), p. 10.
[3] *Ibid.*   [5] *Ibid.*
[4] *Ibid.*   [6] *Ibid.*, p. 13.

tacked. It is a proof of human unreason that the people should seem heroic when they do so, whereas authority, which is the necessary basis of the State, passes for an assassin!

Like Machiavelli, whom he admired, Balzac believed that politically the end justifies the means. In his essay on Catherine de Médici, he bitterly berates the injustice of historians towards her. True, she sacrificed faith, honor, humanity, and every human feeling, including maternal love, to the "reason of state." But Balzac approves her; this is the conduct of a true statesman. No interest must pass before that of the State. Catherine, he says, saw the evils which the spirit of inquiry, as evidenced by the Reformation, was to bring upon Europe, and she was determined to stamp it out in France.

The Edict of Nantes, Balzac considers as a great mistake. Henry IV should not have been satisfied until he had eliminated either all Protestants, or all Catholics from his realm, and restored agreement and authority.

In regarding order and uniformity of opinion as the supreme social ideal Balzac was the predecessor of Charles Maurras. Like him, too, he believed that the Catholic tradition and teaching are the means of attaining this ideal in France. Balzac's chief interest for royalist theory is that like the royalists of the present day he reached conclusions as rigidly authoritarian as those of the theocrats from a practical and observational point of view.

The man of this period whose writings embody most fully the pure legitimist doctrines is Blanc de St. Bonnet. His work deserves more attention than it has received, for, although his point of view is much like that of the theocrats, his philosophy has some originality, both in content and in presentation. He is clearer, less aridly logical, and therefore more convincing than Bonald, and although less brilliant than Maistre, he has something of the latter's fearlessness, and love of paradox. He was a true philosopher, and all his books bear the evidence of years of meditation, and detachment from immediate events. His style has a tendency to lapse into exhortation, and he is inclined to mysticism. Nevertheless, there is something simple and compelling in the expression of his thought. Perhaps because of his extremely reactionary ideas, he was little known, even during his life time, and today he is almost forgotten, yet he influenced both Veuillot, La Tour du Pin, and other Catholic writers.

Antoine Blanc de St. Bonnet was born in 1815. His parents destined him for the law, and he was educated partly at Bourg and partly in Paris. In 1841 he published three large volumes of philosophy,[7] which had some success, and which won him the cross of the Legion of Honor at 29 years of age. His moral philosophy was an attempt to develop the ideas of Ballanche in accord with the doctrines of the Church. Victor Cousin had a great admiration for his work.

St. Bonnet cared little for honors or money, and he disliked the life of the city. He left Paris in 1841, and spent the rest of his life in his native St. Bonnet, occupied with his lands, which he administered himself, with his family, and with the books which he continued to write. This patriarchal existence was quite in harmony with his philosophy. In later life he became increasingly visionary, and he believed that he was the chosen interpreter of God's

[7] *L'Unité spirituelle; ou, La Société et son but au-delà du temps* (Paris, 1841).

thought. In spite of this strain of fanaticism there is much that is interesting in his ideas.[8]

The great question, from a political point of view, he said, is the nature of man. If he is fundamentally good, as some philosophers say, then "socialism"[9] is perfectly logical, but if he is bad, then only Catholic doctrine is just. In reality, Blanc de St. Bonnet said, man, although he is a superhuman being with divine possibilities, is tainted with evil, which has compromised his development, and marred his civil and political life. The philosophers and jurists have imagined a state of nature in which man was good and happy, but since the fall (on which Blanc de St. Bonnet constantly insists) men live in a state, not of nature, but of *justice;* it is natural for them to hate and kill each other. Man was created imperfect, but God put in him the seed of all good possibilities. His soul gradually develops, through labor and pain and from this soul he evolves, little by little, the society in which he lives.

Society is "a harmony of wills, directed to the betterment of man, and of his earthly condition."[10] Its object is to ameliorate human beings, and to create saints. Men are not in the world to satisfy their bodily needs, but to grow nobler, and they associate to learn to love each other better. Society is in men's hearts; it is not a mathematical unity, but a true union.

This society, which is the mother of man, and has the

[8] His works on political philosophy are *De la Restauration française* (Paris, 1851) ; *Politique réelle* (Paris, 1858) ; *De la légitimité* (Paris, 1873) ; *La Loi electorale* (Paris, 1875) ; *Le Socialisme* (Paris, 1880).

[9] Blanc de St. Bonnet used this word loosely. He appears to refer to equalitarian doctrines in general, and not to those of State ownership of the means of production.

[10] *De la légitimité,* p. 358.

first claim upon him, must be organized according to the divine law. Were this law man-made there could be no obligation to obey it, but it is the word of God, not the emanation of human wills. Order comes, not from government, but from religion, which teaches the idea of God and of right. It must exist first of all in the spirits of men, where it is created by common beliefs, habits and laws. If religion were sincerely and universally adhered to there would be no need of government, or of a political organization. It is because evil exists that there are kings, institutions, laws and penalties. Political life is the relation between moral force and evil, between liberty and its abuse.

Since men do not, as a rule, prefer the general good to their own desires, they must be ruled. Violent and evil passions are not to be restrained by liberty or reason. Authority is essential to the existence of society, of which, as its name indicates, it is the "author." No possible principle for this authority, no real basis for government exists outside of God. The State represents the Divine Power, and so it has the right to command.

One power must dominate the others, in order to protect the general interest of society. Sovereignty is the authority which possesses the law; it is the primordial element on which all else depends. Since the law, which is justice and reason, requires power to maintain itself, that power, which is sovereignty, has a divine right. All sovereignty comes from God, who has made kings to administer His justice.

As a result of the Fall, natural law does not suffice to establish society, and a superior family must intervene to protect property and faith. There are races which God has chosen as instruments of his law. Legitimacy, or the right to govern a nation, is tied to such a family, without which that nation could not have been formed. It is not peoples who have taken kings to themselves, but kings who have created the nations.[11] Monarchs are the depositaries of God's power, and the great title of royalty is to represent Him on earth. The authority of the monarch, and his legitimate rights are identical with those of a father over his family; he harmonizes the other powers of society and regulates them. By means of the social hierarchy, the king's authority extends to all his subjects and touches them all. It is through its king that a great people possesses itself, and is conscious of its own personality. Sovereigns must defend the masses against their own pride and self will; they have a charge of souls. The people must not be allowed, under the pretext of liberty, to fall into ignorance and corruption; their own protection demands that they be held forcibly to the true law.[12]

The principle of monarchy is heredity. By election it is men who choose their rulers, but with heredity it is God himself who chooses.[13] Hereditary monarchy is not a property of which the prince can dispose; he is merely the depositary of a principle which is the patrimony of the nation. Kings cannot abdicate their rights.

Society is like an army; all belong in the ranks, in a definite order. The political order, however, is not immutable but progressive. Man has the sublime power of doing good, but also the possibility, though not the right, of doing evil. Since men are morally free they are responsible, and their acts win them merit or demerit. This merit is the

[11] Blanc de St. Bonnet (*De la légitimité*, p. 427) instanced Russia, which only appeared with the Romanovs.

[12] The influence of Bossuet is evident throughout Blanc de St. Bonnet's philosophy, and particularly in his conception of royalty.

[13] Poland, Blanc de St. Bonnet pointed out, died of choosing its kings.

only true source of rights, and society must be based on it, not on the so-called "innate rights" which some people wish to substitute for those of effort and virtue. The first law of society is that men should not be equal, but should be placed according to their merits. It is the rejection of this principle which is causing the decay of Europe.

Blanc de St. Bonnet's ideas on property are the most original part of his political theory. They follow directly from his belief that society exists for the moral development of men. Production and consumption are not ends in themselves; they are means of preparing souls for eternity. Labor and renunciation were ordained for man to discipline and form his soul. The first virtue is to overcome laziness, the second is to overcome greed, and the third to use one's possessions for the common good.

The earth was given to man to develop, and by his efforts he has created the "vegetable soil"[14] which nourishes him, and has modified and improved the climate. This has improved his own blood, and so enabled him to multiply, and to form the nations![15] It is for this reason that each people sees its glory in its territory, which is as inviolable as its soul.

Civilization has its roots in property, which is the creative principle of society. Capital is the result of effort and of self-control. Since its source is labor and renunciation, it is created by morality, and is therefore sacred. It is the evidence of merit and its legitimacy is in its origin, not in its distribution. Blanc de St. Bonnet defines capital as "all that

[14] *De la Restauration française,* p. 15.

[15] Man, Blanc de St. Bonnet said, first appeared in Asia. His personality had to develop before he could approach the temperate zones and the poles!—*De la Restauration française,* p. 21.

man has produced and not consumed"[16] or "the fruit of saving, that is to say, moderation in enjoyment."[17] It is, he says, "the tool, the cow, the ploughed field, the garment, the machine, steam, gravitation, thought . . . all the forces that man has seized and used."[18] It exists in proportion to the labor, the virtue, and the intelligence of man, and its origin is in the human heart. Labor and nature have a limit of fertility, capital has none. Capital by making labor more productive has released humanity from universal and perpetual toil. It has given well-being, and made science, philosophy and education possible. Had no men been freed from bodily work, all would have remained savages or slaves. The savage state in which there is no ploughing or harvesting, is merely the absence of capital. The first kings were simply men who had accumulated capital and who used it to group a society about them. It was Christianity which led to the development of capital by preaching moderation in enjoyment.

Wealth, then, is based on virtue, and all peoples have considered it as a sign of social capacity. If men were all equally sober and hard-working, wealth could be evenly divided, but in every society there are in fact those who produce more than they consume, and those who destroy, and are mere barbarians. Of eight million fathers of families in France, Blanc de St. Bonnet says, six million have some property, and two million have not. If all this property were given to the two million, in twenty-five years everything would have returned to the present condition. Poverty can only be abolished by abolishing laziness and corruption.

Wealth, however, which represents labor and a contri-

[16] *De la Restauration française,* p. 21.
[17] *Ibid.,* p. 22.   [18] *Ibid.*

bution to society, may be destroyed by vice. A man is himself a capital which sin can destroy, and a population may consume the accumulated riches of centuries in a few years. Luxury is the paganism of today. All capital used for other than useful things such as food, clothing, furniture, education, is a burden upon the resources of a nation. Whoever satisfies his needs twice prevents another from satisfying his. The wealth used in luxury should be turned into agricultural capital, for the development of more land. The real object of wealth is not pleasure but the virtue which is necessary for its creation. "Let men keep privation intimately in their hearts!"[19] cries St. Bonnet.

In the organization of society the rights of merit must never be sacrificed. Civilization only exists if the impulsion comes from the best and most enlightened men, that is, from an aristocracy. Aristocrats are those who, though born evil, like everyone, come nearest to what is good. Just as souls rise and develop personality by love and effort, so classes emerge in a nation. An aristocracy has both a social and a political function. It must lead and organize the masses, as well as elevate them morally by its example. There are in the world both moral and material interests. An aristocracy represents the former, and is only the "best" because it has defended these.

The qualities of an aristocracy are not necessarily those of intelligence, for it is an error to place superiority in the mind, rather than in the heart. The virtues of an aristocracy are courage, activity, honor, respect, and piety. It is an infallible sign of decadence when a nation no longer produces such an *élite,* and without it despotism is inevitable.

A hierarchy must exist, it is the very structure of society,

[19] *Ibid.,* p. 65.

and aristocracies can only be preserved by heredity. Families are units, based on continuity. They are one by reputation, destiny, fortune, blood, and the state of mind of a family acts on its civil, economic, and social situation. Its virtues are a common possession. Some families are more civilized, nearer to God than others. Their merit and honor must be an inheritance, or else money will become the chief desire, and men will seek to leave wealth, not virtue or glory, as a legacy to their children.

The aristocracy should form a Chamber of Peers, which will be the protector of tradition, and of the moral interests of society. It will support and modify the royal power, and will keep the spirit of emulation and noble ambition alive. Power is not a favor, and must be given only to those who aid in the formation of society; therefore the peerage today must be open only to high virtue, to territorial wealth, or to public service, such as that of magistrates or soldiers.

In the history of peoples a first aristocracy has usually formed the national territory, and created the laws and doctrines by which all exist. As these first leaders disappear, capital is formed, and a second aristocracy arises. It is inferior to the first, which springs from the people by heroism, whereas the second owes its elevation to labor. Thus the middle classes are always the source of the aristocracies of the future. The *bourgeoisie* must mingle freely with the aristocrats and be ennobled according to its deserts.

Blanc de St. Bonnet considered that the political institutions of every country are formed by its history and traditions, and there must be no written constitution to circumscribe the royal power. He recognized that public rights exist: they are the highest fruit of the social hierarchy, but they belong only to those individuals and bodies which have acquired them during the course of the ages. The parliamentary system is an evil; it must be done away with, and the nation restored to its ancient organization. A well-ordered State is formed of small societies; provincial chambers, magistracies, orders, corporations, which should each have a legal existence and effective means of representation.

There may be an elective chamber, whose function is to look after the economic interests of the country. It must not be chosen by universal suffrage, however. This is "atheism erected into an institution, the demolition of the social hierarchy, man substituted for God."[20] The elective Chamber must be created by indirect election in which all interests will be represented in the order of their social importance. The family is the smallest social unit, and its head, the father, is the communal elector. The communal corporations will choose representatives for the cantonal bodies, these will send representatives to the council of the *arrondissement,* and these to the departmental chamber. Finally the departmental chamber will send deputies to the national chamber.

Blanc de St. Bonnet wished the old guilds (*corps de métiers*) to be revived, and to be represented, but he did not formulate any clear scheme of professional representation, although he urged that the Chamber of Deputies should be divided into two commissions, one to represent agriculture and the other industry.

He was greatly in favor of decentralization. The sovereign, though he makes the laws, must not administer them in detail. Local responsibility gives variety and spontaneity to life, and allows a place for the activity of the family, the profession, and the city. The provinces should be reëstablished administratively, and wider corporative and collective

[20] *La Loi electorale,* p. 12.

interests entrusted to them in order to induce the population to return to the land. There should even be provincial peerages.

It is obvious that Blanc de St. Bonnet's whole philosophy was founded on the doctrines of Catholic Christianity. His views on the relations of Church and State were much the same as those of Bonald and Maistre, that all society is religion realized, and laws and powers proceed from God. But he did not institute a pure theocracy, or give the Church absolute power. Though civil and spiritual society depend on the same truth, their existence is separate. The authority of the king springs from nature, and the Church merely sanctions it, as it sanctions and blesses the institution of marriage. Nevertheless, faith is the sole means of maintaining order and liberty in a free society, and the State should therefore, protect the spiritual power. The Church has its own society and hierarchy, whose independence and free action must be assured.[21]

The system of entire liberty is not favorable to faith. The people, were they consulted, would reject alike the Trinity, confession, humility, chastity, God, king, peerage and police! Their own welfare demands that they should be enlightened and held in the good road. In order to accomplish this all education must be put into religious hands. "What is an instruction," Blanc de St. Bonnet asked, "which speaks to men neither of their souls, nor of their future destiny? Which does not explain to them the meaning of their life on earth?"[22] All teachers should be required to spend three years in the study of theology, and schools, colleges and uni-

[21] Like Maistre, Blanc de St. Bonnet saw in the pope an authority which might rightly judge of a king's legitimacy.

[22] *De la Restauration française,* p. 316.

versities, as well as seminaries, should be directed by ecclesiastics. It is the clergy who form the first and best aristocracy of a nation; they created the wealth of Europe, and to them its regeneration must be confided.

Like Bonald and Maistre, Blanc de St. Bonnet was hostile to freedom of thought. Only God's truth has a right to liberty. Irreligious or immoral books must be forbidden. Men have no more right to circulate harmful literature than to sell poison!

Like the theocrats, Blanc de St. Bonnet believed that Europe was rushing to an irrevocable ruin. The cause of this breaking up of society was man's pride and egoism, which found expression in Voltairian philosophy, and in the Revolution. "A doctrine," he said, "exists which explains the inequality of men, and furnishes them both consolation and remedy. This doctrine has been rejected. The Revolution substituted man for God, and tried to found society on the individual."[23] Men today see themselves as Gods on earth; they think only of enjoyment, and pretend that it is society which has depraved them! "You called men free," he exclaimed, addressing the philosophers, "without asking how they became so! You called them equal without saying before whom they are so!"[24] It is no longer merit, but equality which has become the law of society.

Liberalism is the expression of this error. It is the most terrible illusion which has ever taken possession of men's minds. Some honest people have believed that it was the application of Christianity in politics, and have called themselves "liberal Catholics."[25] This was possible because there

[23] *De la légitimité,* pp. V, 23.
[24] *De la Restauration française,* p. 79.
[25] *De la légitimité,* pp. 96-99.

is an element of truth in the liberal error, namely, that freedom must be kept in view as the goal. It must belong, however, not to the universality of men, but to *acquired merit*.

It is largely the middle classes which are responsible both for this error and for the love of luxury in France. They attacked the property of the nobles partly from envy, and partly in hope of winning luxury and idleness for themselves. But either *all* capital is legitimate, or *none* is. Communism is the logical outcome of the *bourgeois* attitude.

The people served as tools to the middle classes to overthrow the King, and now the middle classes are themselves about to be devoured by the people. The masses have risen against authority, and they will only tolerate the *bourgeoisie* for a short time.

Yet all is not lost. The misfortunes of France are an expiation for her heresy, and she may yet be saved. Democracy, born of pride and envy, is an unmitigated evil, but it is not inevitable. Virtue can save society from it. If France is not to die, a great moral renovation must take place. There must be no compromise with the Revolution. Salvation lies only in a return of the King, supported by the Church, in the rebirth of an aristocracy, the creation of a peerage, a reconstruction of landed property, and a rational form of representation by groups.

Blanc de St. Bonnet was strongly opposed to a "fusion" between the two branches of the Bourbon family. Opposite principles, he said, cannot be combined, as can two rival businesses. The kings of France have themselves been guilty; they encouraged luxury and vice, and tolerated atheism. But God has in reserve for France such a king as she needs. The Comte de Chambord, who rightly refused to become the "legitimate King of the Revolution,"[26] is the greatest exponent of Christian monarchy.

It is evident that Blanc de St. Bonnet's philosophy was a continuation of that of Bonald and Maistre. His political ideal was the organization of medieval Europe, and his economic views were drawn from the patriarchal and rural life which he himself led. There is a resemblance between his social ideas and those of LePlay. Like the early theocrats, he was too optimistic as to the past, and too somber as to the present.

His theory of capital, though visionary, is interesting. It is evident that virtue is not, and never has been, the sole source of riches. Yet the idea that wealth does, on the whole, usually indicate a genuine moral superiority is widely held by men very different from the devout Blanc de St. Bonnet. In fact, it is supposed to be a peculiarly American conception produced by the impact of Calvinism upon pioneer conditions.[27] In the creation of capital the virtues of courage, energy, and intelligence often play a greater part than sobriety and thrift, and a belief in the latter traits as the source of prosperity has been, on the whole, more characteristic of Protestant than of Catholic thought. Economy, however, has certainly played a large part in the formation of capital in France, and the Frenchman's conception of wealth is closely bound up with the ideas of sobriety and saving. Riches, for him, are rather to be amassed, than to be conquered or created.[28]

[26] Quoted from the Comte de Chambord's manifesto of January 25, 1872.

[27] The idea that work is a duty, and that it alone justifies wealth is also current in America.

[28] This fact has been pointed out by Mr. André Siegfried in a recent

St. Bonnet's theory of monarchy is exactly that of the earlier theocrats. The king's right is divine and inalienable. He possesses an absolute sovereignty. No constitution or bodies in the State may question his authority, and political rights or privileges are bestowed by him on merit. That this doctrine should be hopefully expressed in the last quarter of the nineteenth century is a proof both of the conservatism of French thought, especially in the provinces, and of the tenacity of the authoritarian idea.

Blanc de St. Bonnet tried, as had the theocrats seventy-five years before, to refute the doctrines of individualism by the Catholic teaching. No one has expressed better than he did the claims of merit as against those of "natural rights." He admitted the latter if interpreted only as a minimum of protection for the individual against arbitrary action, but he rejected them as the basis of social organization.

He saw life as a means of discipline and development for the soul, and he therefore accepted society in its ancient form. "To deplore the general condition of men," he said, "is to reproach God."[29] This conception of the object of life is a noble one; its ideal is resignation, self-discipline, and service; its aim, as Blanc de St. Bonnet said, is to make saints. Is there a higher ideal? A man as different from St. Bonnet as the American, William James, concluded that the saint, though apparently impractical, is really better fitted as a type to found society, than a more selfish or predatory man.[30] However, it has been said that "one good custom

---

lecture on French characteristics, delivered at the École de la Paix, March 3, 1932.

[29] *De la Restauration française,* p. 238.

[30] William James, *Varieties of religious experience* (New York, 1903).

may corrupt the world,"[31] and too much resignation to existing conditions may also be an evil. It must be admitted
that God's will, even if it is taken as the basis of society, is
not so evident in political matters as Blanc de St. Bonnet
imagined!

A man of much wider reputation, a brilliant journalist
and one of the outstanding figures of his day was Louis
Veuillot. He was not primarily a royalist, and it is to the
history of French Catholicism rather than to that of monarchy that the greater part of his work belongs. But his
conversion to the cause of legitimacy was an event of much
interest for the royalists, and he undoubtedly influenced the
Comte de Chambord, therefore his theory has a place in the
evolution of royalist doctrine.

Louis Veuillot was born in 1813. His father was a work-
man, and he himself was given only the most elementary
education. As a young man he was converted to ardent
Catholicism by a visit to Rome, and this conversion determined his future. His best known books are called *The Per-
fume of Rome* and *The Odors of Paris,* and he declared that
his whole life was expressed in these two phrases. His talent
as a polemist soon enabled him to make his way. He was
for many years the editor of the *Univers,* one of the principal Catholic newspapers, and he made it a power in the
land. It is probable that his influence on the French clergy
is felt even today.

Veuillot was truly a man of the people, as both his religious and his political thoughts testify. His faith was simple and uncritical, he took pleasure in the supernatural, and
he was always eager to believe in modern miracles. His

[31] Tennyson, *Morte d'Arthur.*

sympathy was for the workers, of whom he felt himself to be one, and he hated the sceptical materialistic middle classes. Their leaders, he said, could not understand the needs of the people, and they had deprived them of religion, which is their comfort and support. Liberalism, the philosophy of the middle classes, was his great enemy. Two parties, he said, struggle in the modern world: that of Revelation and that of revolution. The former is Christianity, headed by the Catholics, the latter is liberalism. A third party—that of liberal Catholicism—has tried to conciliate the two doctrines, but it has produced only confusion. It is an error of rich men, impossible to anyone who had lived among the people and seen how difficult it is for truth to descend into the depths! Because of the mistakes of the liberals, socialism will pass like a plough over society.[32]

Just as Benjamin Constant accepted every government so long as it promised to protect the rights of the individual, Veuillot was ready to serve any régime which he believed would favor the interests of the Church. He fiercely opposed the July Monarchy because it was the rule of the middle classes, but he rallied openly, even noisily, to the Second Empire. The war in Italy, and Napoléon III's quarrel with the Pope, however, turned him into a bitter opponent of the régime. He defended the temporal power of Rome with so much vehemence that his newspaper, the *Univers,* was for a time suppressed. As a result of his experiences of democracy and Caesarism he became convinced that legitimate monarchy was the only government which would safeguard Catholicism in France: "A very Christian King!" he wrote

[32] In one of his philosophical dramas he shows Vindex, the rebellious slave, as less guilty than Spartacus, the radical bourgeois.

to a friend in 1872.[33] "How we will astonish the world!
But it must be this, or civilization will fall. The King has
now only the Catholics to rely on, and the *Catholics have
only the King.*"[34]

For Veuillot the basis of political authority is religion.
"Jesus Christ is King of the world."[35] The Church *is* authority, while government is only a function. But God permits temporal powers to exist for the material organization
of society, and for this reason the Church recognizes and
upholds them; it institutes kings to confess and defend the
truth, and to protect the poor. Divine right is the consecration given by Heaven to a race chosen to govern the people.
The divine sanction, however, is not conferred on royalty
alone; it may be bestowed on any government which defends
Catholicism. "I do not believe in the inalienable right of
crowns" he wrote in 1848, "Catholic theology proclaims the
divine right of peoples." Man's first principle must be to
accommodate himself to power, whatever its form, if it
gives liberty and protection to the Church. "Let us fall at
the foot of the cross!" he wrote again;[36] "if God puts a
fleur de lys on it, I will not strike it off, but I will always
pray 'let God decide!' For me the Cross is enough." Nevertheless, Veuillot said that he had always preferred monarchy: "royalty was order, and order is life. When the
French King fell, every throne and cottage trembled to its

[33] "Letter to Comte Guitaut," August 2, 1872, Laurentie, François, *Le
Comte de Chambord* (Paris, 1912), p. 36.

[34] The italics are the author's, not Veuillot's. It must be remembered
that Veuillot died in 1883 before the *ralliement* made such an attitude
impossible to an ultramontane Catholic.

[35] *Mélanges,* 3ème série, V, 366.

[36] To O'Mahony, April 14, 1860.

foundation."[37] It was because the kings of France abandoned their faith that the Monarchy fell, for God allows the spirit of revolt to appear, in order to chastise rulers and peoples.

Royal power, although it is bestowed by God, has also its source in the nation. National sovereignty has always existed, it is not a creation of 1789. Formerly there was, at the head of each people, a man who was the father of his country, the expression of its faith, its memories, its aspirations. Today national sovereignty has disappeared, for the moral and physical being which was France has ceased to exist. What makes a people is religious and political unity, and this has been destroyed.

As to the character of monarchy, Veuillot, like Bossuet, and the legitimists in general, wished it to be absolute in theory, but tempered in practice by laws and customs. Despotism is a dictatorship without brake or restraint, and it is precisely to free themselves from such tyrannies that nations accept kings. Absolutism, he said, is not despotic; though it is independent and sacred, it is limited by other recognized powers, such as those of Church, the magistracies, and the corporations, and it would never try to annul the laws of the realm. The idea of royal power as at once independent and liberal is too little known.

In a collection of articles written during the siege of Paris and the Commune, and entitled *Paris during the Two Sieges,* Veuillot elaborated a sketch of a government, which he called *"Everybody's Republic."* "I believe in the resurrection of France,"[38] was the idea which inspired him. "She dreams of Christianity even in attacking it, and makes revolutions in the name of fraternity." The Prussian cannon,

[37] *Derniers mélanges,* III, 184.
[38] *Paris pendant deux sièges,* p. 372.

which has killed luxury and centralization, may be the instrument of France's regeneration, for France is still the eldest daughter of the Church, whereas Prussia, child of Luther, is the sin of Europe.

The social bases of Veuillot's constitution were religion, property, and family. The political bases were universal suffrage, the heredity of the throne, and the division of the territory into the old provinces. The national unity was to be preserved by the king, by a national court of justice, and by a representative body somewhat like the old States General.

According to Veuillot's constitution the head of the State, whose office was to be hereditary in the male line, was to name his ministers, propose the laws, make war or peace, coin money, convoke the General Assembly, and name its president. The provinces were to be administered locally, each having its own magistrates, budget, university, and militia. The National Assembly, besides the deputies elected by the provincial assemblies, was to include the Archbishops, the Heads of the Militia, and the chief magistrates of each province. Communes and corporations of all sorts, and particularly workmen's unions, being social entities, and property owners, must have a legalized existence, and political representation.

As soon as this constitution was voted, Veuillot wished "Henri de Bourbon"[39] to be invited to accept for himself and his descendants the supreme power. He was to be free to choose his own title, to be crowned at Rheims or at St.

[39] The Comte de Chambord. Veuillot was actively hostile to the "fusion" of the Bourbon family. "There must be no union with the remains of the liberal monarchy," he said.—"Histoire du Parti Catholique." Veuillot, *Oeuvres* (Paris, 1925), V. 409.

John Lateran, as he preferred, and to select the national flag.[40] The Comte de Chambord, Veuillot said, represented the monarchical principle, whose force is immense. His power would be stable, sacred, and truly liberal, because independent.

In his views on Church and State Veuillot was even more theocratic than Bonald and Maistre. His attitude is that of ultramontane Catholicism pushed to its limit. The papacy is the cornerstone of the social edifice, and the pope speaks as master, even to kings. Authority exists only to defend the truth, and, since Catholicism alone possesses this, it is a sign of social decadence to allow other cults to develop. The Catholic Church must be defended, and it must have unlimited rights and powers.

For Veuillot, not even the national interest could weigh against that of Catholicism, and Rome was the final arbiter in all matters. He gave a striking proof of his own submission to spiritual authority in a letter which he wrote to the Pope in 1853.[41] He had had some reason to fear that certain of his policies were not acceptable to Rome, and he hastened to put himself entirely at the disposal of the Holy Father, assuring him that he would never express an opinion which would not have his entire approval. "I have never put anything," he declared, "above Catholic doctrine and Catholic interests."

Veuillot's plan of political and social reorganization was quite in accord with the ideas of legitimists like Blanc de St. Bonnet, but he had greater faith in the people. He imagined that an alliance between king and people, such as

[40] Veuillot (writing in 1870) suggested a black flag with a red cross on it to symbolize the national mourning.

[41] March 3, 1893.

had existed in the early Middle Ages, was still possible, and he apparently believed that a genuine democracy in France would be Catholic and royalist. The character of the National Assembly of 1871 seemed to carry out this expectation, but events have since shown that he was mistaken.

It is an important fact that a man whose aims were exclusively Catholic should have reached the same conclusions as nationalists, like Berryer. These conclusions were much the same as are those of Charles Maurras today. The vital difference between the two men is that Veuillot was a devout believer, whereas Maurras is an agnostic. Thus Veuillot was a submissive son of the Church, ready to modify his policy at the bidding of Rome. From the point of view of the Church such an attitude is desirable, and it is natural that Rome should prefer for its defenders those who, like Veuillot, can be counted on to submit to its authority. To the royalists, however, they are somewhat doubtful allies.

CHAPTER X

THE ROYAL CLAIMANTS: COMTE DE CHAMBORD AND COMTE DE PARIS

The history of the Comte de Chambord is a strange one. He began his life brilliantly as the darling of a nation, and ended it in a long tragedy of exile. No prince ever came so near to occupying a throne legitimately and peacefully only to reject it by his own act.

Henri-Charles-Ferdinand-Marie-Dieudonné d'Artois was the last French descendant of Louis XIV in the male line. Louis XVII died or disappeared during the Revolution, Louis XVIII had no son, and the Duc d'Angoulême, eldest son of Charles X, was childless. The Duc de Berry, Charles X's second son, who was Chambord's father, was assassinated in 1820, and the boy, born seven months later, was called the Child of the Miracle. His birth was hailed with enthusiasm throughout France. He was at first known as the Duc de Bordeaux, but he took later the title of Comte de Chambord because a castle of that name was presented to him by national subscription.

On August 2, 1830, Charles X and his son, the Dauphin,[1] both abdicated their rights to the Crown. Thus, at ten years of age, the Duc de Bordeaux became the nominal King of France, at the very moment when the throne was lost. The whole rest of his life, with the exception of a brief visit to Chambord in 1871, was spent in exile.

The Comte de Chambord was very unlike his parents in character. His father, the Duc de Berry, was a gay and ro-

---

[1] The Duc d'Angoulême.

mantic young man, active, and fond of adventures of all sorts. His mother, Marie-Caroline de Bourbon-Sicile, had energy and courage, but she was ardent, impulsive, and unwise. Her later marriage with Lucchesi-Pali separated her to a great extent from her royal children. Henry V, as his followers called him, was serious, devout and austere. It is in the influences of his early life that the explanation of his character and doctrine is to be found, and these tended to make him both melancholy and distrustful. He was brought up in the somber atmosphere which surrounded Charles X in exile; an atmosphere created by the inertia of the old King and the solemn piety of Madame Royale.[2] Charles X had shown little comprehension of the modern world while he was on the throne,[3] and exile only made him more obstinate in his adherence to his principles. His grandson was educated entirely in the ideas and traditions of the past. His only contact with France was through the visits of devoted royalists who came on pilgrimage to see him during the course of his life-long exile.

His marriage also accentuated the seriousness of Chambord's character. It was an unfortunate union. His wife, the daughter of the duke of Modena, was remarkably plain, and, though extremely devout, was of a somber, and even suspicious nature. Moreover, she had no children, which was, from the legitimist point of view, a great misfortune. Although she was devoted to her husband, she felt her personal disqualifications, and did not want to be Queen of France.

[2] The Duchesse d'Angoulême. She was the daughter of Louis XVI and was married to the eldest son of Charles X.

[3] The most striking proof of this is his lack of appreciation of the probable effect of the ordinances of 1830. He took no precautions whatever to enforce them, or to protect himself from possible revolution.

In so far as she influenced the Comte de Chambord, it was in the direction of rigidity of principles, and mistrust of persons. The social and political conceptions of the Comte de Chambord were also determined in part by the fact that he was a very devout Catholic. As King of France he was, in his own eyes, the eldest son of the Church, and her interests were almost as dear to him as those of his country.

Everything, then, in the life and history of "Henry V" united to incline him towards the more reactionary doctrines of the authoritarian principle which he represented. In this principle he fervently believed, but his convictions were the result of reflexion, as well as of teaching and tradition. He was intelligent, and though not supple in mind, he was gifted with the entire courage of his convictions.

His thought, as it is to be found in his letters and manifestoes, is not always complete, or even clear. It must be remembered that his position was a difficult one. He was not a philosopher, but, in his own eyes, and in those of his followers, a king, and the doctrines which he expounded were certain to become at least the program of a party, and perhaps eventually the constitution of France. He was obliged to take into account the fact that many shades of opinion existed, even among his own supporters, and to avoid compromising the future, and alienating sympathies, by too clear-cut pronouncements on nonessential points. Hoping for a restoration, he wisely tried to leave as many questions as possible to be decided, as he said, "in agreement with France herself."

Chambord never expressed a belief in the divine right of kings. He founded his claim to the throne on the traditional principle of hereditary monarchy, as it had always existed in France. A Christian nation, he wrote in 1871, cannot tear up the century-old pages of its history, and break the chain of its tradition. "My birth," he said, "has made me your king."[4] His right was, above all, national. "Monarchy in France is the royal house indissolubly united to the nation."[5] Caesarism and anarchy result from seeking salvation in persons, rather than in the fundamental principles. He himself represented such a principle. It was "the sacred deposit of the national tradition,"[6] without which he was nothing, but with which he could accomplish anything. The solemn resolution to keep this principle intact, undiminished by any mixture of the elective idea, was always before his mind.

As to the character of monarchy as he understood it, it was to be "tutelary," and "tempered," and he declared that he would never put the royal power above the law, or dream of arbitrary absolutism. "Tempered monarchy," he wrote, "implies the existence of two chambers, one named by the sovereign from among specified categories, and the other chosen by the nation."[7] He was, however, opposed to the supremacy of the chambers, and to the parliamentary régime, which makes the ministers responsible to the elected body. "I do not want," he said, "the sterile parliamentary struggles, whence the sovereign issues weakened and powerless. I repudiate the formula, of foreign origin, which all our national traditions reject, of a King who reigns but does not govern. . . . I want a power strong enough to be able to repair and reconstruct."[8]

During the July Monarchy he was in favor of an exten-

[4] Manifesto of July 2, 1874, addressed to "Frenchmen."
[5] Manifesto of October 23, 1852.
[6] Letter to de Mun, November 26, 1878.
[7] Letter of July 2, 1874.
[8] Letter of July 2, 1874.

sion of the franchise. "I have always shown my conviction," he said, "that the happiness of France lies in a sincere alliance of the monarchical principle with public liberties. I see with the greatest interest the efforts made to obtain the repeal of the unjust laws which deprive the greater part of the people of their *legitimate* participation in the voting of the taxes."[9] He repudiated, however, La Rochejaquelein's demand for an actual appeal to the people. For him the monarchical principle, though it was consistent with public liberties, did not require popular assent. His program was:

a power founded on hereditary monarchy, respected in its principle and its action; free access to all posts and honors; religious and civil liberties safeguarded; the administration progressively decentralized; landed property given life and independence by the lightening of the burdens weighing on it.[10]

This program is an expression of the classic legitimist doctrines, but it is vague. The Comte de Chambord, however, was never more definite in his statements on these general questions. His conception of the monarchy of the future appears to have been neither exactly that of the Restoration, nor that of the old absolute monarchy of Louis XIV, but a modification of the latter. In an interesting letter of 1860,[11] he admitted that reforms had been needed before the Revolution. With time even the best institutions degenerate and abuses appear.

The Duke of Burgundy seemed destined to consummate the secular work of royalty, and to found the peace and prosperity of France on a solid basis, that of the old alliance of monarchy and liberty, those two national traditions which must always lend each other

[9] Letter to the Vicomte de Saint-Priest, January 22, 1848.
[10] Letter to the Vicomte de Saint-Priest, December 9, 1866.
[11] Letter to the Baron de Larey, March 31, 1860.

mutual aid. His premature death was the cause of this long series of disastrous revolutions.

Louis XVI saw that ameliorations were necessary, but the economists of his time gave him bad advice, and their plans failed. The Comte de Chambord himself wished, he said, to take up again the national movement of the end of the eighteenth century.

Two subjects interested Chambord particularly. The first was the social movement, and the condition of the lower classes. He wrote in 1847, "it is for us, the royalists, to head the social movement, to give it a wise and useful direction, and to show the working classes on which side are the real defenders of their interests."[12] In 1865 he wrote a manifesto in the form of a letter on the condition of the workers. In this he pointed out the bad results of individualism and free competition. The development of public prosperity, he said, had created a privileged industrial class which, holding in its hands the existence of the workers, had come to exercise a dominating influence in society. He severely blamed the laws which denied the right of association to working men. "In spite of the generous benevolence of a number of industrial leaders . . . the protection of the laboring classes is not sufficient . . . their moral and material interests have suffered."[13] As a remedy he proposed the right of association, wisely limited and supervised. This, he said, would be the regularization of a situation which actually existed, for there are always associations, but if they are not recognized by law, they are secret, and therefore dangerous. If free voluntary associations of workers are formed for the de-

[12] To the Baron de la Rivière, June 15, 1847.
[13] Letter on the workers, April 20, 1865.

fense of their interests, these "syndicates" can enter into relations with the employers, and settle by arbitration questions regarding the conditions of work and salary. The public authority will have nothing to fear from such associations, for it can oversee and regulate them, and make sure that they do not overstep their rights. Mixed commissions of workers and employers can assemble under the aegis of the State. The voluntary formation of free but regulated corporations is a powerful element of order and social harmony. Such corporations could enter into the organization of the commune, and form the basis of the franchise.

The other problem, closely connected with this, which particularly interested the Comte de Chambord, was decentralization. He treated it at length in a letter of November 14, 1862. The alliance of authority and liberty, he said, is the great problem in France. Despotism corrupts and eventually kills authority. In order to avoid this, the administration of France must be decentralized, but this must be done progressively, and with prudence. By calling all Frenchmen to take part more or less directly in matters touching their common interests both in the commune, the canton, and the department, a better political personnel would be created. This would produce a new social hierarchy, natural and mobile, and favor the "distributive justice"[14] which is real equality. The representative system, he said, has failed because the country was organized to be administered, not governed. The assemblies had been mere haphazard creations, which did not truly represent France. Only by decentralization can the country become conscious of its needs, and representative government be a reality.

The Comte de Chambord was also interested in the condi-

[14] Letter on decentralization, November 14, 1862.

tion of agriculture, but living, as he did, away from France, his opinions on that subject were largely tentative. He urged his followers, however, to live on their estates, and to take the lead, as far as possible, in the better development of agricultural methods.

With regard to the Church, Chambord was quite in agreement with the ideas of his most Catholic supporters. He always insisted on the importance of giving religious education to the people, and of allowing the Church all possible rights and liberties. Moreover he declared himself a firm defender of the temporal power of the Holy See. "The cause of the temporal sovereignty of the Pope," he wrote, "is not isolated; it is that of all religious and social liberty."[15] Even in a manifesto published in 1870, at a moment when France was struggling with Prussia, he declared that those who said that the independence of the Pope was dear to him, and that he was determined to guarantee it, spoke the truth.

During the early part of his life, the Comte de Chambord was opposed to force as the means of a restoration. In 1869 he wrote, "I have always respected France in the experiments she wished to try, and I was resolved not to increase her difficulties."[16] In his manifesto of 1870 (written on the Swiss frontier) he said, "during the long years of an unmerited exile I have never allowed my name to be a cause of division or disorder."[17] After the failure of a peaceful restoration in 1873 he appears to have modified his ideas on this subject. In or about 1879 the royalists raised money, and planned a restoration by a *coup d'état,* with the help of the

[15] Letter to Saint-Priest, December 9, 1866.
[16] Letter to M. . . . November 15, 1869.
[17] Manifesto, October 9, 1870.

army. Chambord seems to have authorized the plan, and to have allowed funds to be raised for the purpose. The project came to nothing.

It is difficult to know how much of Chambord's theory was original and how much was the result of the influence of his advisers. Many of his ideas were like those of Berryer, notably his advocacy of a wider suffrage, and his interest in the working classes and in freedom of association. In later years, Louis Veuillot appears to have influenced him, and the manifesto of 1872 was written by Veuillot himself, the Comte de Chambord, according to Veuillot, only changing a word or two. It was natural that the ideas of the prince should have been formed in part by the opinions of those of his followers who were in contact with France, and knew her political and social needs. That he could at times decide for himself is shown both by his resistance to Berryer's parliamentary policy, after the advent of Louis Napoleon, and by his conduct in regard to the flag. Whoever his advisers were, the ideas which he accepted and expressed were always in accord with the classic traditions of hereditary monarchy.

Two important problems arise in regard to the Comte de Chambord. The first is that of his reasons for refusing to abandon the white flag in 1874; the second that of his opinion as to the heir to his claim to the throne.

The question of the flag has been much discussed. There can be no doubt that it was his determination not to accept the tricolor as the national colors which broke up the royalist majority in the National Assembly and thus made impossible a restoration through that body. Great pressure was brought to bear on him in regard to this matter. His own most devoted partisans implored him, some literally on their knees,[18]

[18] The Duc de Bisaccia. See Pierre de Luz, *Henry* V, pp. 355-56.

to yield the point, and Monseigneur Dupanloup, who had once been his confessor, went so far as to reprove him for his rigidity. He has often been accused since of acting without judgment, of sacrificing the cause of monarchy to an absurd scruple, but these reproaches betray an incomplete grasp of the situation, and a misunderstanding of the nature of the man.

Chambord undoubtedly felt that to keep the white flag, the standard of his ancestors, was a point of honor, and the tricolor was associated for him with all the crimes of which his family had been the victims. But there is more behind his refusal than this aversion, or even the point of honor. To yield to the National Assembly in the matter of the flag, a question on which he had already declared himself,[19] was to admit, at least tacitly, its right to bestow the throne upon him. It was to abandon a position of authority, and to accept by implication the supremacy of the elected body, and its power to determine the ruler. This was contrary to the essential principle of hereditary monarchy as he understood it.

Chambord's mental evolution had been increasingly anti-parliamentary. Until the Empire he had tolerated a legitimist opposition in the Chamber of Deputies, and his confidence had been given to Berryer, the leader of this party. After 1852, he became more and more distrustful of the representative system as it then existed, and forbade his followers to participate in it. The National Assembly of 1871, although its majority was royalist, was a product of this same system, and a large part of that very majority was Orléanist, that is to say, liberal. To owe his throne to such an assembly, to allow it to dictate to him in a matter where he held his honor to be engaged, and to accept the symbol of ideas which were

[19] Manifesto of July 5, 1871.

contrary to all his principles was impossible to the Comte de Chambord; it meant his becoming "the legitimate King of the Revolution."[20] Chambord believed in the principle which he represented, of an inalienable and hereditary right, inherent in his person, and independent of all consent. His whole aim in occupying the throne of his fathers would have been to realize, by the authority of this principle, the reforms which he considered necessary. This principle once abandoned, would not the concession forced upon him in regard to the flag have been but the first of a series of compromises which would have made him into the constitutional monarch, who reigns but does not govern? He wrote to the Marquis of Foresta in 1879: "The country expected a King of France, but political intrigue had resolved to give it a mayor of the palace."[21]

It is evident that in refusing to accept the demands of the royalist majority, the Comte de Chambord did not realize that he was destroying all hope of his own restoration. Ill informed as to the real condition of opinion in France, he thought that if he could appear in the Assembly he would at once be acclaimed as king. That such was his belief is proved by the fact that a few days after the proclamation of the septennate, he made a secret visit to Versailles, in order to persuade the President, Marshal Mac-Mahon, to appear with him before the Assembly. But the newly-elected President felt that his honor was engaged to the Assembly, and refused to see the claimant whom he nevertheless considered to be his king!

[20] Manifesto of January 25, 1872. This is the manifesto which was inspired, and partially written by Louis Veuillot.
[21] Letter to the Marquis of Foresta, July 26, 1879.

As to the question of the heir to the throne, the Comte de Chambord never expressed himself officially. There can be no doubt that his *entourage* hated the Orléans family, but he himself was a generous man, and he does not seem to have shared this feeling. In August 1873, the Comte de Paris visited Chambord at Frohsdorf in order to effect the reconciliation, the "fusion" so often discussed. In receiving him, the Comte de Chambord exacted from him an express admission of the hereditary principle. The statement which was first proposed by "Henry V" contained the words: "The Comte de Paris, in visiting him [Chambord] will declare that he comes not only to greet the head of his House, but to recognize the principle of which the Comte de Chambord is the representative, and *to resume his place in the family.*"[22] For the last phrase, which would have left his position as heir to the throne entirely undefined, the Comte de Paris substituted the words "He wishes France to seek its salvation in a return to this principle, and comes to the Comte de Chambord in order to assure him that he will find no competitor in his family." This statement, it will be noticed, implies that the Comte de Paris had the right to speak for his whole Orléans branch of the family, because he was its head. The speech, thus modified, was accepted, and recited word for word at the meeting, according to the testimony of all the witnesses.[23] The men who were present agree that during their interview the Comte de Chambord said, in the course of conversation, "The king has his ideas, the heir to

[22] Pierre de Luz, *op. cit.,* p. 370-75. See also Robinet de Clery, *Les Deux Fusions* (Paris, 1908).

[23] Pierre de Luz, *op. cit.,* p. 374; René de Monti, *Souvenirs du Comte de Chambord* (Paris, 1930), p. 105; Vannsay, *Procès verbal.*

the throne may have his own." This remark, and some others made during his last illness to an intimate,[24] appear to imply that he considered the Comte de Paris as the next claimant to the throne. The fact that he again received the Orléans princes when he was dying, in spite of the efforts of some of his followers, and the opposition of the Comtesse de Chambord, and that he showed particular tenderness to the Comte de Paris, points in the same direction.[25]

It would, in fact, have been inconsistent with the Comte de Chambord's conception of the royal prerogative to have named his political heir. The principle of hereditary monarchy is that succession is automatic; the king is not called upon to pronounce in the matter.

At the death of Chambord in 1884, however, a small number of his adherents refused to recognize the claims of the Comte de Paris, and considered that the Spanish prince, Don Juan, was the heir to Chambord's political rights.[26] They were known as the "Spanish whites."[27] The theory on which they relied was that the right which is vested in the person of a king is not a personal possession of which he can dispose, and though he may himself abdicate, he cannot renounce the claims of his posterity. When the Duc d'Anjou mounted the throne of Spain he solemnly forswore all rights to the French crown for ever, for himself and for his descendants. This renunciation had been embodied in the treaty of Utrecht (1713), which ended the war of the Span-

[24] René de Monti de Rezé, *Souvenirs du Comte de Chambord,* pp. 138-39.

[25] Pierre de Luz, *op. cit.,* p. 458.

[26] Members of this family of Bourbon-Parme were the personal heirs both of the Comte and the Comtesse de Chambord. Even the Château de Chambord went to them.

[27] Blancs d'Espagne.

ish succession. But if a king cannot legitimately renounce the claims of his posterity, then the rights of the descendants of the Duc d'Anjou, Louis XIV's own grandson, preceded those of the Orléans family, who descended from Gaston d'Orléans, Louis XIV's younger brother.

That the throne of France can only be occupied by a Frenchman, is, however, the theory almost universally accepted by French royalists. The "Spanish whites" were too few and too insignificant to play any real part in the history of French royalism, and the vast majority of the legitimists recognized the Comte de Paris as the new king. Thus, with the death of the Comte de Chambord, the long separation of the royalists into two parties, with rival claimants, which had done so much to prevent a restoration, came to an end.

The new pretender was the grandson of Louis Philippe. His life represents in some respects a curious parallel to that of the Comte de Chambord. His father, the Duc d'Orléans, was killed in an accident in 1842, so that the Comte de Paris became heir to the throne when he was only two years old. The revolution of 1848 drove his grandfather from France when he was eight years old, and he spent his youth in exile. He was educated in England and Germany, traveled a great deal, and wrote a number of books and articles on his travels. He studied the conditions of labor in England, and published a small book on the subject in 1873. He and his brother, the Duc de Chartres took part in the war of Secession in America, on McClellan's staff, and actually fought in the battle of Malvern Hills, and the retreat of Chickahominy.

The Comte de Paris had sound political judgment. The initiative of the reconciliation with the Comte de Chambord was his own, and, as we have seen, he showed great tact and presence of mind in the negotiations which preceded his visit to his royal cousin.

He had been brought up in the Orléans traditions of liberalism and constitutional monarchy, but he was not a theorist, and his letters and public pronouncements contain for the most part only the most conventional royalist doctrines. In this his wisdom is evident, for if at the death of the Comte de Chambord both authoritarian and liberal royalists were to unite in his support, it was necessary that his official views should be acceptable to them all. Although he undoubtedly remained fundamentally liberal he made some effort to reconcile, as far as possible, the two systems.

He considered that the royal right was originally based on a national compact.

The Capetien Monarchy made the unity of France because it had as its origin a real national pact, concluded in the first hours of their history between those who represented the new-born France, and the family whose lot it was to be united to the nation during good and ill fortune.[28]

Two points on which the Comte de Paris insisted particularly were the power of the monarchical principle to furnish a strong and stable authority, and its ability to accommodate itself to democracy.

Only the national monarchy, traditional in principle, but modern in nature, of which I am the representative, can reduce disorder to impotence, assure political and religious liberty, and restore authority and the public fortune. It alone can give our democratic society a strong government, open to all, and superior to parties, whose stability will be a guaranty of peace.[29]

[28] Protest of June 2, 1886. See *La Monarchie française* (Paris, 1907). This is a collection of royal speeches and letters, including those of the Comte de Chambord, the Comte de Paris, and the Duc d'Orleans.
[29] Protest of June 21, 1886. See *La Monarchie française* (Paris, 1907).

In 1887, he repeated: "The traditional monarchy can adapt itself to modern institutions. It will give to our democratic society the element of moderation which the Republic lacks." These speeches are liberal, but his criticisms of the parliamentary régime were of a nature to please authoritarians. The monarchy alone, thanks to its origin, he said, would be strong enough to conciliate universal suffrage with the guarantees of order which the country, disgusted with the parliamentary régime, demands. Under the Republic, the chamber governs uncontrolled; under the monarchy the king governs, with the help of the two chambers.

Another point which he greatly stressed was the protection of religion. "For Christian France," he said, "the monarchy is necessary." It would give Catholics an effective guaranty against the return of oppressive laws. In France the Republic will never be Catholic.

These ideas are general enough to allow some latitude of interpretation, and to be in accord with royalist tradition as a whole. They are remote from the theories of Blanc de St. Bonnet, or of Louis Veuillot, but they are not unlike those of Chateaubriand and Berryer. Royalists might not unreasonably claim that monarchical doctrines like all living things, must have a right to adapt themselves to the realities of a changing world.

At the death of the Comte de Paris, in 1894, his son the Duc d'Orléans became the pretender. This prince accepted the support of the Action française and showed sympathy for their ideas. His successor, the Duc de Guise, the present pretender, has followed the same policy.

CHAPTER XI

THE RALLIEMENT: ITS DOCTRINE AND ITS EFFECT ON ROYALIST IDEAS

The Catholic Church has never advocated in its doctrine one form of political constitution above another, and in practice it has been able to accommodate itself more or less readily to the form of government existing in each country, so long as the public authority did not actively oppose its interests.

The Church teaches that civil power is of divine origin. The Catholic conception is expressed by Saint Thomas of Aquinas in syllogistic form. (*Major*) Man is created by God to live in society; and families, tribes, nations, which are the forms of civil society, have a natural origin. (*Minor*) To live in society, a superior authority is necessary, in order that each member may be controlled for the common good. (*Conclusion*) Since God has willed the end, which is society, he also willed civil authority, which is the means.[1]

This authority was communicated to the nations[2] by God, and, since the nation as a whole cannot exercise it directly, it communicates it to persons who exercise it in the common interest. To do so is so sacred a duty that the nation takes back, or can take back its right, even in an hereditary monarchy, when the depositaries of sovereignty become impotent to fulfill their mission, or fail in their duty, and no longer labor for the common good.

[1] *Summa theologicae,* IA 2, Quaestio XCVI, art. iii, ad Tertium.

[2] To the nation as a whole, not necessarily to the individuals who compose one generation. See Chénon, *Théorie catholique de la souveraineté nationale* (Paris, 1898), p. 13.

This doctrine, its implications, and the circumstances under which it is applicable have been much discussed, and it is, of course, contrary to the theory of the divine right of kings.[3] It was certainly held by many of the fathers and doctors of the Church, including Saint Augustine,[4] Saint John Chrysostom, Saint Thomas Aquinas,[5] Gerson, Bellarmin, Suarez, Molina and others,[6] and has been expressed by several popes.[7]

In practice, also, the Church has naturally preferred and supported those governments which have favored its interests; so much so that it has become in some cases more or less identified with them. Such has been the condition in France. The Revolution was based on theories of individualism and freedom of inquiry which were in opposition to Catholic doctrine, and it early became actively anti-clerical. Throughout the nineteenth century this anti-clerical spirit continued to be more or less characteristic both of liberalism and of the republican ideal.

At the Restoration the interest of the Church and the Monarchy alike was to reorganize society on a conservative basis, and in this task they gave each other mutual support. Thus the union between Catholicism and royalism, which had existed before the Revolution, was renewed.

It would be inexact to say that all Catholics were then, or

[3] See works of Chénon, and of Feret, mentioned in bibliography.
[4] *Confessions*, Lib. III, Cap. viii. [5] *Summa theologica, loc. cit.*
[6] See Abbé Feret, *Le Pouvoir civil devant l'enseignement catholique* (Paris, 1888), for a compendium of authorities on this subject. Also *Le Droit divin et la théologie* (Paris, 1874), and the answers of Tancrède de Hauteville, *L'Union,* August 27, 1874, and Coquille, *Le Monde,* Sept. 4, 1874. There is a résumé of the material in Chénon, *op. cit.*
[7] Nicholas I wrote during his struggle with Lothair II, "See if these kings are true kings and princes . . . if they govern their people well. . . . If not they must be considered as tyrants, and openly resisted."— Baronius, *Annales ecclesiastiques,* An. 863, cap. lx.

at any time, monarchists, or to suppose that the Holy See and the French clergy as a whole held the Catholic cause to be indissolubly bound to that of legitimate monarchy, but in the eyes of the public the two ideas were closely connected.

When the Monarchy of the Restoration fell, the Church did actually suffer, in some measure, for its affiliation with the dynasty and the party of reaction. As time went by, and the July Monarchy was succeeded by more revolutionary régimes, the Republic and the Empire, it is easy to see how disadvantageous for Catholicism was its identification in the popular mind with the royalist cause.

The Comte de Chambord's refusal in 1874 to renounce the white flag made an immediate return to monarchy improbable. The Republic seemed more and more likely to endure, and what, then, would be the position of the Catholics if they remained attached to a party which permanently opposed the existing form of government? Such an attitude might not only provoke, but more or less justify, acts of aggression on the part of the Republic, including even the suppression of the budget of the Church.[8] This budget, which had, in a measure, replaced its prerevolutionary wealth, was then thought necessary to the existence of the Church in France.

There were, moreover, elements among the Catholics, and particularly in Rome, which were hostile to a royalist restoration in France.[9] A national king, if he were strong, might, it was feared, try to revive the old Gallican tradition.

The nineteenth century had witnessed the development both of liberal Catholicism, and of the social Catholic move-

[8] Mermeix, *Le Ralliement et l'Action française* (Paris, 1927), p. 77.
[9] Many Catholics were Bonapartists. For the influence in Rome see Léon de Cheyssac, *Le Ralliement* (Paris, 1906), p. 24.

ment in France. Leo XIII wished to replace the fallen temporal power by an apostolic royalty over intelligences. He hoped to win the working classes back to the Church, and he was much interested in popular Catholic movements. His famous encyclical on the condition of the workers[10] was the signal for a new activity among the Catholics. Social Catholicism in France was not essentially republican; on the contrary, many of its leaders were royalists, but it might be thought that here, also, too close an association between monarchy and Catholicism would limit the influence of the latter among the lower classes.

For all these reasons Leo XIII wished to detach the French Catholics from their close association with royalism. In 1879 he made an effort to win the Comte de Chambord to this policy. The papal legate, Monseigneur Czacky, approached the Comte de Dreux-Brezé, Henri V's political representative, and the Comte de Blacas, one of his intimates. To both these men he said that the pope had no further hope of a restoration in France. The republican current, he thought, was sure to grow stronger. The legitimists, if they continued to struggle for the monarchical principle, would see the number of their followers diminish, and their great moral influence would be lost. He hoped, therefore, that they might recognize existing facts, cease to combat the Republic, and unite with all other Catholics to defend only the interests of the Church.

The Comte de Chambord rejected this proposal with great decision[11] and Leo XIII made no further effort until after the death of that prince. "Henry V," even during his lifetime,

[10] *Rerum novarum,* 1891.
[11] When he received it he actually telegraphed to Dreux-Brezé "Tenez bon."

was an almost mythical person. His misfortunes and the genuine nobility of his character entitled him to respect, and he was in the eyes of many the very Christian prince "par excellence"; the defender, and almost the martyr of the idea of Christian monarchy. His devotion to the temporal power,. and his constant declarations in its favor, even at the most difficult moments[12] entitled him to special consideration from the papacy.

With his death in 1883, however, the situation changed. The Comte de Paris, his successor, although like Chambord, he united his cause to that of Catholicism, had not the same claims to the gratitude of the Pope, and his traditionally liberal opinions made him unwelcome to many Catholics. Moreover, his chances of mounting the throne appeared to diminish after the elections of 1885, which, although they showed the strength of the conservative elements in France, yet again gave the victory to the Republic.

The Boulangist episode in 1888-1889 indicated that the French were still inclined to favor a personal government. Boulanger was merely a popular soldier, but the royalists hoped to find in him another General Monk, and they and many of the Catholics supported him because he promised a return of authority, and the end of parliamentary squabbles and scandals. He had, however, no real capacity nor courage, and he fled when he felt himself in danger. This flat failure covered his supporters with ridicule, and served further to discredit both royalists and Catholics. The Pope might well feel anxious as to the future of Catholicism in France!

The first open move in the papal policy of rallying the Catholics to the Republic was a toast proposed by Cardinal Lavigerie at a banquet given by him, as archbishop of Al-

[12] See above p. 173.

giers, to the officers of a French squadron then visiting that port.[13]

> When the will of a people has been clearly asserted and the form of the government is not in itself contrary to the principles by which Christian and civilized nations live . . . the moment has come . . . to put an end to our divisions, and to sacrifice all that honor and conscience will allow . . . to the well-being of our country. Outside of this resignation, this patriotic acceptance, nothing can be done to preserve the world from the social peril, or save the religion of which we are the ministers. In what I say I am sure that I shall not be contradicted by any authority.

Lavigerie had recently been to Rome, and there could be no doubt that his speech was at least approved, if not inspired, by Leo XIII.

Although it found some immediate approbation and adherences, Lavigerie's toast was, on the whole, ill-received both by the royalists and the republicans. The question first raised was by what authority he took such action, and certain churchmen asked the pope whether Lavigerie's words were to be considered merely as a personal opinion, or as the instructions of the Church. On December 5, 1892, Cardinal Rampolla, Leo XIII's Secretary of State, wrote an answer which confirmed the sympathy of Rome with the attitude announced in the toast of Algiers, and on February 16, 1892, the Pope himself published an encyclical, to the archbishops, bishops, clergy, and all the Catholics of France, to the same effect.

In this encyclical Leo XIII began by exhorting "not only all Catholics, but all wise and honest Frenchmen to set aside every source of political dissent, and devote their strength to the pacification of their country." Religion alone, he con-

[13] November 12, 1890.

tinued, can create the social bond. When families, while keeping the rights and duties of domestic society, unite to form civil society, their object is not merely to increase their material welfare, but to perfect themselves morally. Without this moral improvement society could scarcely be said to be of benefit to man.

Morality implies a dependence on truth, which is the light of the spirit, and on the good, which is the object of will. It supposes God, and, with God, religion. The Catholic religion, as the true Church of Christ, possesses more than any other the power to regulate life in the individual, and in society. France gives a striking example of this, for, as a Catholic country it rose constantly in moral, political and military power. For a Frenchman to renounce such glory would be to deny his country, and with French Catholics, the first object must be to preserve their religion, the more so as it has been so fiercely attacked.

The Church does not wish to exercise a political domination in the State; this is an old calumny, which was preferred against Christ himself, but, in order to protect the interests of religion, other considerations must be held as secondary. Theoretically, one form of government may be better than others, but in practice any form is good, if it genuinely serves the common welfare. The Church, therefore, disregards the form of the powers with which she has to deal, and considers only the religious interests of the peoples of which she is the guardian.

Individuals are bound to accept the government under which they live, and the Church, holding that power derives from God, has always reproved subversive doctrines, and condemned the men who rebel against legitimate authority. She has done so, even when the holders of that authority used it against herself.

Each people has its own form of political power, born of the ensemble of its history and its nature, but human societies are transformed by time. It is only the Church which is immutable. Changes may cause anarchy and disorder, and nations have therefore the right to reëstablish the public peace, and to create new governments when necessity justifies them. On such occasions the novelty lies in the political form of the civil power, or in its mode of transmission, it does not affect power, considered in itself. That remains worthy of respect, since it is constituted for the common good. In other words, the civil power, whatever its form, is always from God. Therefore, to accept it is not only allowed, but imposed by the interest of the social welfare.

It is said that the Republic in France is anti-Christian, and so cannot conscientiously be accepted by Catholics. There is, however, a great difference between the constituted power and legislation. Under the best form of government there may be detestable legislation, and, on the other hand the most imperfect government may make excellent laws. Legislation is thus a ground on which all good men may unite to combat abuses. The respect due to authority does not forbid this, nor does it imply an unlimited obedience to every measure proposed by government. Law is a prescription of reason, promulgated for the common welfare by the holders of power. Legislation which is contrary to this welfare can never be approved, and it is a duty to oppose it. To this category belong all laws which are hostile to God and to religion.

The encyclical was followed, on May 3, 1892, by a letter to six French cardinals, who had announced their adherence to the papal policy.[14] The encyclical, Leo XIII said, had already done much good. The conservative forces of France,

[14] They were Desprez (Toulouse), Lavigerie (Algiers), Place (Rennes), Foulon (Lyons), Langemieux (Reims), Richard (Paris).

which had been paralyzed and rendered sterile by their disunion, could now unite to support the cause of Christ. The necessity of a civil power, he continued, to direct the wills of its subjects derives from the needs of the general welfare, and the reason for accepting this authority is that the common good must prevail over all other interests. When an authority actually exists, the general welfare soon becomes bound up with it, and it must, therefore, be respected.

Human institutions do not always keep their vigor, and unexpected changes may take place. Monarchies may fall, or be dismembered, and dynasties may replace dynasties. These changes are not always legitimate in their origins, but the supreme criterion of the common welfare and public tranquillity imposes their acceptance, once they are established. Thus, the rules of the transmission of power may be suspended or abolished, yet conscience demand submission to the constituted government, in the name of the sovereign right, indisputable and inalienable, which is called the social welfare. Legislation, however, need not be accepted, and in this direction there is room for men to use their influence and authority to ameliorate matters.

Men who subordinate all to the triumph of a party, even if it seems to them to be the one best fitted to defend religion, are making politics, which divide, pass before religion, which unites. "It has been said," the Pope added, "that we act differently in France and in Italy. Not so. Our object in speaking to French Catholics is to safeguard religious interests. It is these interests which inspire us also in Italy . . ." We make all converge to one object; religion, and, by religion, the salvation of society, and the happiness of peoples.

On June 22, 1892, Leo XIII wrote to Monseigneur Fava, Bishop of Grenoble, to complain of attacks on his policy.

We do not seek to dabble in politics (*faire de la politique*) but where politics are closely bound to religious interests, as they are in France, the pope has a mission to determine the conduct which best safeguards the supreme interest—that of the Church.

France, he added, is menaced with complete de-Christianization, and French Catholics must seek the concord and coöperation of all honest men. In writing to Monseigneur Perraud, on December 20, 1893, the Pope repeated: "We claim the power and duty of choosing the means best adapted to the circumstances of time and place, to procure the good of religion . . . We are pained to see that many reject our advice."

In 1897, in a letter to Cardinal Matthieu, Leo XIII declared that he had added nothing to the teaching of the great doctors of the Church, but had merely appropriated them to circumstances. To sacrifice interests and personal attachments for the sake of assuring the welfare of tomorrow is wiser and more praiseworthy than to struggle in the void, to the detriment of religion and the Church.

The encyclical, and the letters which followed it, not only repudiated the connection between Catholicism and the royalist cause, but enjoined Catholics to accept the Republic. This action was based on the traditional doctrine of the Church that all forms of government are acceptable, so long as they promote the general welfare. The encyclical, however, seems to consider the security of religion as the only criterion of that welfare, so that the conclusion might be drawn that the interest of the Catholic Church can alone justify resistance to any government, or even political action in general.

The doctrine that *de facto* governments, whatever their origin, must be obeyed, implies the acceptance of all usurpations, however unjust, if they prove successful, and the

Church has, in fact, recognized many governments of doubt-ful antecedents.[15] This indifference as to the form and origin of a régime implies a pragmatic, almost an amoral point of view with regard to civil government, which is strange in the papacy, the defender of morality. It follows naturally, how-ever, from the fact that the religious interests of the people are always the paramount consideration of the Church.[16] In examining the doctrine of the encyclical the question arises whether men should be willing to sacrifice what they believe to be the advantage of their country to the interests of re-ligion. In other words, are Catholics morally obliged to fol-low the line of political conduct which is most favorable to the Church, even if they hold it to be bad for their country? To a devout Catholic the true interest of his country must seem to be closely bound up with that of religion, but it is difficult for the average man to admit that the latter should always be his first concern. The doctrine of the encyclical, on this point, does explain, to some extent, the anti-clerical-ism of certain French patriots.

A second question is whether Catholics are free to decide themselves as to what is the best policy in the interests of religion. Leo XIII denied that the Church sought to exercise political domination. This was, no doubt, true, but he claimed the right to direct the conduct of Catholics, in matters where the interests of the Church were affected by politics. The proof that he considered the admonitions of the encyclical as more than mere advice is to be found in the letters which followed it, especially the one to Monseigneur Fava. It is

[15] It recognized both the Directory and the Empire.

[16] This attitude of serene indifference to the temporal power was that of Christ himself. It is implied in "Render unto Caesar that which is Caesar's."

difficult to draw the line as to where such a right begins, and the whole episode of the *ralliement* is an example of the influence which Rome does, at times, exert on Catholics, in regard to political matters.

The distinction drawn by the encyclical between the form of government, and legislation, is valuable, but it cannot be carried too far. If governments are poorly constituted, or have won their way to power by violence, their legislation is very apt to be affected thereby.

There is a certain contradiction between the teaching of the encyclical with regard to the duty of opposing abusive laws, and the respect for, and obedience to, authority which it enjoins. Theoretically, it is possible to respect a form of government, and yet refuse to obey its laws, but in practice no government can afford to allow such a distinction, and most rebellions have, in fact, begun as protests against definite laws, rather then against a form of government.[17] Resistance to the law is very apt, if successful, to lead to a change of political régime. The encyclical, however, spoke only of opposition, and there was no question of active resistance to the laws of the Republic either in the mind of Leo XIII or of his listeners.

It is interesting to see that the past glories of France, and her former commanding position in Europe, which the royalists always attribute to the influence of her kings, are considered by Leo XIII to be due to her Catholicism. So long as the union of royalism and Catholicism lasted, it was not necessary to question whether it was her religion, or her form of government which had made the France of Louis

---

[17] An example is our own War of Independence. Even the French Revolution was, in the beginning, a struggle for legislative reform, rather than for the overthrow of the régime.

XIV so great; the two appeared to be interdependent. There is much in the writings of the royalists, especially of Bonald, Maistre, Berryer and Blanc de St. Bonnet,[18] which agrees with the statement that the strength of France was due to her religion, and that it was the disappearance of faith which caused her relative decline in Europe, but this theory is refuted by her enormous power and influence during the Napoleonic era.[19]

The doctrine of the encyclical as to the origin and object of society, which is the traditional teaching of the Church, is identical with the ideas of the theocrats, and with those of most of the royalist philosophers. This is a proof of the genuine connection between the two ideas which made it so difficult to separate them.

The encyclical, and the letters which followed it, were a heavy blow to the monarchists. It is not possible to discuss here their actual effect on the royalist party,[20] but it is certain that many of its influential members followed the Pope's advice. The most important adherence was that of Albert de Mun, the founder and leader of the Catholic working men's circles. De Mun had been a fervent royalist,[21] but his great interest was the development of social Catholicism, and he hoped that the acceptance of the Republic might be helpful to

[18] Chateaubriand expressed the same idea many times in *Mémoires d'outre-tombe.*

[19] It is obvious that neither Catholics nor royalists took into consideration many factors which determined the relative "greatness" of France in the seventeenth century. See below, p. 222-23.

[20] Léon de Cheyssac gave some information on this subject in *Le Ralliement* (Paris, 1897), pp. 105-25.

[21] He had said "The King is the law. Legitimate monarchy is the condition necessary for the safety of France." See *Bartelme, Le Railliement* (Paris, 1897), p. 12, and P. T. Moon, *The Social Catholic Movement in France.*

this. On January 24, 1892, he wrote to the reverend Father Didon a letter which was a formal adherence to the policy outlined in Lavigerie's toast, "I do not hesitate to say," he wrote, "that I am ready to conform my attitude to the advice given on February 25,[22] with so much authority." He repeated "There are men who, because they are Catholics, make the defense of religion and of popular interests their first preoccupation."[23]

The *ralliement* went through a number of phases, and various efforts were made to put the papal advice into effect, but in spite of all these defections, the royalist party did not disappear, for many of its members were unwilling to abandon their ideas, and the cause which they considered to be the hope of France.

Shortly after the toast of Algiers the Comte d'Haussonville made a speech at a banquet at Nîmes, where 3,000 royalists were present, in which he developed the chief royalist arguments against the *ralliement*. The Republic, he said, would never be favorable to Catholicism; it had not taken the way of conciliation, and would repulse those who rallied to it. The policy of disarmament is one of abdication. The words of Monseigneur Lavigerie need only be taken as advice, for the Church, though it preaches submission to the established powers, does not take part for or against a dynasty, and it cannot teach adherence to the Republic as an article of faith. Each man has a right to fight for the cause which is dear to him. Conscience will not allow the royalists, after denouncing the Republic as intolerant, and reproaching it with driving Christ from hospitals and schools, to bring it their adherence. There is in monarchy a superior principle,

[22] A. de Mun, *Discours* (Paris, 1891-94), p. 127.
[23] *Ibid.*, p. 108.

which France cannot repudiate without losing all hope of
rising beyond a certain level.

We are monarchists not only from fidelity, and respect for the past,
but because we love France . . . We will not allow ourselves to
be placed under the alternative of renouncing our religious convictions, or betraying our country . . . If anyone seeks to impose
on us as Catholics the moral obligation of becoming republicans,
we shall have to answer *Non possumus*.[24]

In a further speech of July 19,[25] he pleaded that Catholicism
should not be separated from the conservative interests to
which it is allied.

The Comte de Paris approved the speech at Nîmes, and
declared that it could leave no doubts in the minds of the
royalists. He described the *ralliement* as "dangerous and
chimerical,"[26] but refused to make any remonstrance to the
Pope, for to do so would imply the right of the Holy See to
intervene in French politics which the Comte de Paris denied.
He wrote (on January 13, 1892) to General de Charette that
he did not ask the Pope to pronounce in favor of the monarchy, or to recommend monarchist candidates to Catholics
at the elections. All he asked for was neutrality. The royalists, in addressing the clergy, wished to prove to them on
the one hand that the Republic will always disappoint those
who do not recognize that it is the irreconcilable enemy of
religion, and, on the other that a national monarchy would
give Christian France all the guaranties she justly claims.
Even if there should still be an anti-clerical chamber under
the monarchy, the minority would then have an effective
protection. It is unjust, he continued, to treat as Gallicans

[24] Speech made at Nîmes, 1891.
[25] Toulouse, 1891.
[26] Letter to Colonel de Perseval, February 21, 1891. *La Monarchie
française,* p. 178.

those who do not blindly accept the advice of the Holy See on purely political matters. The conscientious duties of a Catholic may easily be reconciled with the duties which his political convictions impose on a monarchist. Experience will prove how imprudent it was to separate Catholic interests from the conservative cause, for nothing can be done for religion, or for the preservation of tradition in France, save by the monarchy.

Many royalist papers rallied to the Republic, but a few held firm. One of the most important of these, the *Gazette de France,* published immediately after the encyclical[27] the opinion of several influential monarchists among whom were Cazenove de Pradine, Audren de Kerdrel and Delahaye. The arguments advanced by these men were that the Pope has not the right to dictate to the conscience of patriots in political matters, that monarchists cannot adopt a line of conduct opposite to what they have always held, without losing all claims to respect, and that the Holy See did not require them to enter the Republic, but merely advised them not to combat it by force. On May 10 the editor of the *Gazette de France* declared that the royalists must close up their ranks, and look to the future, when the king would be called on to play his part. The restoration once accomplished, the papal blessing would not be wanting! According to certain royalists the theory of the *ralliement* resembled the heretical idea of the lesser evil; "let us submit to our enemies, lest they do us greater harm."[28] On the whole, however, the royalist opposition to the *ralliement* was largely a passive one. Astonishingly little was written in open refutation of the papal advice, and the reasons advanced for resistance were, in general, prac-

[27] February 22, 1892.
[28] *Gazette de France,* January 6 and January 9, 1898.

tical, rather than theoretic. The most active opposition came from the Bonapartist Cassagnac, whose paper *L'Autorité* was extremely vigorous in its attacks on the papal doctrines. This was natural, for the Empire was always less submissive to the Church than was the Monarchy.

It might have been supposed that in answer to the papal opposition to the old alliance, some royalists would have suggested the possibility of a non-Catholic or even anti-clerical monarchy. This idea was advanced by a journalist, Urbain Gohier,[29] but it found no echo. The royalists in general merely kept their old position, and continued to claim that in hereditary monarchy lay the salvation of France and the safety of the Church. Their arguments were mainly confined to the inexpediency of the *ralliement* and sought to demonstrate its certain failure. They did not openly attack Leo XIII, or do more than respectfully set aside his advice.

There are several reasons for this reserve. In the first place, while Catholics were not all royalists in 1892, almost all royalists were Catholics. They might, therefore, treat the encyclical as mere advice, and so neglect it, but they could hardly contest its doctrine, or criticize its author. There is a marked contrast between the attitude of the royalist leaders, in this respect, and the violence of the Bonapartist Cassagnac. Moreover the royalist's ideas as to the object of society, and its organization, their respect for order and authority, and for the family, are essentially Catholic. They could not separate their cause from that of the Church without denying the religious philosophy which was the basis of their

[29] Urbain Gohier, *L'Armée contre la Nation* (Paris, 1899). Gohier's monarchical opinions were somewhat uncertain. He afterwards joined the staff of the *Aurore,* a paper founded by Clemenceau to defend Dreyfus.

whole political and social system. This was true even of the liberal royalists, in spite of the greater individualism of their ideas.

Yet, while the encyclical did not provoke much doctrinal reaction, it had a great effect on royalist theory. The Pope had reminded men that the Church, though it considers authority sacred, does not admit that kings have any particular divine sanction, nor that they are the only source of authority. The conception of sovereignty as vested by divine right in kings had already almost disappeared, and the *ralliement* gave it the death blow. It therefore became necessary for royalist philosophers to find some other basis for the authority of the monarch. As for the political consequence of the *ralliement,* all that can be said is that it failed to accomplish the chief object of Leo XIII, which was to prevent the separation of Church and State in France.

CHAPTER XII

LA TOUR DU PIN

During the nineteenth century the growth of democracy and the industrial revolution gave rise to problems of social organization and of the distribution of wealth, which became the chief concern of theorists. In the political field liberalism had created the parliamentary régime, which gave increasing scope to democracy, but it appeared impotent to deal with these economic and social questions. Both socialism and communism professed to have found solutions, the one in State ownership of the means of production, the other in an entire economic equality. The royalists proposed their own solution of the social problem.

The social and political system which the royalists advocated was based on traditional ideas and institutions, modified to meet the new conditions. Traces of this adjustment are to be found in the works of the men whose ideas we have already examined,[1] but certain aspects of the royalist doctrine were most fully formulated by La Tour du Pin. It was in the social field that his chief contribution lay, but his ideas formed a whole, of which monarchy was a vital part. For this reason, he did not, like his friend, Albert de Mun, rally to the Republic.

Both chronologically and doctrinally La Tour du Pin stands between the legitimist philosophers of the nineteenth century and the Action française, as a sort of connecting link. He was to a certain degree affiliated with the latter; some of his articles were published in their newspaper, and

[1] Notably in those of Berryer, Chambord and Louis Veuillot.

his social doctrines are taught at the Institut d'Action française, but he did not wholly identify himself with the party.

Charles Humbert René de La Tour du Pin-Chambly de
la Charce was born in 1834, and died in 1924. Thus his active
life included a large part of the nineteenth, as well as the
first quarter of the twentieth, century. His family was a
very old and very noble one, descended from the Scottish
Douglases, whose arms they bore in their escutcheon. René
de la Tour du Pin was educated at home in the family traditions of courtesy and duty. One of his youthful memories,
which always influenced him, was the words of his father,
as he showed his son their domain: "Never forget that you
will only be the administrator of these lands for their inhabitants."[2] La Tour du Pin was devoted to his home and his
land, and liked to call himself a peasant.

Life, according to the ideas in which he was brought up,
was service, and the military profession was a part of his
family tradition. There had been fifteen generals in the La
Tour du Pin family before the Revolution, and a regiment
had borne their name. Moreover, since the Revolution the
army was the only career which seemed possible to sons of
the old royalist families. There they could still serve their
country. La Tour du Pin went through St. Cyr and also
the general staff college. He was an excellent soldier, and
saw active service in the Crimean and Italian wars, and in
Algeria, as well as in the war of 1870.[3]

After the end of the Franco-Prussian war he was appointed military attaché in Vienna. While he was there he
often visited the Comte de Chambord at Frohsdorf, with the
knowledge and tacit consent of his superiors. He was a roy-

[2] Charles Baussan, *La Tour du Pin* (Paris, 1931).
[3] He wrote several books on military life.

alist by birth and tradition, and by reasoned conviction, as
well. He had a deep admiration for "Henri V," and often
discussed with him his social ideas, on which, as Chambord
expressly declared, they were in perfect agreement.[4]

La Tour du Pin left the army in 1882.[5] From that time
on he worked to spread the social and political ideas in which
he believed. He helped to found a review called *Tradition-
Progrès* and contributed to many other papers and magazines, including *La Revue catholique,* and, later, *L'Action
française.* Although he was extremely active in the foundation of Catholic working-men's circles, and closely associated
in them with de Mun, he did not follow him in the matter
of the *ralliement,* but, as he said in his old age, he "ended his
life in fidelity."[6] The war of 1914 ravaged his home, but he
lived to see the beginning of its reconstruction. He died in
Lausanne in 1924.

La Tour du Pin was not an individualist. He agreed with
Blanc de St. Bonnet, whom he admired, and often quoted,
that men associate not to produce more, but to learn to
love each other better. Man is essentially a social and historic being; he is born into a domestic society, and lives in an
historic one. His condition is due to his past, and the development of his life is closely associated with other men.
No individual exists, there are only members of society. This
social man is subject to immutable laws, given by God, which
are contained in the decalogue, supplemented by the law of
love. Individualism is the absence of the social concept, the
ignoring of the divine law. Its result is the disappearance of

[4] Baussan, *op. cit.,* p. 75.

[5] The reason appears to have been that he spoke of a restoration in
terms which led his general to suggest his resignation. Baussan, *op. cit.,*
p. 11.

[6] *Ibid.,* p. 98.

all social authorities, whatever their origin. It is the curse
of modern society.

The social body is like a real body, with vital organs,
which are the family, the home, property, and groups of
all sorts, professional or local. By substituting the individual
for the group, the Revolution sowed disorder everywhere. It
weakened the family, destroyed the corporations, suppressed
the provinces, and usurped the sovereignty of the State. This
was the consequence of the rupture with religion, of which
economic and political liberalism was the cause. The declaration of the Rights of Man was an expression of individualism,
and, although it was the preamble to a constitution, it contained no mention of the social body! Only by returning to a
better organization, in which the individual will cease to be
the basis of everything, can the present social disorder be
eliminated.

La Tour du Pin did not discuss the question of sovereignty
in the abstract; he merely said that authority is essential to
the existence of society. It is not a necessary evil, nor is it
the delegation of the sovereignty of individuals, a mandate
given by those who are to be subject to it, and revocable by
them; it is a national right, the consequence of the historic
traditions of a people. A nation is a living thing, a being
which endures for centuries, and from its needs develops the
authority which is necessary to it.

The right of the king is born of the needs of the people.
This is a dominant principle, and it is that of the French
national and traditional monarchy. In France the kings gen-
erated the whole constitution, and created the nation. Their
historic right flows from its maintenance of the integrity
of national existence. La Tour du Pin expressly said that
this is not the theory of divine right, which implied an inde-

pendence of history, and was solely determined by the order
of primogeniture in the royal house.

The French king was invested by God, for men of old
recognized that it was divine action which created the historic right. The king was also acclaimed by the people, but
they did not pretend to have thereby created his right, they
merely recognized it, for it was not dependent on a compact,
or contract, but on consent. The representatives of the public
liberties which the centuries had developed, in acknowledging the king, did not give themselves a master, but
recognized a protector. During the centuries institutions and
customs changed, but nothing interrupted the historical continuity of the royal right. It was the fundamental law of the
land.

The essential traits of the French Monarchy were that it
was national, military, and tempered. The first implied that
France could only be governed by princes of its own blood;
the nation was incarnated in the House of France. The second trait resulted from the national needs; the kings of
France have always been under the necessity of being soldiers, and the military profession was held in honor because
of its utility. As to the third trait, the French monarchy was
never entirely absolute.

The character of the Monarchy was formed gradually.
The steps in its evolution were the baptism of Clovis, the
election of Hugh Capet, and the consecration of Charles
VII. Thus, the first principle acquired was the Christianiza-
tion of the supreme power; an essential matter for a Christian State. The second was the consent of the nation through
its representatives: bishops, nobles, and people; and the third
was the establishment of the hereditary succession in the male
line, according to the Salic law. It was Jeanne d'Arc who

caused this third principle to be definitely recognized. The king was created by right, by consecration, and by acclamation, as the ritual of the "sacre" shows.

According to the national right the king both reigned and governed. The monarch chose his ministers freely, but they were merely the executors of his will, and did not share his sovereignty. The royal power could not be divided, but some of its attributes were delegated permanently to special bodies, such as the council of state, the court of accounts, and the high court of justice.

The royal sovereignty, although it was indivisible, was limited by the laws of the land, and by the rights of the people in their estates. The old constitution was, as Le Play advocated, democratic in the commune, aristocratic in the provinces, and monarchical in the State.

La Tour du Pin distinguishes between the national monarchy and the *ancien régime*. The fundamental laws of France were the historic right of the dynasty, and the right of the people to consent to new laws. Thus an accord between the prince in his council and the people in their estates was an essential trait of the national monarchy. The *ancien régime* tended to be absolutist and Caesarian. The king gradually absorbed all powers into his own hand. This tendency was not of medieval origin; it followed the treaty of Westphalia, and was a consequence of the wars of religion.

As a result of the growing absolutism of the *ancien régime,* some constitutional modifications had become necessary, but the "satanic ferments"[7] of the Revolution prevented Louis XVI from carrying them out. The Revolution did not mitigate the absolutism of the central power, it only trans-

[7] *Vers un ordre social chrétien* (Paris, 1907), p. 462-63.

ferred it to the masses, or to their representatives. The Comte de Chambord perceived this, and wished to take up the movement of 1789, which had been interrupted by violence. In the States General of 1789 the old French constitution was soon forgotten, although the mandate of the delegates had only been to amend it. The abolition of royalty was not a normal product of historic evolution; it was the result of the revolutionary philosophy, which was anti-national. No really national constitution can issue from this poisoned source.

At the Restoration the returning King did not dare to take up the old traditions, but tried to create new ones. This was difficult, for, as the Comte de Chambord pointed out, the nation was organized not to be governed but to be administered. To govern is to coördinate the social forces in a collective action for the common interest. These forces must be organized and represented. The question at the Restoration was how to obtain such representation in a country in which it had been destroyed. To provide it, artificial classes based on property qualifications were created, and an arbitrary choice was made of hereditary peers. Thus the parliamentary régime was instituted.

The King believed in the prestige of his crown, and thought that in the parliament he would merely have a council, but it gradually became evident that he had given himself masters. These were absolute, in spite of their liberalism, and moreover they were incompetent and irresponsible. The parliament was a mere simulacrum of representative government, and it gave birth to a power which was always ready to seize the government, but was never able to give it a continuous direction.

The failure of this so-called representative régime in

France, La Tour du Pin says,[8] is the most outstanding fact of contemporary history. It has not spared France a single revolution, nor preserved a single public liberty. It has not even delayed, as it has in some countries, the progress of the social revolution. This was because it had no solid basis in the social conditions of France.

An analysis of the social body shows that families and social groups are the true elements of representation, and therefore complete individualism is destructive of a representative system. The Chamber of Deputies, elected by a narrow franchise, did not constitute a real democracy, nor was the Chamber of Peers a true aristocracy. The King lost all authority, and the formula of a king who reigns, but does not govern, made monarchy so despicable that even a republic became acceptable.

Men must have certain personal rights, and also certain common rights, due to the social organization, which it is the duty of government to recognize. These rights are a part of the national constitution. Whether codified or not, the real constitution of a country is what is traditional, permanent, and essential to the principles of its political institutions. It is an historic product; the sum total of solutions given to the eternal problem of reconciling authority with the desire for liberty.

In the past this problem was less acute, for men had a different conception of liberty. To us today liberty is individualistic and means the absence of restraints; to them, because they were more truly Christian, it was social, and meant the free play of the institutions which ensure social justice, that is to say, an equitable distribution of the burdens and advantages of society.

[8] *Vers un ordre social chrétien,* p. 411.

The true basis of such institutions is the association of men according to their functions. Thus only is the sense of social solidarity developed. To be genuine, a representative system must make room for all social collectivities. Both the feudal and the corporative régimes were just such organizations of men, not according to classes, but according to functions.

A political body should represent, not individuals, but social bodies, organic elements, such as bishoprics, fiefs, cities, communes, corporations. When laws are to be elaborated, it is only from such organized bodies that one can expect competence, independence, and prudence. When classes and interests are represented there is a constant current, and no violent movements occur, but when the parliament is based on an unorganized universal suffrage, only opinion is represented, and all is ephemeral—it is a mere demagogy.

La Tour du Pin was favorable to the creation of an aristocracy. There have never been closed castes in Christian countries, he pointed out, but only classes. These will always exist, for a society necessarily develops an aristocracy, which is the mainspring of its civilization. If society is not to be a chaos, a natural selection of families by means of heredity must be allowed to take place. The hereditary possession of the land is the truest source of distinction and authority; it alone can create a genuine nobility.

When a parliament represents permanent forces, as it does in countries like England (where the absolutism of the *ancien régime* did not penetrate), when a peerage is a real House of Lords, that is to say, of those possessing great fiefs, and representing the families which have always shared in the sovereignty, the result is good. But in France the nobility had ceased during the *ancien régime* to be a political order, and had become a mere social class. This was one of the reasons why at the Restoration it was so difficult to reconstruct a representative system.

In addition to the peerage, which already represents the class of landowners and the profession of soldiers, there are three types of interests which should be represented. They are (1) the taxpayers, (2) constituted bodies in the State, and (3) professional associations. As to the first category, the family is the primordial unit of representation, as it is of society. Each head of a family has a right to select mandataries who will consent to taxation. Widows and unmarried women should here have in this respect equal rights with fathers, for they represent a family. Electoral colleges may be formed of these heads of families. They should be divided into three classes, according to the amount of taxes which they pay, and the burden should be distributed equally among these three groups.

As to the second category, churches, universities, and legal bodies, as well as the professional corporations, must have representation. It cannot be regulated, however, as in the case of the taxpayers; it must be based on the hierarchical principle which is the very structure of these bodies.

Most important of all is professional representation. The corporative régime must be introduced into all occupations, and become the basis of economic, social, and political life. All occupations create common rights and interests, and the associations which arise from these should be organized, and erected into political as well as economic units.

The representatives of the taxpayers would constitute the administrative organs, which would be autonomous in the communes, and in the State would exercise a control over the use of public monies, through a chamber of deputies, which would vote the budget. The budget, however, should normally be voted for a number of years ahead, unless there is some unusual expense to be provided for.

Another chamber should exist, formed by the representatives of the social bodies, which would have the right to be consulted on all technical and economic matters. This would secure a balance between the opinion of the moment, represented by the taxpayers' delegates, and the permanent interests of the country, represented by the delegates of the organized bodies. The consent of both chambers would be necessary for measures which concerned all.

The chambers are not, however, to have a supreme authority, either in legislation or in administration. It is the king in his council who governs, and the States, Provincial or General, have merely rights of consent and control. They are not to sit in permanence, or be convoked regularly, for this would lead to a divided sovereignty, and perpetual struggle.

This political structure as conceived by La Tour du Pin was founded on the corporative organization of industry, professions, and the land. His ideas with regard to this corporative régime are precise. What should the contract of labor provide for the worker, for the owner, and for society? he asked. This contract is an exchange of services. Both capitalist and laborer must procure a living from it, each according to his condition, and a living implies a home and the means of rearing a family.

The corporative régime is not socialistic; it admits that inequalities of social condition must be respected. Its basis is the fact that labor and capital are mutually dependent. Its principle is the admission of a right and a duty for each member of the association, and of reciprocal rights and duties between the association and the State. The corpora-

tion is, like the commune, a state within the State, a social
institution, with a fixed place in the community, and obligations to it.

In the Middle Ages the land was for the peasant, and
the tool for the worker. Today the laborer has no real rights,
no guaranty of fixed work, no safe tomorrow. Socialism,
on the contrary, gives no rights at all to capital. The corporative régime gives rights to both.

A corporation should include all who are engaged in a
given industry, in whatever capacity, for they are all interdependent, and the salary or profit of each, according to his
place will depend alike on the state of the industry.

The fundamental functions of a corporation are: first, the
formation of a corporative patrimony, i.e., an insurance
fund, to be levied partly on the profits of capital, and partly
on the wages of labor, and to serve both as a protection for
the workers, in old age and illness, and as a reserve for the
industry itself, to enable it to survive times of stress; and
second, the verification of professional capacity, both of
workers and directors, and the supervision of the quality of
production. This will limit, but will not do away with competition, and access to trades and professions. It will protect the
public and safeguard the skill which is the laborers' capital.
A third function would be the representation of each element in a corporative government. This will allow disputes
as to wages and the conditions of labor to be settled by those
who are actually interested in the industry in question, either
as workers or as owners.

The land, like the tools of industry, must yield the means
of subsistence to those who cultivate it. It belongs to the
poor as well as to the rich. Society has rights in it, and the
individual only a tenancy.

In every case the duties, not the rights of property owners should be stressed. Property is the basis of society only if it is reasonably accessible to all. The masses to become conservative must be given a stake in the community. Liberalism destroyed the old corporations, in which everyone had some interest, and free competition lowered the standard of living, and did not respect the needs of family life. The State exists only to protect society, and if misery becomes so great that a large number of members do not want society to be preserved, the State will not be able to act.

La Tour du Pin saw the need of decentralization. He thought that it could best be realized by means of indirect professional representation. All professional associations should send delegates to a local syndical chamber, in which owners and workers would be equally represented. These local chambers would send delegates to a body which would have its place of meeting in the chief town of the *arrondissement*. These in turn would send delegates to provincial chambers. Thus agriculture and industry, producers and retailers, as well as the liberal professions, would each possess a provincial chamber, and these chambers could unite, when necessary, to discuss their common interests. They would then form a body much like the old Provincial Estates. These chambers should be presided over by a permanent official, emissary of the central power, and there should also be a central office in each province to permit the government to keep in touch with the local corporations.[9]

La Tour du Pin was hostile to the liberal conception of a free Church in a free State. In practice, he said, this had

[9] For a discussion of the theories of de Mun and of the social Catholic movement in France see: Parker T. Moon, *The Labor Problem and the Social Catholic Movement in France* (New York, 1921).

proved unfavorable to religion. The Church once had the right of ministry, that of teaching, and that of administering justice where its interests or its members were concerned. Today only the first of these is left, for the Church's judicial power has disappeared, and her right to teach is strongly contested.

Both the idea that religion is a private matter, and the belief that the Church should be submitted to the control of the State are errors. "Man," he said, "is a religious being, and the social order always corresponds more or less closely to a religious idea."[10] Religious society is the best society, and its precepts must be practiced. No attack upon it must be allowed. All that is not Christian in the spirit and habits of society must be banished. Dissidents may be tolerated, but they should be treated, not as members of the community, but as strangers.[11]

He was extremely hostile to the Jews, and to their influence. He pointed out that they always form a people apart, and that their social ideal, which is entirely materialistic, is not that of the rest of the nation. They try to gather the means of production into their own hands, and use them for the benefit of their own race, without any sense of general social responsibility. "France," he said, "is a country conquered by the Jews."[12]

Like the theocrats, La Tour du Pin considered man as an essentially social and historic being. He believed that men's possessions and their activities are only justified in so far as they serve the common welfare. He was severe in his judgment of capital as it exists today, but he was resolutely opposed both to its destruction, and to its transfer to the

[10] *Vers un ordre social,* p. 165.
[11] *Ibid.,* p. 214.   [12] *Ibid.,* p. 341.

State. Men must be owners, but ownership means responsibility, rather than enjoyment. But, he did not, like Bonald and Maistre, wish to crush all personal initiative under the weight of an absolute and unlimited authority, and a series of unvarying rules. He understood the value of spontaneous and voluntary action.

The chief originality of his thought lies in his insistence on the corporative organization of society. Common rights, common duties, common responsibilities seemed to him to be the natural basis of human association, and he saw in a series of hierarchies, professional, industrial, and communal, the means of increasing the social sense, which is so readily lost in an individualistic society ruled by an unlimited central power, even when that power is democratic. He also hoped by this means to substitute coöperation for competition in the economic field.

In this system the monarchy was to furnish the essential unity and the permanent direction. The State, incarnated in the king, was to be a benevolent protector, and to coördinate the activities of these various bodies in view of the common good.

These ideas are reasonable and attractive. They might, if put into practice, modify to some extent the intensity of class hatred by offering new fields of activity to ambitions, greater protection to the workers, and more opportunities for contact and comprehension between men of different rank. Professional *esprit de corps* might conceivably come to replace class consciousness. The greatest objection to his system is the enormous, the apparently insuperable difficulty of establishing it in a society already organized on another basis.

La Tour du Pin's conception of monarchy was essentially a rational one. He did not share the mysticism of the theocrats and Blanc de St. Bonnet in regard to the origin of sovereignty. Like the royalists of today, he considered that the claims of the king have a double justification in history and tradition on the one hand, and in the needs of the nation on the other. More liberal than the theocrats, he held, as did Royer-Collard, that the royal power, although it could not be divided, should be limited. In a society so highly organized, and possessing so many liberties and rights as that which he advocated, a strong central authority would be easy to bear, and would indeed actually be necessary to the unity and safety of the State.[13]

His views on French history, while sometimes questionable,[14] are far clearer and more critical than those of the theocrats. His résumé of the development of the principles of the French Monarchy, and his distinction between the true character of that Monarchy and the absolutist and centralizing tendency of the *ancien régime* are novel and interesting. It cannot be admitted, however, that the reason which he gives for this growth of absolutism (that is to say, the disorder caused by the wars of religion) was the only, or even the most important one.

La Tour du Pin's ideas were not original; they were a synthesis of the doctrines of authoritarian royalism. In his general conception he was influenced by the theocrats, by Blanc de St. Bonnet, by the Spaniard Donoso Cortes, and by

[13] In attempting a work of decentralization Charles Maurras perceived this very point, and it was one of the considerations which led him to become a royalist.

[14] His opinion of the French nobility before the Revolution is probably too favorable. He refuses to take the great nobles into consideration at all, and is very lenient to the small country gentry. This is not in agreement with the careful studies of Tocqueville on the subject. See A. de Tocqueville, *L'Ancien Régime et la Révolution.*

Le Play. All of these thinkers he frequently quoted. His social doctrines, and his program of a corporative society he held in common with Albert de Mun, whom he considered as his leader in this field. Both were, no doubt, inspired in part by the social Catholic movement in Germany and elsewhere, although their theories were somewhat different.[15] But this synthesis, as expressed in his principal work *Vers un ordre social chrétien,* is admirable. It is clear, stimulating, and logical. Its basis is the Christian view of life, but, unlike the theocrats, whose point of departure was the same, La Tour du Pin saw the real problems of modern society, and instead of idly regretting the past, he suggested new solutions, in accordance with the Catholic point of view.[16] The book contains the greater part of what is living and valuable in the theory of authoritarian royalism.

La Tour du Pin's life was a remarkably complete one; he was in turn a soldier, a diplomat, a landowner, a social worker, and a philosopher. In all these characters he showed himself courageous, generous, and devoted to that ideal of service to mankind which was the essence of his thought. Both as a man and a philosopher he was representative of what is best in the royalist tradition.

[15] They are perhaps even more closely related to "guild socialism." Cf. Arthur J. Penty, *A Guildman's Interpretation of History* (London, 1920) ; also Parker T. Moon, *op. cit.*

[16] His article on capital, which is a vigorous criticism of present-day conditions, as based on "usury," was the object of episcopal criticism. See *Vers un ordre social,* pp. IX, 70.

CHAPTER XIII

ORIGIN OF THE ACTION FRANÇAISE: NON-ROYALIST SOURCES

It has often been said that there are two nations in France: the one conservative, traditionalist, and Catholic; the other individualistic, democratic, and anti-clerical.

Various theories have been advanced to account for this division. Among the most interesting are those of a Swiss writer, Professor Seippel.[1] He believes that the two currents in French thought are due on the one hand to the Roman tradition of absolutism, inherited by the Catholic Church, and on the other, to a survival of the old Gallic spirit of independence and individualism, which found expression in the Reformation. These explanations are very questionable. Divisions exist in all nations where there has been a revolution violent enough to cause a change of régime. It is undoubtedly true, however, that the intellectual and emotional cleavage produced by the Revolution has been so profound that it has endured up to the present time, and may be said to have divided France into two separate nations.

The influence of time would naturally tend to reduce such differences. A middle party, combining some elements of each of the others might be expected to develop, and gradually to absorb all but the extremists of both sides. In France, however, the liberals, who formed such a middle party, did not succeed in absorbing either the radical republicans on the

---

[1] Paul Seippel, *Les Deux Frances et leurs origines historiques* (Lausanne, 1905).

one hand, or the reactionaries on the other. On the contrary, the *juste milieu* tended to disappear, leaving irreconcilable adversaries face to face. Two nations, resulting from two different philosophies, continued to oppose each other throughout the nineteenth century. The struggle had various phases, more or less acute, but, even in periods of relative calm, a deep distrust separated them. Only a spark was needed to cause distrust to flame into violent conflict, and this spark was furnished by the Dreyfus case.

It is difficult to realize the immense importance which this matter assumed, or to gauge its true significance. This lay not in the question of Dreyfus' guilt or innocence, or even principally in the matter of right or justice, but in the fact that the *affaire* was a battle between two philosophies, two traditions: the one Catholic, conservative, and nationalist, the other anti-clerical, individualistic, and pacifist. All France was divided into two camps. Homes were broken up, old friends became enemies, and even today a deep bitterness of feeling exists among some of those who remember that time. The anti-Dreyfusards included the greater part of the monarchists, the clericals, the army, and a vast majority of the nationalist and conservative elements of the country, while a feeling of common danger united the parties of the left, even including the socialists, in the defense of the Republic.

The partisans of Dreyfus triumphed in the judicial struggle, and their hero was rehabilitated and promoted. But the affair had revealed the two nations to each other. The victors had been seriously alarmed, and they determined to use their strength in the political field to try to crush their adversaries once and for all. They carried through an anticlerical and antimilitary policy which resulted on the one hand in the disestablishment of the Church, and on the other in the shortening of the time of military service, and other measures weakening to the army.

The inevitable reaction to such measures was a vigorous revival of nationalism. The situation of France in Europe was precarious. Germany was still a menace, as the Moroccan episode of 1905-1906 showed. Russia, France's ally, had suffered a military collapse in her war with Japan. It was natural that patriots should feel great alarm at attacks on the army made at such a time.

The most influential leaders of the nationalist revival were Maurice Barrès, the writer, and one-time protagonist of individualism, and Paul Déroulède. These men, and those who followed them criticised the anti-national policy of the government, and urged a revival of patriotism. They did not attack the republican régime itself.[2]

A group of men appeared, however, who were not content merely to attack the ministers, but passed from a criticism of the republicans to the arraignment of the Republic. They attributed the harm done to the army, and the weakness of the government in the Dreyfus affair not to individuals, but to the form of the government.

Finding it difficult to express these views in the conservative papers and magazines, which were for the most part either republican, or so mildly royalist as to be afraid of vigorous conclusions, they founded an organ of their own, a monthly review, which they called the *Action française*.[3]

[2] Déroulède was not averse to overthrowing the government by force, and appealing to a plebiscite, but he always declared himself a republican.

[3] The *Action française* became a daily newspaper in March, 1908.

Among the original members of this group were Charles Maurras, Henry Vaugeois, Lucien Moreau, and Maurice Pujo. Jacques Bainville, Leon de Montesquiou, and Leon Daudet soon joined them. These men were not, for the most part, royalists by tradition, but, starting from various points of view, they had all come to reject the parliamentary and republican régime. Nationalism was the basis of their thought, and they considered political problems solely with regard to the advantage of France.

The nationalism of the Action française is essentially cultural and intellectual. It is scarcely possible to find in the writings of Maurras, Montesquiou, or the others, a reference to the economic advantages of national strength. They wish France to be powerful not in order that Frenchmen may be more prosperous, but in order that they remain French.

The rationale of their nationalism was clearly formulated in a statement of policy made on November 15, 1899, which lays down the following basic propositions: first, that society is essential to man and that his greatest interest lies in its preservation; second, that the nation is today the most complete, stable, and extensive form of society. Since the old association known in the Middle Ages as "Christendom" is dissolved, nationality is the absolutely necessary condition of human existence. If the nations were to disappear, the spiritual and material intercourse of humanity would be compromised, and civilization would recede. Nationalism, therefore, is not a matter of sentiment, but a rational obligation. Third, that France is a state which is menaced by the rivalry of factions. Frenchmen must, therefore, resolve all questions solely with regard to the interest of the nation, and they must be grouped, over and above their religious, political or economic opinions, according to the intensity and depth of their faith in France. Fourth, it is the duty of all Frenchmen to formulate these truths as publicly and as often as possible.[4]

Thus, for the Action française, the nation is the necessary and final form of modern society. In this opinion they are in agreement with thinkers of many groups, including the Jacobins, radicals, and even the socialists. The basic difference between them and the parties of the left (who adhere to the revolutionary doctrines, but who are often patriots and nationalists) lies in their belief in the value of tradition, and their wish for solidarity with the prerevolutionary past. Like Barrès,[5] they pointed out that the individual is only a moment in a long culture, a gesture among the many gestures of a force which has preceded, and will survive him.[6] Men and nations are alike conditioned by their past, by the work of bygone generations, and though they create, in turn, the lives of future generations, they cannot do this arbitrarily, by a mere act of will or reason; they must follow the lines which experience, as crystallized in custom and tradition, has laid down for them. "The problem for individuals and for nations," Montesquiou said,[7] "is not to create themselves as they would wish to be (an impossible task!) but to keep themselves as the centuries have predestined them." From these three postulates: Man's need of society, the nation as the inevitable social group, and the

[4] These articles were adopted and published on November 15, 1899, by the adherents of the *Action française* (then a monthly review). For a list of those who signed it see *Au Signe de Flore* (Paris, 1931), p. 27.

[5] Maurice Barrès, *Un Homme libre* (Paris, 1912).

[6] Léon de Montesquiou, *Les Raisons du nationalisme*, pp. 15-16.

[7] *Ibid.*, p. 21.

determining force of the past, the nationalists of the Action française derive the absolute duty of protecting and developing the nation, along the lines of its history and tradition.

In the opinion of these men, French culture and character are the highest development of civilization. Maurras considered that seventeenth-century France combined the intellectual liberty and fecundity of Greece with the Roman spirit of order and discipline. "The French," he said, "are a people who, even more than the Romans, incorporate discipline with instinct, art with nature, thought with life." This culture, this mastery of life by thought, must not be allowed to perish.

During the reign of Louis XIV France was undoubtedly the dominant power in Europe. Both in population, riches, military strength, and civilization she was superior to the other western nations. Her situation in comparison to that of other powers is today greatly diminished. The populations of Germany and Russia exceed, and those of England and Italy approximately equal hers; nor are her wealth and her military power so markedly superior as they were in the seventeenth century. Frenchmen, in thinking of their country, must inevitably look for the causes of this decline.

The geographic situation of France has been favorable to her unity and to her cultural development; but centrally placed, with access both to the Atlantic and to the Mediterranean, yet divided from her southern neighbors by mountain ranges, she has always been exposed to invasion from the North. Even before the Roman conquest, the hordes of barbarians began to pour across the Rhine into Gaul, and they have continued to do so until today. The frontier cities of northern France have suffered from the invaders in every age. This constant menace made unity and centralization peculiarly necessary to France. Her kings saw this, and the powerful organization which they created had, no doubt, much to do with the superior position of France in the seventeenth and early eighteenth centuries. But other nations, although they were slower to reach unity under a strong government, have gradually developed along the same lines. Russia entered the orbit of European politics; England grew in strength, and has increased her influence on the continent almost continuously since the beginning of the eighteenth century. During the nineteenth century Italy and Germany achieved unity, and in both cases this was followed by a great national development.

In addition to the inevitable growth of other nations, many factors might be suggested which have probably contributed to the changed position of France in Europe. The men of the Action française, however, attributed her relative decline solely to the social and political disorganization caused by the Revolution, and its doctrines. The philosophy of individualism, they say, gave birth to a spirit of envy and revolt, which culminated in the destruction of the existing society by the Revolution. Many Frenchmen came to hate their past, to despise their own traditions, customs and ideas, and to look to other nations for new theories and institutions. These borrowed forms were not adapted to the needs of France, and they have weakened her so much that nations which had no such inner struggle to contend with have surpassed her in their development. The men of the Action française, therefore, wished to unite all who truly love France, her culture, her tradition, her past, in demanding for her a better political system, and one more in conformity with her national character and history. This, they considered, is to be found in traditional authoritarian monarchy. France was prosperous and powerful under her kings; let her return to the political and social régime which was so advantageous to her, if she wishes to recover her former security and strength!

They saw that in order to combat the revolutionary ideas a body of doctrines was necessary, and they took from various sources those ideas which were in harmony with their general scheme or thought. They referred to the theories of monarchy as developed by Bonald, Maistre, Balzac, and the Comte de Chambord, and to the social theories of La Tour du Pin. They pointed out also that many French thinkers of the nineteenth century who were not actually royalists, nevertheless developed antirevolutionary doctrines in various fields which agree to a large extent with the classic monarchical theory.

The most important of these non-royalist sources of the thought of the Action française is positivism. Comte proposed to apply the methods of scientific induction to society, and to ascertain from a study of the nature and history of man certain social and political principles which would have the invariability of the laws of nature. Now most of the royalists had believed in the existence of such immutable laws; they were a part of the thought not only of Bonald, Maistre, St. Bonnet, and the other authoritarians, but of Chateaubriand, Royer-Collard, and Guizot. These men, however, all had religious convictions; for them the laws of society, though they were "natural," had their sanction in the will of God, and were expressed in Revelation. Thus a certain mysticism tinged the convictions of the early royalists; they derived their premises partly from their faith.

The thinkers of the Action française also believed in immutable laws, which govern the development of society. They regarded the establishment of order through authority, the ascendency of an *élite*, and adherence to tradition as among the basic postulates of a sane social evolution. Only by these means, they felt, can the true character of France be preserved, and her integrity and power be secured. But, unlike the former royalists, several of the leaders of the Action française were agnostics; they could not accept Revelation as the sole basis of moral and political dogma. Positivism had, therefore, a double advantage for them. In the first place, if, by the application of a scientific method, definite laws governing the development of society could be found, these laws would be incontestable. They would have the validity of evident and verifiable truth, and would thus be as convincing to agnostics as the laws given by Revelation are to believers. Such laws, Comte, and with him men of the Action française, claimed to discover by the methods of positivism.

Comte, Maurras said, perceived that science has remained ordered and serene. This, he believed, was because general principles had been established in that domain, whereas this has not been done in the political and social field. He therefore undertook to create a science of "sociology," which would discover and formulate general laws in this domain also. Positivism, Maurras declared,[8] is a "doctrine of observation."[9] Ethics require sociology to exist. Men must induct in order to deduct, and so to build, and must foresee, in order to be able *to do,* for man is made to be active, and convictions, in the form of dogma, are necessary to support his good impulses.

[8] "Le Dilemme de Marc Sangnier," *La Democratie religieuse* (Paris, 1921), pp. 34-36.
[9] "Doctrine de constatation," *ibid.,* p. 35.

In the second place, the laws deduced by Comte are in harmony both with the teachings of Catholicism, and with the doctrines of French traditional monarchy. The positivist ideas as to the constitution of society, legislation, the family, education, and the necessity for a general authority all agree with Catholic and royalist theory, and therefore seem to give it a scientific confirmation. Royalists, Maurras pointed out,[10] may be Christians "first of all," that is to say, they may invoke the design of God (divine right) in justification of monarchy; or they may be positivists, and appeal to natural law and history. The great mystics, Joan of Arc, Saint Theresa, Saint Francis, were all instinctive positivists, for they observed and questioned nature, and used this knowledge, by the aid of God, for achievement.[11]

This agreement in social doctrine between positivism and Catholicism indicates a possibility of alliance. Positivism, Maurras says, is solely occupied with phenomena; it does not inquire into causes, or ultimate realities. It can, therefore, be respectful of the Church, and, although it will not accept its revelation, it will not attempt to interfere with it in the spiritual domain. Comte himself wished for an alliance between the positivists and the Jesuits. He saw that the idea of God may lead to anarchy. This is, he said, inherent in a non-Catholic attitude towards religion, for men who are in revolt against society will pretend to justify their conduct by claiming a direct contact with Divinity. The Church is the ally of order, and it should be treated accord-

[10] "Le Dilemme de Marc Sangnier," *Le Democratie religieuse* (Paris, 1921), pp. 34-36.

[11] It is interesting to compare this with Bergson's theory that the superiority of the Christian mystics lies precisely in their power of accomplishment. See *Les Deux Sources de la religion et de la morale* (Paris, 1932), pp. 242-52.

ing to its own wishes. The religion of humanity, which creates enthusiasm by placing at its center the greatest *knowable* thing, Man, will replace faith for those who cannot believe in the dogma of the Church. This point of view is in perfect harmony with the ideas of Maurras, and it is well adapted to the needs of a party which tries to unite Catholics and non-Catholics in common action. France, Maurras admitted, will long be divided as to religious beliefs, and a *modus vivendi* must be found. Christian socialists and monarchical positivists can agree on *what is to be done*, and on the application of social doctrine, for they are in agreement as to the value of Catholicism to the nation, and to humanity.

The chief attraction of positivist doctrine for Maurras and his followers was its respect for order. Comte hated anarchy. Progress he considered to be simply a gradual development of the order which is inherent in the very nature of life. Submission is the basis of this development, and the only means of reaching perfection. Like the theocrats, Comte denied the right to an independent morality, and made duty depend on dogma. Free thought appeared to him, as to many of the royalists, to be contrary to a true social organization. He called it a "mental insurrection of the individual against the race." Man, he said, has the power to become good, but it is society which enables him to do so. It is society which is all-important. The living are governed by the dead. They must submit to the social authority, and dedicate themselves increasingly to humanity. These ideas are valuable to nationalists like the men of the Action française, for they lead to the sacrifice of the individual to the group, and both Maurras and Montesquiou quoted them repeatedly. It must be noted, however, that they did not share

Comte's broad view of humanity. Maurras said that by this term only an *élite* is to be understood.

Comte's criticism of the principles of the Revolution is also in accord with royalist theory. Men, he said, do not consent to enter society; they are essentially a part of it, and their debt to it always exists. The individual has duties, of which he should be reminded, rather than rights, of which he should be told. A "right" is only a fact which has been crowned by assent of history, that is to say, proved good. Comte declared that all choice of superiors by inferiors is deeply anarchical. It is obvious that these are the same arguments used by the royalists against Rousseau. Tradition and positivism, Maurras declared, have together destroyed the idea of a "State of nature."

As to Comte's attitude towards monarchy, Maurras asked how he could be considered a republican, since his commonwealth excluded a parliament, centralization, and plebiscites? Comte, he said, admitted the advantage of a government where authority is transmitted by the same means as property, that is to say by heredity. He also pointed out that in 1855 Comte spoke of the monarchy as a last means of safety if parliamentary anarchy should return.

In developing the conception of a science of society, Comte made a great contribution to human thought. He opened new paths for investigation, and suggested the means by which men may hope some day to regulate their conduct according to the laws of their nature. Sociology, however, is not an exact science. It requires the aid of psychology, which was scarcely born in the lifetime of Comte. Even today, seventy-five years after Comte's death, sociologists differ radically both as to the laws of society, and the methods by which these laws are to be determined. As a matter of fact,

Comte deduced his political principles from general considerations, based on the study of history, very much as
political theorists had always done. For this reason they
cannot be said to be scientifically established, as are the laws
of chemistry or physics, which have been verified by experiments that can always be repeated. Yet it is not the most
substantial part of Comte's work, that is to say, his conception of a science of society, which Maurras stressed, but
rather his much more debatable political system. Maurras
expressly declared that the "politique positive" is superior
to the "philosophie positive." This is probably because Maurras is himself a systematic spirit. The groping methods of a
youthful and inexact science, like sociology, are not congenial to him. His mind requires definite laws on which to
build and these are not easy to combine with a genuine em-
piricism.

Comte was undoubtedly a great thinker, and his scientific
method gives an appearance of authority even to his most
questionable conclusions. Therefore in positivism Maurras
found what he wanted; a system which claims to be as precise and all-embracing as that of the *Summa theologica,* but
to be based on a rational study of fact.

The immediate aims of the Action française were political,
but its leaders recognized that the changes in government
which they hoped to effect must be accompanied by a social
reorganization. They insisted on the social and economic
weaknesses of liberalism and democracy almost as much as
on their political faults. In this respect they found support
in the work of the economist Frédéric Le Play, and, like
many of their royalist predecessors, they often referred to
his authority. Le Play considered, with Bonald, Maistre, and
many others, that the family, not the individual, is the social

unit. For many years he studied the social and economic condition of families in various countries. On the basis of this careful examination of facts he criticized the social results of the Revolution. Systematized liberty, providential equality, and the right of revolt were, he said, the revolutionary doctrines, and they are destructive of the family. From his studies Le Play also deduced certain principles which he considered necessary to the success of a social group. His criteria of success were prosperity and continuity, but he stressed the moral as much as the material benefits of these. The most important principles in which he believed were paternal authority, religion, an absolute sovereignty (whether held by one or by several persons) and the existence of property, in its three forms: communal, family, and "patronal," that is to say, corporative.

He divided families into three types: the patriarchal, in which all the branches remain under one roof and one authority; the "branch" family, in which the younger members detach themselves, but where the family property remains with the parent stem; and the "unstable" family, where all the members separate, and the family property is divided among them. This latter type of family, Le Play said, is revolutionary. It is unstable, and it leads to the loss of family responsibility and traditions. Its results are immoral, for it isolates the individual in youth and in old age, just at the times when he most needs support. In order to strengthen family ties, and to prevent the undue growth of individualism, Le Play wished marriage to be made inviolable, the authority of the father to be increased, and the freedom of testation returned to him. The suppression of this right by the Revolution he believed to be the cause of the low birth rate in France.[12]

[12] It is not certain that France actually has a markedly low natality.

Le Play defended property in the interest of the family as Bonald had done. Only the possession of property, and the right to hand it on can give continuity to family life. Men must be able to own their homes, and to keep them as an inviolable center around which their children may gather. It is better for the individual that such a center should exist, even if, as a younger son, he is obliged to make a sacrifice for its preservation.

This insistence on the family, and the means which Le Play proposed for ameliorating its condition are in complete agreement with Catholic teaching and with the ideas of many of the royalists, such as Berryer, Blanc de St. Bonnet, and La Tour du Pin. The freedom of testation, and the authority of the father were always demanded by royalist philosophers. In addition, Le Play's objective method, his subordination of abstract justice to practical utility, and his refusal to consider heroic humanitarianism as a reliable human motive had an especial appeal to the rational "positivism" of the men of the Action française. Their great respect for tradition and for the past also allied their thought to his.

The Action française found support for its historic point of view in the authority of Fustel de Coulanges. His method, which comported a great respect for contemporary texts, and his belief that history requires the help of tradition in the interpretation of the past, agreed with their ideas.

Fustel de Coulanges was not a believer in democracy. He pointed out in *La Cité antique* that the rule of the masses, of mere number, leads to the appearance of a plutocracy, or a tyranny. He considered that the wish to take part in public affairs is an artificial one, not natural to the average man. He denied that the living have an absolute right over the works of the dead, and said that political institutions are not the result of will whether that of a man or of a nation.

"Peoples" he wrote, in the preface to the *Histoire des institutions de l'ancienne France* (edition of 1875), "are governed, not as they wish to be, but as the sum total of their interests, and the basis of their opinions demand that they should be."

He provided the men of the Action française with a conception of patriotism in full accord with their own point of view.

Real patriotism is not merely the love of one's own land; it is the love of the past. It is respect for the generations which have preceded us . . . Our historians have taught us to curse them . . . they have broken with French tradition, and yet they imagine that a French patriotism can still exist.

He declared that the first duty of a great people is to love themselves, and he considered that the French did not do so sufficiently. He felt, as did Maurras, that an excessive admiration of foreign thought was one of the symptoms of national sickness.

Fustel de Coulanges, the royalists say, helped by his historical teaching to free Frenchmen from the influence which German thought had acquired over them during the nineteenth century. He admitted the practical sense of the Germans, and the utility of their historical and scientific activities, but he said that a truly scientific spirit is much rarer in Germany than is commonly supposed. French historians had been too ready to accept the German point of view; they were too apt to take the part of the German Emperors, invaders and despoilers of Italy, against the Church, and even against their own kings.

He denied that Gaul was enslaved by her Germanic invaders, and that the French nobility descended from a race of conquering strangers, as revolutionary thinkers had affirmed. He considered that French history shows a unity of development; there was no revolution at its beginning, no victors or vanquished, but a rapid fusion of races, with little changes in institutions. He believed that among the Germanic races progress had always come from without; during 800 years they made no advance in civilization, and at last it was Charlemagne who imposed it on them by force. Like most of the royalists, however, Fustel had little belief in the part played by great men in history, and he minimized the personal rôle of Charlemagne. These ideas give a fitting historical basis to the cultural nationalism of Maurras, Bainville, and their colleagues.

The philosophical anarchist, Pierre-Joseph Proudhon, is also among the nineteenth-century writers referred to by members of the Action française as contributing to their doctrines,[13] although they made many reservations with regard to his thought. Maurras and Dimier pointed out that there is a great deal of disorder and contradiction among his ideas. Maurras criticized his method, as being purely doctrinal, and said that, like the eighteenth-century philosophers, he made the mistake of considering not so much what is, as what *ought to* be. Moreover, Proudhon suffered from the fact that he was a man of limited education, and knew little history. Nevertheless, the royalists found some support for their own ideas in his theory.

Proudhon, they said, really understood the necessary lines of French policy. He had a clear perception of the national interest, and he saw the danger of Italian and German unity for France. In 1859 he took up a Catholic and clerical posi-

[13] A "Proudhon Club" was founded by members of the Action française, and Jacques Bainville dedicated his book *Bismarck et la France* to Proudhon's memory.

tion, and defended the temporal sovereignty of the Pope, in the name of the French interest, to the great indignation of his friends of the left. His books on Germany and the Rhine, and on Federation, and Italian unity[14] gave the French solution of these European problems. In fact, in spite of his averred anarchy, Proudhon was a nationalist.

Moreover, Proudhon was both antiliberal and antidemocratic. He detested the Jacobins, and was hostile to freemasonry, and to St. Simonianism. He attacked Rousseau's doctrine of the social contract, and his powerful criticism of it, although based on highly individualistic grounds, was agreeable to the men of the Action française because it undermines the liberal and the democratic positions. Proudhon pointed out that the social contract, as defined by Rousseau, limits itself to attributing political rights to men, but does not take into account their economic needs, and that it gives no guaranty or protection to the individual, or to minorities. It is, in fact, he says, an alliance of those who possess against those who do not possess. There is some agreement here between Proudhon's criticism and the royalist objections to liberalism and democracy.

Proudhon was a federalist, for he was an enemy of the State, and he saw in decentralization a means of weakening and limiting its power. The present-day royalists also advocate a régime of regional decentralization, the possibly centrifugal tendencies of which they hope to neutralize through the monarchy, for they see in the king a central power working for cohesion and protecting the integrity of the nation both at home and abroad. Proudhon was not so logical, and

[14] *France et Rhin* (Paris, 1868) ; *La Fédération et l'unité de l'Italie* (Paris, 1864).

his nationalism would seem to be at loggerheads with his whole system of individualism.

Proudhon also defended the right of revolt.

A revolution is, in the order of moral facts, an act of sovereign justice, proceeding from the necessity of things, and consequently it contains its own justification, which it is a crime for a statesman to resist. . . .[15] Let the fanatics of authority declaim against conspirators. To conspire may be an heroic act or a villany; the most holy of duties or the worst of felonies. All depends on the cause, the circumstances, the object, and also the successful result.[16]

These ideas are not far removed from those of Maurras and his colleagues. They believed that a *coup d'état,* and the use of force are justifiable when the interest of the nation requires the substitution of a good government for a bad. This attitude was natural in the anarchist, Proudhon, but it is illogical in men, who, like Maurras, are essentially authoritarian, and who deny the right of the people to dispose of themselves. Bonald pointed out the weakness of such a position. Who is to decide what government is good or bad, or when circumstances justify a revolt? Every party, when it is out of power, will declare, perhaps even genuinely believe, that the nation is in peril, and every government necessarily considers itself to be legitimate, and to have the right to defend order and liberty.

Proudhon was an iconoclast; he was opposed to almost all the ideas and institutions of his day, and he was powerful in attacking them. It must be admitted that he was much less able in constructing. His mind was not systematic, and there is so genuine a contradiction among his ideas, that his authority can be invoked by political groups otherwise poles

[15] *L'Idée de la Revolution au dix-neuvième siècle,* p. 35.
[16] *La Federation et l'unité de l'Italie,* p. 9.

apart. The men of the Action française made use of his thought in so far as it was directed against their enemies, and minimized that part of it which is opposed to their own ideas.[17]

In Taine the present-day royalists see one of the most influential inaugurators of the "counter-revolutionary" movement in French thought.[18] His great work *Les Origines de la France contemporaine* made a deep impression when it was published, and has continued to be widely read. A close examination of facts led Taine to oppose the favorable view of the revolution which was current in the middle of the nineteenth century, and which Michelet and Thiers had fostered and propagated. These historians had painted the men of the Revolution with an enthusiasm which Taine criticized. He pointed out, on the contrary, the thinness of their rhetoric, and the weakness of their ideas, and he emphasized in particular the lowering in quality of French political assemblies after 1789.

Like Bonald and Maistre he saw the folly of imagining an abstract Man, with no location in time or space, and of making general laws for his benefit. "There are," he said, "Frenchmen, Englishmen, Papuans, but there is no abstract 'Man.' "[19] To real men the State[20] is essential. It is a per-

[17] Thus Dimier declares that Proudhon's famous paradox: "Property is theft" (*La propriété c'est le vol*) is only the expression of a pamphleteer determined to push to the utmost limit the part of a reformer.— Louis Dimier, *Les Maîtres de la contre-révolution* (Paris, 1917), p. 247.

[18] Dimier declared that the intellectual counter-revolution in France dates from 1876, when the first volume of the *Origines* appeared. The Action française, he says, was constituted out of the forces awakened by Taine.—*Les Maîtres de la contre-révolution en France*, p. 156.

[19] Taine, *La Revolution*, I, Book II, chap. ii.

[20] "La chose publique" is the expression used.

petual foundation, to which successive generations have each brought their contribution, and in which individuals have only a life tenure. If one of these tenants, whose duty it is to administer the trust for the general good, through presumption, irresponsibility, haste, or partiality jeopardizes the sacred interests entrusted to his care he injures both his predecessors, whose sacrifice he renders vain, and his successors, whose hopes he frustrates.[21] In a well-known allegory Taine compared the French State at the Revolution to a ship whose passengers, profiting by a mutiny of the crew, had undertaken to navigate according to their own theories, and had forced the captain to give the orders which they dictated. The shipwreck which inevitably resulted they attributed to the ill will of the captain and the crew.

Taine was a freethinker,[22] but he saw the social value of the Church, and its close connection with tradition and order.[23] This point of view bears a certain resemblance to that of the Action française, although Taine did not have Maurras' intense admiration for Catholicism.

The agreement of adversaries, and of those who are in a different camp is always a precious tribute. That a spirit so penetrating as Taine's should have been led by the methodical study of history to believe in the *raison d'état,* which liberals rejected, and so to criticize both the deeds and the results of the Revolution, is a potent argument for the modern royalists.

For the same reason Renan is often quoted by the men of

[21] *La Revolution,* I, Book I, chap. ii, 2.

[22] In spite of his unbelief Taine asked to be buried according to the Protestant rites. In France to be buried without religious ceremony is a political gesture. It is a final declaration of anticlericalism, and this Taine wished to avoid.

[23] *Ibid.,* I, Book II, chap. ii, 4.

the Action française, for, although they repudiate his religious doctrines with indignation,[24] they find much in his political and social thought which agrees with their opinions. A great deal remains to be said as to Renan's political theory and it is difficult to determine exactly what were his ultimate convictions. He was intellectually eclectic. He dallied with opposing ideas and systems of thought, absorbing each in turn so completely, and expressing it so convincingly as to make it appear his own; but he often subjected these same ideas to an acute and devastating criticism.[25] It is probable that his thought underwent a certain evolution. As a young man he had been deeply impressed by German philosophy, but the Franco-Prussian war modified his view of Germany. In the same way the strain of idealism in his nature, turning to humanitarianism, seems to have inclined him at one time to feel some sympathy with the revolutionary ideas, but events led him to conclude that revolutionary democracy in both its aspects, that of anarchy and that of Caesarism, led France to the abyss. Thus, there is a marked difference in point of view between *L'Avenir de la Science,* a book written in 1849, and *La Reforme intellectuelle et morale de la France,* which was published after the Franco-Prussian war.[26] The latter might be supposed to be the expression of Renan's mature judgment, yet he deliberately published *L'Avenir de la science* for the first time in 1881! Renan was certainly aristocratic in temper, but he was also

[24] See Dimier, *Les Maîtres de la contre-revolution,* for a vehement expression of this feeling.

[25] In certain of the philosophical dialogues it is very difficult to be sure which speaker expresses the author's own opinions.

[26] Some of the articles collected in this book had appeared a little earlier. The one entitled "Le monarchie constitutionnelle en France" was published in the *Revue des deux mondes* on November 1, 1869.

a realist, and, moreover, profoundly, though amiably, sceptical. These characteristics made him tolerant of all ideas, but
devoted to none.

He seemed, however, on the whole to have had a certain
sympathy for hereditary monarchy. Writing on the *coup
d'état* (1851) he said:

Would you believe that, in the fever of the first few days, I almost
became a legitimist, and I am still tempted to be one if it can be
proved to me that the hereditary transmission of power is the only
way of escape from Caesarism—that fatal consequence of democracy as it is understood in France![27]

In the *Dialogues philosophiques* he said, "Royalty shows us
. . . a nation concentrated in an individual, or, if you like,
in a family, and so reaching the highest degree of national
consciousness, since no consciousness is equal to that of a
mind." He considered the best electorate inferior in quality
to the worst king. There are many passages in *La Réforme
intellectuelle,* and in the articles published in the same volume, as well as in *Questions contemporaines* which attest a
belief in the excellence of constitutional monarchy or plead
in favor of the old dynasty. After 1870 he proposed that
France should follow the example of Prussia after Jena, and
recreate a military monarchy.[28]

It is to the *Réforme intellectuelle* that the royalists usually refer, for it contains a scathing criticism of the Revolution. "By decapitating her king," Renan wrote, "France committed suicide." Like the royalists, and like Taine, Renan
thought that the Revolution had brought not liberty, but an
increase of absolutism. He felt, as they did, that its errors
arose largely from the predominance given to abstract right

[27] Letter of January 14, 1852.
[28] He was, however, soon convinced that a restoration was impossible.

over historic rights. Irrational institutions, he said, which are the result of time and evolution, are usually superior to those created by abstract reason. The Revolution severed France from her past, it cut the generations in two, and made the will of a mechanically-computed majority the sole source of public laws. Democracy, he said, is incompatible with the security of the nation. Egoism, the source of social-ism, and envy, the source of democracy, can create only a weak State, incapable of resisting strong neighbors. "There is," he wrote, "an essential contradiction between the idea of social justice and that of national power. Patriotism lessens when socialism prevails."[29] All these ideas are in agreement with those of the royalists.

Among their contemporaries the man who perhaps in-fluenced Maurras and his colleagues most was the nationalist, Maurice Barrès. Barrès began his career as an individualist,[30] but he was an ardent patriot, and he was among the first to develop the idea of a nationalism which should be philo-sophic, as well as political and economic. He soon felt the need of authority in the State, and of direction from above. He was a Boulangist in 1889, and, like Maurras, he was led by the Dreyfus affair to inquire into the moral condition of France. Two problems seemed to him vital: how to protect her from her foreign enemies, and how to preserve her tradi-

---

[29] *Les Apôtres* (Paris, 1866), p. 374. That a widely humanitarian view of justice is incompatible with patriotism is the belief of Maurras. It must be admitted, however, that the Jacobins were intensely patriotic! Socialism in France has usually been international in tendency, but that socialism is not incompatible with an intense nationalism seems to be proved by the character of Soviet Russia.

[30] Maurras says that at 20 Barrès was a sentimental nihilist. Being well-born, however, the *quality* of his mind led him to recreate his intellectual world.—*L'Enquête sur la Monarchie,* p. 487.

tional personality. In his novels *Les Déracinés, L'Appel au soldat, Leurs figures* (which are often quoted by Maurras) he offered as a solution a combination of nationalism and decentralization. The ideas exposed in these books are that patriotism is compounded of love for one's own home, and of the past; that Frenchmen must have a local home in the common *patrie;* that reason must command in the State, and that this reason must be national, not cosmopolitan. Yet his nationalism did not lead Barrès, like Maurras, to become a royalist. "I can understand," he wrote,[31] "that an intelligence judging *in abstracto* may adopt the monarchical system," but he believed that for monarchy to be realizable it was necessary that some ruling family should unite a great majority of the electorate in its support. This, he said, was not the case in France. Moreover, he despaired of recreating an aristocracy to support a monarch. In short, he differed from Maurras rather in his idea of what was possible than of what was desirable.

It is evident, even from this brief survey, that all these writers, although they did not consider themselves royalists, did, to a greater or lesser extent, combat the doctrines of the Revolution. In calling them the masters of the counter-revolutionary movement, Dimier scarcely exaggerated. The work of Maurras and his collaborators has been to assemble these ideas into one body of thought. The peculiarity—whether it be a strength or a weakness—of the system thus created lies in the fact that the corner stone of the whole edifice is the monarch.

Many conservative thinkers in France feel a certain sympathy with the Action française group and agree with some part of its social and political program, but criticize it for its

[31] Letter to Maurras published in *Enquête,* p. 135.

adherence to the monarchy, which is, they say, an outworn tradition. Whatever the practical justification of this criticism may be, it does not take into account the logical foundation of Maurras' thought. His nationalism has led him to demand a return to the structure of the past, and to urge decentralization, a reorganization of society on the corporative basis, a strengthening of the family versus the individual, combined with an authority strong enough to regulate all the elements in the State, and to be absolute master of the national forces, and the national foreign policy. This combination can scarcely be secured without a king. Thus, the synthesis of conservative and antirevolutionary thought which is the doctrine of the Action française leads logically to the idea of monarchy.

CHAPTER XIV

L'ACTION FRANÇAISE: CHARLES MAURRAS

Political parties in France today differ less from each other in fundamentals than they did during the nineteenth century. At that time their divisions were, on the whole, the result of genuinely different political theories. The legitimists, the Orléanists, the Bonapartists, the republicans did not merely struggle blindly for the possession of power; they each had a distinctive political philosophy and system which they hoped to make prevail.

During the sixty-two years of the third Republic these older parties have, for the most part, become so weak as to have almost no share in the parliamentary life of France. A great majority of the senators and deputies, and their electors are republicans of some sort, and whether they call themselves "republican nationalists," "moderates," "radicals," or even "radical socialists," they do not differ from each other greatly as to political theory; they are separated by shades of opinion, and by questions of means and persons rather than by opposing views as to the form of government. Even in the matter of the religious question, which is the chief ground of dissension between the "right" and the "left," none of the existing parties (except perhaps the communists and the royalists) would today advocate extreme measures either for or against the church. The only parties which still possess definite political and social theories are the extremists; on the one hand, the socialists and the communists; on the other, the royalists of the Action française. Thus the reactionary Action française is the only party which can claim to offer to conservative opinion a body of doctrine, and a positive theory of action.

The Action française is both more and less than a political party. Its parliamentary strength is at present nil, for it has no representatives either in the Senate or in the Chamber of Deputies, but, its political influence, though it is indirect and even occult, is undeniable. It is, in fact, chiefly an organization for propaganda and for counter-revolutionary action. Propaganda is particularly important to it since it aims not to reform or modify the existing régime, but to overthrow it, and effect a complete political and social reorganization of France.

Its chief organ of propaganda is a daily newspaper, called *L'Action française,* of which Charles Maurras and Leon Daudet are the editors-in-chief. This paper, which is remarkably well written, able, and perfectly fearless, exerts a considerable influence on a certain part of public opinion, especially on the youth of the *bourgeois* classes. Its attacks, often violent and unmeasured, but always brilliantly conducted, and always founded on a view of the national interest, have also at times (and particularly during the war) influenced the parliamentary leaders. It is, however, not so much in this newspaper, which is chiefly an instrument for polemical discussion and controversy, as in the books of Maurras, Montesquiou, Daudet, Moreau, Dimier and Bainville, that the political theory of the Action française is to be found. Among the men of talent who belong to this group, the profoundest and most systematic thinker is Charles Maurras. In his works the body of doctrine and all the ideas of the party are expressed.

Maurras was born in 1868 at Martigues, in the department of the Bouches-du-Rhone. His family, which belonged to the modest *bourgeoisie,* had long been established in Provence, that part of France which is most distinctly Mediterranean in character and culture. Thus Maurras is, by race and by early association, emphatically what is called "Latin"[1] —a fact which his personality and his mind alike attest. He received his education in Catholic institutions, and the beauty of the religion in which he was brought up has kept its attraction for him, so that he writes of it with a sort of nostalgia. Nevertheless, he early lost his faith, and this fact has been of great importance in his life.

An element which has also had some part in his formation is the fact that, in consequence of a youthful malady, he is extremely deaf. He can hear only when addressed directly by one person at a time and he is thus excluded from all the casual contacts and remarks which are so often a source of information and enlightenment. Such isolation from a large part of normal human intercourse may deepen the current of a man's thought, but it also deprives him of certain elements of criticism, and so, by lessening his contacts with reality, may lead him to be somewhat dogmatic in his conclusions.

Maurras denies that he was "born a royalist,"[2] but some of his ancestors were attached to the monarchy, and his mother had been brought up to hold the Revolution in horror.[3] At all events, Maurras himself had no definite political opinions when he first came to Paris, and seems, indeed, to have felt a certain contempt for politics.[4] Had he remained

---

[1] An amusing instance of the Latin tradition is to be found in the fact that his mother, and all her brothers and sisters received names from Plutarch. Maurras himself was christened by the curious family name of Photius.

[2] *Au Signe de Flore* (Paris, 1931), p. 1.   [3] *Ibid.,* p. 4.

[4] He took part, however, at the age of 19 in a demonstration against

a critic and *litterateur* it is probable that he would have won a fame and a practical success which his political activities have made impossible, for he is among the greatest living masters of French style. But he is not an eclectic, like Renan. His temperament drove him to look for certainties, and once he had acquired political convictions he was ready to do battle all his life for their sake.

Two lines of approach led him to a belief in monarchy. The first was his love of his own province. Like Mistral, Amouretti, and many other Provençals, he was eager to defend its treasures against what he calls "Jacobin uniformity," that is to say,[5] the standardization of democracy. His coming to Paris gave increased force to this feeling, and he became a *Felibre*.[6] With him, regionalism was the first step in the direction of royalism.

But, though he wanted a revival of local life and freedom, Maurras is an ardent patriot. The men of his generation, whose youth was darkened by the results of the Franco-Prussian war, are particularly sensitive to the weakness of France in Europe, and to the diminution of her influence. Maurras' perception of these things was stimulated by a trip he made to Greece in 1896. Just as he saw his beloved Provence more clearly when he looked at it from Paris, so he realized the situation of France with greater intensity from abroad. The voyage to Greece had for him a double lesson: on the Acropolis he felt the glory and divinity of a civilization of which he holds France to be the child and heir, and

Monsieur Grévy apropos of the Panama scandals. *Au Signe de Flore* (Paris, 1931), p. 16.

[5] *Ibid.*, p. 32.

[6] A "Felibre" is a partisan of the renaissance of the Provençal language.

in modern Greece he saw many signs of the waning of French influence.

This inferiority seemed to him to come, not from any intrinsic defect in the French people, but from a lack of unity in the national will resulting from the absence of a national authority. He came to the conclusion that England and Germany owed their coherence and force to the fact that their governments were dynastic. In contrast to them France, as he expressed it, seemed to him to be an orphan![7] The experience of foreign travel crystallized his ideas. "Evidence," he wrote, "at last forced me to admit that . . . if France is to live, the king must return. . . . The decision of my intellectual royalism was taken."[8] This decision was only translated into action a year later. The Dreyfus affair convinced Maurras of the urgent necessity for a change of régime, and, abandoning his purely literary career, he made "politics first" his motto. Since then almost all his activity has been in the field of political philosophy and propaganda.

Maurras has keen sensibilities, and an ardent and enthusiastic nature. His temperament is that of an aristocrat and an artist. Intellectually he has the Latin passion for clarity and logic, and, as he is fearless, and even combative, he likes to carry his theories to their utmost limits. In his method of thought he is a "positivist"; he examines political facts from a realistic and pragmatic point of view. But he is over-anxious to establish fundamental laws, and to reduce human affairs to the precision of logical formulas, and so is apt to be led into extremes.[9]

[7] *Au Signe de Flore,* p. 47.   [8] *Ibid.,* p. 49.

[9] "In aesthetics and politics he knew," he said, "the joy of seizing the evidence of fundamental thoughts."—*La Démocratie religieuse* (Paris, 1921), p. 463.

His loss of faith has left him profoundly, but calmly, sceptical. There is no trace of mysticism in his thought, and he does not even seem to feel the need of it, as averred sceptics often do.[10] Positivism, and Comte's religion of Humanity have supplied him with a philosophy which he finds sufficient. Yet, in spite of this scepticism, Maurras is not a materialist. His fundamental conception of life is aesthetic. This world, beyond which he does not look, he finds to be full of beauty, and beauty he adores. Deprived of Christian mysticism, and subjected to the intellectual discipline of a classical education, and of positivism, his natural enthusiasm and ardor have been translated into a devotion to Latin culture and the classic spirit. In his conception of the "good life" Maurras is a humanist; he believes that it depends on moderation, discipline and choice, together with respect for the past. These are the qualities which appear to him to have built the Parthenon, and which characterize French civilization. "Beauty is order—it is harmony—it is wisdom."[11] For him, thought is supreme. Life and vitality have no value in themselves; they are only good when they are disciplined, and used constructively. "It is not its heart, but its head which distinguishes the human race."[12] His conception of the value of life as consisting in a disciplined harmony leads Maurras to love order for itself, and to feel a passionate devotion to the French civilization which, he feels, has come nearest to

[10] He was "saved," he said, from mysticism by his passion for literary criticism, and by his French patriotism.—*La Démocratie religieuse*, p. 462.

[11] *Anthinéa* (Paris, 1926), pp. 215-16.

[12] *Romantisme et révolution*, p. 256, note VI. This conception of beauty is evident in his aesthetic judgments. He dislikes all that smacks of "romanticism," that is, sensibility for its own sake. Even the artist must submit to a technique which he has not invented. He is ruled by the intimate laws of beauty, and does what he likes, but not *as he pleases.*

embodying his ideal. "France, of old," he has said, "had the true classic spirit; it was more sensitive to the relations between things than to things themselves."[13] The French alone have a feeling for perfection.[14] This is the result of the Latin discipline; "the Roman man is the child and heir of all civilization."[15] The French are more civilized than the Germans. Were this not so, the Germans would have been justified in invading French territory.[16]

Maurras' philosophy is strongly anti-individualistic. *Man, he says, needs man.* We are born of love, to love, and our hearts and souls are not really our own, they belong to others in undivided community. Our hunger and thirst for one another, in friendship, in love, and in wider communions, is the chief part of ourselves. Even hate is a testimony to our need for each other. We require each other materially, too. It is as if life were made on purpose for love, and, though the effort to realize this ideal may be hopeless, the impulse towards it is too great to be resisted.

Does the individual produce society, or society the individual? Since in the animal kingdom, two individuals are needed to produce a third, Maurras concludes that society, which is the series of the generations, produces the individual.[17] An association is not the sum of the associated, but

---

[13] André Chevrillon has expressed a very similar idea in comparing the Anglo-Saxons to the Latins. The former, he says, see and feel the concrete; the latter are more alive to abstract relationships. The ones are seers, the others thinkers.

[14] *La Musique intérieure* (Paris, 1925), p. 42; and *Quand les Français ne s'aimaient pas,* p. 110.

[15] He calls Leibnitz, Goethe, Heine, Schopenhauer and Nietsche "barbarians more or less romanised."—*Quand les Français ne s'aimaient pas* (Paris, 1916), p. 28.

[16] This point of view is much like that of the "Pan-Germans," although the rôles are reversed.

[17] *La Démocratie religieuse,* pp. 314-15. This reasoning is only an

their mother. The error of liberalism consists in demanding freedom for the sake of *individuation;* that is to say, for the upbuilding of the individual for his own sake, without recognizing that it is only through society that individuals can develop. If the value of life lies in the contribution of each individual, then laws, habits, institutions, customs, and the chosen and filtered products of generations are useless. If nothing is more sacred than the individual, he should never be brought to justice, and everything, including society itself, can be put in peril for his sake!

The individual is not even the social unit, for, Maurras says, "since human society produces the individual, it cannot be composed of what it produces."[18] Human society is composed of families, who find it natural to live together in groups, and who may produce men some day, by virtue of society. Society only *lives* metaphorically, but this existence governs the interest of many living beings; it is superior to the individual, and the proper order is society first, and then man. In the political field individualism gave birth to the Revolution; in the religious field it produced the Reformation; and in the aesthetic field it created Romanticism. All three are antisocial, and are to be condemned.

Can man really live socially? Can he live for others? In order that he may do so, his social instincts must become habitual, and they must be supported by institutions which will humanize him, for the most social man is also the most truly human. How, then, shall human associations be or-

---

arbitrary answer to the old question of whether the egg produces the chicken, or the chicken the egg!

[18] *Ibid.,* p. 315. This is entirely sophistical. One of the characteristics of living things is that they do produce or, more exactly, reproduce that of which they are made!

ganized? Life, Maurras says, may be ruled according to some mysterious and all-wise plan, but that plan, even if it exists, cannot be known. Fate and ruin are neutral; they do not spare what is valuable to man. Yet thought, art and civilization begin by an act of faith in the immutable essence of things, for we believe that like causes always produce like results. Acting on this practical belief, science has deduced many of the laws of nature, and in the same way, the laws of society can be discovered. There are a small number of these political and social laws governing all human associations, which can be determined with certainty from history and from experience, and according to which society must be organized if it is to be prosperous.

The object of society in general is association for its own sake, but the material aim of particular societies is prosperity. Therefore, the first question to be asked in regard to social organization is: "What is favorable to the subsistence of a given social group?" Societies normally follow a curve of development and flower, but they can die, or be killed by violence. Order is the essential condition of their continued existence, and therefore it is more important than the liberty of individuals. For order to be maintained, the submission of the individual is absolutely necessary. Individualism, in the sense of the right of self-determination, is contrary even to the interests of the individual, for it creates an anarchy which destroys the society by which he lives.

How can the submission of the individual be procured? In the first place by unity of ideas and customs among the members of a community. In society the present is always based on the past, and social unity is the result of common traditions and habits. Therefore, to maintain these common traditions is to create, and to lay the basis for future creation, whereas to impair them is evil, for the harmony which produces the good and beautiful is the result of a long evolution, and if it is destroyed, it will not return. In accordance with this Maurras considers, as did the theocrats, that tolerance is not desirable. It is incompatible with the ideal of national unity of thought and belief. He admits that a certain degree of curiosity and open-mindedness are necessary elements of thought but curiosity places everything on the same level, and this spells disorder. Truth must exclude.[19] A State which wishes to grow must have a rule, an inner discipline: "One must come out of liberty as out of a prison."[20] Intellectual tolerance, he says, is not natural to Frenchmen; they are always proselytes either in religion or in other domains: "those who do not burn for ideas, and feel a secret fanaticism for abstract types are not truly Frenchmen."[21]

In order that the submission of the individual may be assured, there must also be an authority in society. It follows from the preceding arguments that the source of this authority is not the assent of individuals, but the demands of the general welfare. True sovereignty exists by a right which is inherent in human needs, and power becomes legitimate because it is useful. To the proved necessity a holy sanction is given, but this mystical sanction is common to all ideas of right, such as the right of a father, of an owner, of a worker. The usefulness of government has always been the justification of the law's constraint, and even the ages of faith demanded that power should insure the common good.

Rousseau, Maurras says, tried to identify the lawmaker with the man for whom the law is made, but this is a soph-

[19] *Ibid.,* pp. 267-68.
[20] *Quand les Français ne s'aimaient pas,* p. 207.
[21] *Ibid.,* p. 214.

ism; the success of majorities is merely the success of force, and it is endured, but not accepted. "If political science exists, it proves that society did not spring from a contract, but from necessity. . . . Law arose from the nature of things, and not from the general assent; it was discovered, not decreed."[22] Order does not arise spontaneously in society; authority precedes and creates it, and authority must exist for the common welfare, and the defense of the nation.

The modern form of social organization is the nation. Catholic Christendom was a wider form of association, but it ceased to be a political reality with the triumph of the Reformation. "For good or for ill," Maurras says, "the future is to the nations. . . . Nationalism is the modern imperative; it wins adherents every day, and it will soon penetrate both Asia and Africa."[23] The nation is not a mere sum of voters or citizens; it includes the dead, as well as the living, and also the land itself, with its influences, its treasures, its language, its spirit. It is a superior, an almost eternal moral entity. The influence of the nation is all-powerful upon the *élite* who alone are capable of a real political consciousness. The necessity of saving the labor of their ancestors, and of preserving the source of their intellectual and moral, as well as their material being, makes this *élite* consider the nation as a work of art, for which they gladly spend their efforts, and even their lives. Thus the nation perfectly fulfills the needs of human organization, for it both favors a homogeneity of thought and custom among citizens, and stimulates the individual to sacrifice himself to the community.

Maurras points out that life, a continued existence, is the first essential for all societies. Therefore durability is the

[22] *De Demos à César*, pp. 117-19.
[23] *Enquête sur la Monarchie*, p. CXVII.

greatest good for every nation. The public safety is the vital matter, which all governments must first of all insure. "The legitimate government is the one which saves us. The usurper is the government which ruins us."[24] Democracy has not furnished the necessary safety to France, and therefore is to be condemned.

Maurras' criticisms of democracy and the Republic have probably been the most influential part of his work. These criticisms are of two kinds: in the first place he combats the theory of democracy, and in the second he attacks its practical results. Democracy, he says, is government confided to a majority in which all are considered as equal. This is absurd, for equality does not exist in fact. Men are equal before death, but not before life, nor has modern progress by giving them more things, equalized them. On the contrary, material prosperity, socialism (which Maurras says, is essentially aristocratic) and the fusion of races have all made for a general "hierarchization." Some people say that there is a social democratic State, in which individuals, added together, make a conscious force. But to organize this number is to destroy its democratic character, for democracy and organization are antithetical. All organisms are formed of elements differentiated for a purpose, and the higher the organism the greater the inequality. "If equality is justice, animals are monuments of injustice!"[25]

Democracy, at best, can only exist in humble communities, where society is not complex, and always under miserable conditions. Wealth and civilization inevitably bring inequalities.[26] If political equality were to spread, it would lead to

[24] *Enquête,* p. CIX.
[25] *De Demos à César* (Paris, 1930), p. 23.
[26] *Ibid.,* p. 82.

social and economic equality, and so to universal poverty. Nature herself says: "inequality or death."[27] Therefore, the people should not be encouraged to think of equality and the dominance of numbers as good.

Those who favor a Republic pretend that it rests on the stable basis of the national will as expressed by elections, but objects so precious as the national life and welfare cannot be allowed to depend on the undisciplined wills of individuals, who will not look beyond their own immediate interests. The voices of incompetents in great numbers cannot suffice to resolve delicate problems. Nationalism is, on the contrary, a revolt against the revolutionary error of the "Rights of Man." Sovereignty must be snatched from the inert and unforeseeing masses in the name of a national right which does not belong to one generation, but to the entire nation, both past and future.

Political institutions must be judged, not according to their theoretic merits, but by their practical results, and therefore, Maurras says, his criticisms of the Republic are chiefly directed to its obvious bad results. What, he asks, have been the benefits of democracy for France? What is vital to the life of the individual is liberty; what is vital to the political life of the nation is authority, and the Republic has failed to supply either. It has shown itself inadequate both in its internal and in its foreign policy. Within the country, it has weakened the foundations of social life: religion, property, and the family. It destroyed the old economic order, based on the free corporations, and it has put nothing in its place except the vicious policy of economic *laissez faire*. It swept away the remains of the old local liberties and rights, and it has never been able to accomplish

[27] *Ibid.*, p. 142.

anything in the way of decentralization. It has also signally failed to respect the rights of minorities, for, in the war of parties, the individual has been poorly protected against the political passions of the parliament. The Republic, in fact, has shown itself more absolute, and more arbitrary than the Monarchy ever was.

Yet this government, so absolute and so unscrupulous, has never obtained the authority born of unity of will. Maurras points out again and again how democracy has fostered discord among Frenchmen. Its very theory excludes a unity of government or policy: every man thinks that he and his friends are the wisest, each seeks to seize the power, and the result is a perpetual struggle. The Republic has been the predominance of party interests and passions over the interests of the nation. Political men have consistently sacrificed the good of the community to their own success, or to that of their party. There can be no authority, or continuity of policy in governments which depend on election; they are "mere phantoms." The ever-changing ministers in a Republic cannot even know their own departments, and there is no tradition, no control to guide them. Cabinets have no unity of views, and they are hampered by their own lack of authority, by the necessity of parliamentary maneuvers, and by their dependence on public opinion. It is to this absence of unity and identity, this lack of stable authority, that the misfortunes of France are due.

The foreign policy of the Republic finds no greater favor in Maurras' eyes. In a series of volumes, of which *"Kiel et Tangier"*[28] is the first, and perhaps the most important, he criticizes the conduct of foreign affairs by the Republic, both in general and in detail. French statesmen, he says, have

[28] Paris, 1905. Republished, with additions, in 1913 and 1921.

not taken a boldly national stand, for until 1914 they allowed Germany or England to dictate their conduct almost continuously, so that France appeared to be governed from Berlin or London. That a great power should dismiss its foreign minister as Delcassé was dismissed, at the bidding of an enemy, was a disgrace. The Republic claims to have won the war, but it only did so by suspending republican forms everywhere, and establishing a military dictatorship. In obedience to the demands of public opinion it stopped the war too soon, and in making peace it failed to secure the safety of France, for it allowed Austria-Hungary to be dismembered, but left Germany intact.

There have, Maurras admits, been reactions, attempts at a revival of nationalism, in what he calls the "Poincaré experiments,"[29] but they have been abortive for lack of "sovereignty." The Republic is doomed always to fall back into the weaknesses and errors which result from its false theories, and the struggles of persons and parties. Maurras concludes that from the national point of view, which is the only position for France, the Republic is a signal failure, and that no government which can be trusted to follow a strong and consistent national policy can issue from the present régime; therefore the authority of the State should be vested, not in the people, but in a family, which will truly represent the national interest. France can still be saved, but only by a return to monarchy: "to personify the nation, we must have a king."[30]

Maurras does not claim that monarchy exists by virtue of an especial "divine right." All legitimate power, he says, is based on "beneficent force."[31] The ownership of power

[29] *Enquête sur la Monarchie,* p. XVII. [30] *Enquête,* p. 78.
[31] *De Demos à César* (Paris, 1930), p. 93.

is justified by its results; the tree must be judged by its fruit.[32] Thus, Hugh Capet and Bonaparte both seized the power, but the former laid the basis of French prosperity and power, and founded a dynasty which endured for 800 years, therefore he was a legitimate king, whereas Napoleon, who led France to eventual ruin, was an usurper. The authority of the French kings was exercised in God's name, but all rights are divine for those who believe, and those of royalty have their particular source in an *historic* right. History, Maurras says, demonstrates that institutions, on the whole, do not change, and the three races of French kings have shown a resemblance which proves that the essential condition of existence for France is monarchy. Because of the great variety of interests in her wide territory France is not adapted to a republic, and it was for this reason that the Gauls, although they were brave, did not succeed in making a nation. Frenchmen can devote themselves to an idea, but only a king can furnish them with the wide conception of a national State, for which they will sacrifice all aims of party, province, or class: "without a king, Frenchmen have nothing real in common."[33] In the Middle Ages anarchy overthrew order, in spite of the intense religious spirit of the times. Since human justice exists to realize order and the public good, new methods were needed, and hereditary monarchy was evolved. French unity was not inevitable; it was created by her kings. France was born of the Capetian organization, and the royal tradition is that of a strong France in a divided Europe.

Monarchy may have three forms: it may be (1) plebisci-

[32] This, as Maurras pointed out, is also the theory of the Church. *De Demos à César*, pp. 149-51.
[33] *La Démocratie religieuse*, p. 60.

tary, (2) elective, or (3) based on force. The French monarchy is of the latter type. The king's power may be ratified by the suffrage of the people, but it does not depend on this for its authority. Its original foundation is force, and acceptance merely follows. The particular advantage of the French monarchy is that it is hereditary in the male line. Heredity of power in the State is the secret of prosperity, and even in successful republics it has played a great part, for it furnishes the necessary element of foresight and responsibility. The work of a dynasty is like that of one man whose life would be sempiternal. This is what is lacking in France today, for there is no one at present who represents a thought of the future. A chief is needed on whose disinterested foresight men can rely.

Hereditary power, Maurras says, is more impersonal, and awakens less envy than other forms of power, for in the throne the past is respected. Moreover, hereditary monarchy is an institution which puts the public interest under the safeguard of an egoism, for the king's advantage is identical with that of his country. It is not the personal character of the king which is important, but his authoritative position. There have been, according to Maurras, a remarkable number of able kings in France (for talents, including that of statesmanship, are apt to run in families), but even bad kings have done little harm.[34] Succeeding princes have had different characters and ideas, but all have been nationalistic and the Monarchy has shown a remarkable continuity of policy.[35]

---

[34] *Enquête,* p. XCII. Even the evils of the reigns of John II and Charles VI, Maurras said, are to be attributed to the efforts to establish an elective and parliamentary régime! *De Demos à César,* II, 185.

[35] *Enquête,* p. XCV.

As to the character of the monarchy which he would wish to restore, although he does not call it "absolute," Maurras does not deny that it would be "authoritarian." The king will not need to *solicit* either obedience or commandment, nor will he have to *impose* them, for both will belong to him naturally, and by right. The restored monarchy may at first take the form of a dictatorship, but this would only be a passing phase. Yet the new monarchy must not be "constitutional," as was the liberal monarchy of Louis Philippe; the parliament must be done away with. Liberalism attacked the power of the State, without restoring the liberty of the citizens: it weakened the government in its foreign relations, where it should have remained strong, but left it all-powerful in civil life, where liberty is necessary. Democracy confused *representation* with *government,* whereas the formula of the royalists is: "authority above, liberty below." "To the king in council, government. To the people in their assemblies, representation."[36] The latter will express the wishes and preferences of the people, and the former will execute them, in conformity with the public good. Thus, the State will have councilors, but only one master, and the "Republic, one and indivisible" will be replaced by many small republics, under a single permanent power: the king.

To the monarch will be given absolute control over all that concerns the nation as a whole: army, navy, foreign affairs; and he will also have the right to regulate and supervise all the other authorities. The State will be master of its own affairs, and the various associations, professional, local, and so on, will be master in theirs, subject to the coördinating power of the Crown. The State will be free, Maurras says, since the local powers, civil and administra-

[36] *Ibid.,* p. CXXVII.

tive, are to be revived, but it will be strong, since it will be rid of the tyranny of parliament. The royalist program will realize this by means of three measures: (1) The heredity of the throne; (2) the destruction of parliament; (3) moral, religious, professional, administrative and territorial devolution.

Maurras believes in the aristocratic principle. The king will not rule alone, but by means of an hierarchy; he must consult and use other men and therefore an *élite* is necessary. Birth, race, and privilege, with the fineness of quality which they give, should not be separated from the profession of serving the State, for if they are, they lose their value, both for the nation and for themselves. Political families are not subject to the same objections as professional politicians, since they have already been selected by heredity, and have given guaranties of responsibility. France in modern times has not had such great families, but Maurras denies that the preëxistence of an aristocracy is necessary to monarchy, as Barrès affirmed. Should the king return, a new aristocracy could readily be created out of the sound elements of the nation. Yet the king would not be obliged to favor and depend on the old nobility, as some people fear. Maurras points out that, as a matter of fact, the kings of France were always at odds with the nobles; they were the "fathers of the people" rather than the protectors of the great.

It is not, however, by the creation of an aristocracy, still less by a parliament, that the authoritarian character of monarchy is to be tempered, and the necessary element of liberty to be assured; it is by decentralization. The State today, Maurras says, is encumbered with a quantity of business which does not properly belong to it; it has become a schoolmaster, an architect, and even a manufacturer of cigarettes and matches! The present system has given all responsibility to the central power, which is overwhelmed with a mass of details, and is like an athlete holding up so heavy a weight that he is often obliged to let it fall. The Monarchy had already gone too far in the direction of centralization, but the Empire and the Republic have aggravated this evil. The consequence is that local spirit has disappeared, and, with it, the sense of civic responsibility. The communes and the smaller cities have degenerated because they have had neither authority at home, nor discipline from above to make them grow wisely.

It is difficult, if not impossible for the Republic to decentralize. In the first place, if there is no permanent chief, centralization is necessary to preserve the unity of the nation: "France is the political achievement of the monarchy. Without a king she runs the risk of suffocating, or of breaking into pieces."[37] Moreover, centralization is useful to the politicians of a republican régime: it creates a series of links, running from the elector, through the functionary, to the deputy, or minister, and it puts many possibilities of patronage into the hands of the deputies. Only the monarchy will decentralize. It would be its natural policy to strengthen all institutions, such as provinces, communes, families, syndicates, which lead people to take an interest in the national life. All these organizations should be free and autonomous, under the guidance of the State. Only the military forces should remain entirely in the hands of the central power.

Maurras' program of decentralization demands: (1) that

[37] *Ibid.,* p. 51. This objection to decentralization is a very real one. The events in Brittany in 1932 where a group of separatists destroyed a monument commemorating the union of Brittany to France, gives it point.

the provinces should be restored; (2) that the universities should be rendered autonomous; (3) that the family should be strengthened by the suppression of the law of equal inheritances;[38] (4) that the patrimonial tenure both of land and of industry should be encouraged; (5) that syndical autonomy should be allowed; (6) that religious congregations should be authorized. Cities, provinces, and associations, professional and religious, will each be powerful in regard to what concerns itself, but weak in regard to the general direction of affairs. In this way two types of authority will exist: the local and the royal. The monarchy, so organized, would be strong in its own domain, but unable to undertake anything against the individual. Instead of being the subject of a monster state which regulates everything itself, the citizen would be a member of all sorts of free communities, the family, the commune, the corporation, etc.

Maurras' attitude towards Catholicism and the Church is an important part of his political theory. Although he does not believe in what he calls the "beautiful poem" of Christian theology, he is deeply devoted to Catholicism, both as a way of thought, and as a social force. In the first place, it appeals to his aesthetic sense; its organization, power, and unity attract him, and he is impressed by its moral beauty, by its conception of ideal perfection, and by the agreement of its teachings with public and private needs. "Catholicism," he writes, "is an order and a harmony. It is an hierarchy of thought and spirit, as well as of persons. . . . It is the ensemble of its principles which is superb."[39] The Church alone creates real "free thought,"[40] for its disciplines are rational,

[38] It must be remembered that in France a father can only alienate a part of his possessions from his children.
[39] La Démocratie religieuse, pp. 17-19.
[40] Ibid., p. 218.

and all in it springs from reflection. Moreover, Catholicism is Latin: "Tradition is the dearest of goods to a civilized man," Maurras says, "and it is incarnate in Catholicism."[41] He is, he says, a son of Rome because Rome made France, and saved him from being a Norwegian, a German, or a Swiss. "I am Roman because I feel human, for Rome is all civilization and humanity."[42]

Metaphysics are repugnant to Maurras,[43] and he feels a deep mistrust for the mystical and emotional elements in religion.[44] Only the discipline of Catholicism can purge these unsocial elements of their dangers; the feeling soul must be ennobled by the thinking soul, and "God is love" must not be allowed to become "Love is God."[45] A non-Catholic believer has no outer authority to refer to, and private conscience is terribly unrestricted, hence anarchical. Moral anarchy may even be drawn from an individual reading of the Gospel,[46] and many most harmful people, like Rousseau and Tolstoi, have been non-Catholic Christians. Liberalism is Judeo-Protestant, and the Reformation in France was anarchical: "All who are non-Roman are deniers. . . . All that is positive is Catholic." Luther and Kant caused a mental and moral regression,[47] and the equilibrium of humanity was shaken when "German Man" suppressed the cult of the virgin, and belief in the saints, and in purgatory. Maurras concludes that "non-Catholic Christianity is odious."[48]

[41] *La Démocratie religieuse*, p. 464.
[42] *Ibid.*, p. 26.   [43] *Ibid.*, pp. 462-63.
[44] *Ibid.*, p. 433. This attitude is evident in all of his books. See *Romantisme et revolution*, chapter on Chateaubriand and *Chemin de Paradis—enquête sur la Monarchie*, p. 10 (Preface of 1909).
[45] *La Démocratie religieuse*, p. 19.
[46] *Romantisme et revolution*, p. 245.
[47] *La Démocratie religieuse*, pp. 41, 308.   [48] *Ibid.*, p. 41.

Catholicism covers all, and saves all. "This intellectual order," Maurras says, "is practical. Moral life is seized at its source, arrested, guided by a master hand." Such a discipline of the heart goes deeper than the heart itself to the deepest habits of life. In Catholicism, philanthropy and love are kept from excesses, feeling is subjected to thought, even mysticism is regulated and obedient to law. The laws of conscience must be defined in order to formulate the relations between men and society, and at the same time a living authority is needed to resolve these questions. Catholicism alone unites these two things: "man finds a tribunal for his least complaints . . . and society a body which can settle disputed questions."[49] The Church insists upon the place of man in the world, and shows him that he has made neither the law of the universe, nor his own law. It excludes individualism in the name of the broadest love of all, and requires humility.

Maurras naturally recognizes and values also the social action of Catholicism. "The Church," he says, "is the city of order, and it is no offense to consider it as the keystone of society."[50] It teaches authority, hierarchy, order, and peace. Since it does inspire respect for property and for fatherly authority, and the love of concord, why is it blameworthy for those who care for these things to be grateful to it?

Maurras considers that there is a fundamental antagonism between individualistic democracy and Catholicism. He declares that the only stable policy of the Republic has been anticlericalism. Should not those who are opposed to the Revolution in all its forms unite against the common enemy? France, he says, will long be divided as to religious beliefs, and a *modus vivendi* must be found. There is much in com-

[49] *La Démocratie religieuse*, p. 23.   [50] *Ibid.*, p. 41.

266   L ' A C T I O N   F R A N Ç A I S E

mon between positivists and Catholics; they agree as to the constitution of society; they both reprove an independent morality; they both make "duty depend on dogma."[51] Although they may differ as to religion, they think alike as to the value of Catholicism to the nation and to humanity, and therefore they can meet on the ground of the useful, and agree as to the policy to be followed with regard to religion. It is essential to both that this union should exist. How can Catholics find peace in a nation where there is no religious unity unless they have the support of those who agree with them in political and social matters? Nationalists, on the other hand, must remember that should the folly of the republicans draw on France a dismemberment like that of Poland, the Catholic structure would probably be the means of an awakening of the nation. Religious, social and national defense go hand in hand. The religious policy of France should be an homage to the services and virtues of the Church; it must be treated according to its own wishes and allowed to be autonomous, but respected and supported by the State.

Maurras reprobates Gallicanism.[52] It is advantageous both to society and to the State that the Church should have a center, and that that center should be in Rome. Spiritual society must have a chief, and he should not be a national one. Were an autonomous clergy to reject the Roman pontiff, they would lose the immense advantage of the Roman tradition, and its authoritative interpretation of Scripture. The Bible would then become the only source of authority, and

[51] *La Démocratie religieuse,* p. 505.

[52] *Ibid.,* p. 274. It is not certain that Maurras' attitude on this question would be as firm today as it was before his experience of Roman authority.

that is Jewish. Its influence on the Protestant clergy, Maurras says, has been unfortunate: "to avoid a Latin authority," he exclaims "would you become Semitic?"[53] With regard to the *ralliement,* which he calls "an immense error," Maurras says that Leo XIII miscalculated its effects; he did not understand the true state of things in France or realize that the first assemblies had been royalist. Belgium made him fancy France more Catholic than it actually was.

Maurras was anxious to unite Catholic and non-Catholic conservatives in the Action française, and therefore he undoubtedly wished to avoid a conflict with the Church. Even before conflict ocurred he often repeated that he, personally, never touched on theological matters. The Action française, he said, always maintained a respectful attitude towards the Catholic hierarchy; neither discussing them, nor arguing with them. This is true, yet reasons exist which make it probable that such a conflict could not have been avoided indefinitely. In the first place, Maurras' fundamental attitude towards Catholicism cannot be approved by the Church. He denies the truth of revelation, and seems almost to dislike the spirit of the Gospel,[54] yet he accepts the spiritual authority of the Church, which is founded on that Gospel, and wishes to impose it on others, for the sake of its social value. This point of view, which implies that the absolute truth of religion is unimportant, is only possible to a spirit so profoundly sceptical as entirely to reject all possibility of a su-

[53] *Ibid.,* p. 24.

[54] In the *Chemin de Paradis* (Paris, 1895), he says that there are two Christs, two Gospels, one within and one without the Church. Moral anarchy is drawn from an individual reading of the Gospel. It is the Protestant Jesus who perverted Tolstoi, Lammenais, de Vogüe. See also quotation on p. 273 from the *La Démocratie religieuse.*

pernatural reality, mystically revealed.[55] It is comprehensible that ardent believers should be shocked to find such a man among the defenders of the faith.

In the next place, the Catholic Church disposes of an enormous power over its members, since they believe that it alone can open for them the doors of eternal life. This supreme motive for submission will be lacking in a non-believer, however attached he may be to the Church as an institution, and there will always be a question as to how far he will obey orders of which he disapproves.[56] For this reason the Holy See is somewhat mistrustful of the support which it may receive from non-Catholics. It prefers, at all events, to keep the political and social guidance of the faithful, as well as their religious instruction, in its own hands, or in the hands of those who are directly affiliated with itself.

The Action française is a political organization, but it has been active in propaganda and teaching, and it has acquired a considerable influence over the youth, and particularly the Catholic youth of France. It was inevitable that this influence should excite a certain jealousy among purely Catholic teachers. It is true that the men who taught subjects in any way akin to theology or religion in the "Institut d'action française" were Catholics, as were also many members of the editorial staff of the newspaper. Maurras says that these men were never troubled by heresy, or evil influences in the *Action française,* and in 1927 he declared that their spiritual guides did not consider that they had suf-

[55] For an interesting discussion of this see René Gilloin *Trois crises* (Tours, 1929).

[56] An instance of this is the contrast between Maurras' attitude towards the Vatican, when he found himself in conflict with it, and the complete submission of Veuillot under somewhat similar circumstances. See p. 169.

fered.[57] Nevertheless, they were not laboring primarily for the glory of the Church, but to bring about a restoration. Since the Church has never been willing to identify its cause with any political system, it could scarcely allow the men of the *Action française* to appear to speak in its name.

Moreover, the reasons which in 1894 led Leo XIII to initiate a policy of reconciliation with the Republic were still cogent in 1926. It is true that, as the royalists point out, the *ralliement* did not produce the desired effect of appeasement and union; anticlericalism continued to be active in France. But today, anticlericalism has, apparently, done its worst, since it has disestablished the Church, broken up the religious orders, put education into lay hands. These measures have not been as fatal as it was feared they would be, for French Catholicism is still very much alive. Rome has apparently accepted them, for the moment, as unavoidable facts, and a period of relative calm has followed. There are no signs of the immediate disappearance of the Republic, and in the last few years it has been somewhat more conciliatory in its attitude towards the Vatican than it was at the beginning of the century.[58] Therefore it is comprehensible that Pius XI should have considered that the French Catholics still have more to hope for from the Republic than from the royalists.

In addition it is to be noted that the present papal policy is markedly international and pacifist. It would perhaps be too much to suggest that Pius XI wishes to restore the papacy to its old situation of international arbiter, but it is certain that he has showed himself hostile to nationalism. He would, therefore, naturally feel a greater sympathy for

[57] *L'Action française et le Vatican* (Paris, 1927), p. 98.
[58] France now has an ambassador accredited to the Holy See.

the Republic, especially when it is represented by internationally-minded men like Briand, than for the aggressive nationalism of the royalists.

Then, too, Maurras has been the merciless enemy of liberalism in all its forms, and has thus earned the dislike of the liberal Catholics. The intransigence of his ideas, and the violence of their expression are somewhat out of tune with the moderation and spirit of diplomacy which has usually characterized the Church. For all these reasons, a conflict between the Vatican and the Action française was almost inevitable; it is, in fact, remarkable that it was so long delayed.

In studying the conflict itself, it is hard to escape the conviction that it was intended entirely to destroy the Action française. Many of the accusations brought against Maurras are unfounded. For instance his enemies declare that he wished to propitiate Catholicism and the Catholics merely in order to strengthen the royalist party; that he used the Church, but did not serve it. To anyone who studies his writings with impartiality (a thing which his adversaries have not always done) it is evident that this is unjust. Maurras' admiration for Catholicism is deep and sincere. The Church in his eyes is not merely an instrument for enforcing the order which he desires, but an essential part of that order itself. Its dogma, its ritual, its hierarchy, its moral and intellectual discipline, as well as its authority, are all dear to him. He considers it as the supreme source of the Latin culture which is more precious to him than anything else. It may be questioned whether a man can truly love and understand a religion in which he does not believe, and whether, in rejecting the supernatural belief which is its very soul he does not lose the power to judge and the right to defend it.

But, even if this is admitted, Maurras must be absolved from a purely utilitarian motive in defending Catholicism.

An instance of the injustice amounting to animosity which is evident in the charges brought against Maurras is to be found in the criticisms of Monseigneur Andrieu, Cardinal of Bordeaux. Not content with calling the *Chemin de Paradis* and *Anthinea* (two of Maurras' earliest books) licentious, atheistical and blasphemous, Andrieu declares that Maurras condemns systems which make the effort for virtue the rule of life, and that he wants to free society from all moral constraints.[59] There is no justification for this statement. The works of Maurras prove the contrary, as should be evident from the above analysis.

It is doubtful whether submission on the part of Maurras would have been acceptable to Rome, but in any case it was inevitable that he and his colleagues should have refused to yield. Although years before the conflict Maurras wrote that "the Church has the right to mix in affairs of States,"[60] even then he added: "if the king is the only condition for the elevation of France, no rallying, no objurgation, no devotion to the Church can count."[61] However genuinely attached Maurras is to Catholicism, the first object of his devotion is France: her interests are paramount, and it is one of the fundamental tenets of his creed that they should prevail over humanitarian ideals.

The Pope has the interest of Christendom in his keeping, but the political interests of France escape him . . . The deference due to authorities sacred in their own sphere does not oblige one to follow them in what is injurious to one's country . . . If, in the ecclesiastical sphere, a vast plan of world peace is being made, in

[59] *L'Action française et le Vatican*, p. 157.
[60] *La Démocratie religieuse*, p. 273.
[61] *Ibid.*, p. 189.

which France is sacrificed, the *Action française* is here to oppose it.[62]

The political independence of citizens, he points out, is a doctrine proclaimed even by the encyclical of Leo XIII. This independence would be illusory if the Church had the right to impose on the faithful obedience in every political matter in which the pope judged that the good of religion or of souls, was involved. There is *no* political affair which has not its repercussion on the interests of religion or of souls. Thus to extend the indirect power of the Church would give to the Roman pontiff enormous pretentions which he has always repudiated. Maurras concluded by echoing the "non possumus" of Haussonville. The *Action française,* he said, by its resistance is maintaining the conception of a rightful independence of national policy before the religious hierarchy. The Catholics, if they accept their political direction from Rome will lose all credit, and be considered as mere agents of the Vatican.

The action of Rome in regard to the Action française has been much more drastic than was the attitude of Leo XIII toward the royalists at the time of the *ralliement,* and therefore the question of the degree of obedience which the pope may demand from Catholics in political matters is more obvious; it is, in fact, the crux of the whole matter. "It is not allowed to Catholics," Pius XI said in a consistorial allocution of December 20th, 1926, "to belong to enterprises which put the interests of a party above those of religion, nor to expose themselves to dangerous doctrines, nor to sustain, encourage or read papers published by men whose writings we disapprove. It is not suitable that the French should be divided among themselves because of political questions."

[62] *L'Action française et le Vatican,* p. 132.

These very definite prohibitions have since been enforced by forbidding priests to give absolution to those who confess to reading the *Action française,* and, in some cases, by refusing Christian burial to its active members. The *Action française* is not a religious paper; its objects are purely political, and it does not profess to discuss theology or dogma. It is impossible to know until it is published whether there will be heretical material in any given number—yet these numbers are condemned beforehand. The allocution of Pius XI says: "Let each, however, keep the legitimate and honest liberty of preferring some government which does not contradict the divine order," but it is hard to see how, under these conditions, a "legitimate and honest liberty" of judgment is left to those who obey him. If a Catholic honestly believes that the Action française is the one hope of political salvation for France (and a certain number of Catholics undoubtedly did and do so believe), he is relentlessly driven to choose between the good of his country, as he sees it, and the commands of the pope; a terrible dilemma!

An interesting part of Maurras' work deals with the possibility of bringing about a restoration. One of the most frequent objections to the monarchist movement is that a restoration is impossible, but this, Maurras declares, is not true. In the first place, if, as he believes, a return to monarchy is the only hope of restoring to France her strength and prosperity a restoration must be looked on as necessary, however difficult it may be to achieve. In the next place, such a restoration would be much easier than people imagine. For the king to return, it is not necessary that he should have crowds of followers; he needs only the support of a few resolute leaders. History has usually been created by energetic minorities, which the masses have always followed.

The revolutionary ideas are today attacked from all sides; there is a tendency in France to return to tradition; an opinion exists in favor of hereditary rights, and of the family, antiparliamentary feeling is growing, and decentralization is increasingly demanded. Does the people really care for its sovereignty? Many significant facts, Maurras says, seem to show that it has become sceptical and contemptuous of the elective system. Once it is placed before a restoration as an accomplished fact, it will not stir.

In order to bring about such a restoration the first thing to do is to create a royalist state of mind. Once public opinion is formed, a single blow will reëstablish the monarchy. Men readily agree on working to form such a royalist opinion, and the propaganda and activity of the Action française are directed to this end. The Republic must be attacked at every opportunity; her statesmen must be ridiculed and discredited, both by personal and general criticisms, and a policy of "favoring the worst" must be followed.[63] Accordingly the Action française is much more violent against moderate or conservative men than against the socialists or the communists.

It is evident, however, that the monarchy cannot be restored either by election, or by the mere spreading of ideas. Force is necessary, and its use is legitimate, since the good of the nation is at stake. Civil war, which is justly feared, would not be likely, for if a man appeared who was not afraid to speak boldly he would rally first the opposition, and then the inert masses. A violent solution would even

---

[63] "La politique du pire." In its electoral campaign, when its candidate failed, the Action française usually recommended its followers to give their votes to the men of the extreme left, in order to defeat the moderate candidates.

be popular, for French hearts always dream of a chief who would dare! France likes authority, and a strong arm.[64]

What is necessary for a restoration is a small band of watchful and resolute men, ready to seize any opportunity. This may come in the form of a military mutiny, of a popular rising, or of a plot made from above. The latter method of overthrowing the government is much the hardest, for it requires a maximum of secret action, but it is also the best. These things are not impossible, Maurras declared. In 1889 the Elysée was open to Boulanger, and he found no real resistance anywhere. Déroulède also could have been master of Paris in 1898. These two men lacked a doctrine to support them in whose name they could act; they therefore hesitated, and so failed. But a successful blow is not impossible. Suppose, Maurras said, that a Paris regiment revolts, as a result of anti-Jewish propaganda in the army. It goes to the Elysée. Can it be stopped? No, for the troops sent to stop it let it pass. The watchful conspirators are ready to profit by the resulting panic, and in a few hours everything will be over, and the king proclaimed.[65] What is necessary, is a doctrine, and a chief who will be ready to profit by a moment of national emotion, and to answer the appeal of the country in its peril. Such a chief exists, as the royalists know. He is the representative of the family which created France.

[64] *Enquête sur la Monarchie,* p. 418. "Elle aime la poigne."

[65] These are not idle dreams, Maurras declared—such things have happened. He cited the revolt at Béziers in 1907 when the troops allowed the mutineers to pass between their lines.—*Enquête sur la Monarchie,* p. 565.

CHAPTER XV

L'ACTION FRANÇAISE: OTHER MEMBERS OF THE GROUP AND CRITICISM OF THE MAURRASSIAN DOCTRINE

"Integral nationalism," as its adherents call the political philosophy of the Action française, with all its fundamental doctrines and their theoretic consequences, has found complete expression in the more than twenty volumes of Maurras' works. The party has included a number of other able men, who have expressed the same ideas with talent, but there is little if any theory to be found in their works which is not included in those of Maurras.

The most important theorist among Maurras' colleagues was Léon de Montesquiou. Like Maurras, Montesquiou was an admirer of Comte,[1] and was led by a combination of positivism and nationalism to become a royalist. He was a militant member of the Action française and took part in the organization of the party forces, and in many of their active manifestations. He developed in a series of volumes the theory of the supremacy of the national State, and the necessity of the submission of the individual to the public good, with all its implications and consequences. Like Maurras he pointed out the need of a supreme authority vested in a king, of decentralization, of a social reorganization, the value of tradition, and of Catholicism, and the errors, both practical and theoretic, of republican democracy. His doctrines do not differ in any way from those of Maurras, but he showed greater moderation in their expression. Had Montesquiou

---

[1] He wrote several books on positivism.

lived he might have made further and more original contributions to the theory of nationalist royalism, but he was killed in battle in 1916.

The most conspicuous leader of the Action française, a man who is probably more widely known than Maurras, is Léon Daudet, the son of the famous novelist. He is a prolific writer, and, in addition to his daily articles he has published several novels, and many volumes of essays and memoirs. Daudet is not a political theorist; he is a polemist and pamphleteer. By temperament he is peculiarly well fitted for this rôle, for he is both fearless and ruthless, and he has enormous vitality, a wide culture, and a trenchant wit. It is, however, in part at least by deliberate intent that Daudet has used his powers chiefly in the field of personal attack. In the preface of one of his books *The Stupid Nineteenth Century,* he points out that if one wishes to destroy false ideas it is not enough to attack the doctrines themselves, and that those who, from laziness or fear, are satisfied with abstract discussion, will accomplish little in the practical world. In order to overthrow a harmful philosophy, the men who support it must first be demolished. Accordingly he has made this his task, and, in the work of discrediting the Republic and its leaders he is easily the chief force of the Action française. Almost every prominent figure of the régime has been the butt of his cruel, but inimitably witty, shafts, and there is no man in France today whose pen is more dreaded. The doctrines which Daudet's books contain, however, are those more completely exposed by Maurras, and therefore they require no separate analysis.

Jacques Bainville is one of the ablest members of the group of the Action française. He joined it as a very young man, and has remained faithful to it at the cost of a considerable sacrifice, for his remarkable knowledge of foreign affairs, his brilliant intelligence, and his command of style might have won him a high post, if he had renounced his royalist convictions. Like Daudet, Bainville has made little original contribution to political theory proper,[2] but he has expressed, in a series of books, the French nationalist interpretation of history, and so has furnished an historical basis to certain of Maurras' ideas. Although he is both an ardent nationalist and a convinced royalist, Bainville has a moderation and clearsightedness which are sometimes lacking in his colleagues. For this reason even those who disagree with his historical theories cannot afford to disregard them.

Several other members of the Action française have written books which contain political theory, and which are useful for an understanding of the movement. Among them Henri Vaugeois, the original founder and editor-in-chief of the newspaper, the *Action française,* and Louis Dimier should be mentioned. Their doctrines, however, are echoes or applications of the Maurrassian theory, and do not present any original features.

The Action française has made a number of converts among men of letters. One of the first of them was the critic, Jules Lemaître. More important to the royalist cause was the adherence of Paul Bourget, because he used the psychological novel and the drama of ideas as a vehicle for expressing the doctrines of the party, and so conveyed them to a wide public. Thus *L'Etape*[3] was written to show the tragic result of the loss of religious and social tradition on family

---

[2] *La Tasse de Saxe* (Paris, 1928) is a discussion of political and social questions in the Voltairian style.

[3] *L'Etape* (Paris, 1902).

life. *Outre-mer*[4] and several other of Bourget's books of essays are in close harmony with the Maurrassian point of view. Bourget has ceased to support the Action française since its quarrel with Rome.

Charles Benoist, former editor of the *Temps,* ex-deputy, friend of Poincaré, and at one time Minister of France at the Hague, was also converted to royalism, after the war, and became a warm supporter of the Action française. He has recently told the story of his gradual evolution towards royalism in his memoirs, and he has published a series of articles on the subject in the *Revue universelle*[5] which have caused a certain sensation in French intellectual circles.

The Action française has no political power, no wide influence, and little or no chance of practical success, at all events in the near future, yet it commands the loyalty and self-sacrificing devotion of a number of men, some of them of first-rate ability. It is the only party in France, except perhaps the Communist party, which possesses troops, few but resolute, who are ready to expose their lives for their beliefs. Without exaggerating its importance, it must be admitted that it is undoubtedly a living intellectual force in France today.

It is difficult to determine exactly what degree of influence the Action française does exert on French thought, but it is certainly greater than the actual strength of the party would seem to imply. Many Frenchmen who do not actively adhere to the royalist program, feel a certain sympathy with all or with part of Maurras' ideas, and his criticisms of the Republic from a nationalistic point of view bear weight with

[4] This book antedates Bourget's adherence to the Action française.
[5] *Revue universelle,* July 1 and July 15, 1932.

many who do not agree with his conclusions. The reasons for this influence are evident. A certain number of people in France today are dissatisfied with democracy and the parliamentary régime; to them the Action française offers not only a forceful criticism of the existing government, but an alternative program, based on a body of doctrine. This is important, for in France ideas can inspire real enthusiasm.

His theory, Maurras declares, is not new; it is merely a reformulation of the traditional wisdom of his royalist predecessors. There is some truth in this, for his arguments against individualism and democracy are essentially the same as those of Bonald, Maistre, and the other authoritarian royalists, his conception of monarchy is based on the ideas of Berryer, Veuillot, and the Comte de Chambord; and his social theory is taken from La Tour du Pin. He has, however, assembled these doctrines into a coherent system, the most complete and logical since that of the theocrats, and he has supplied them with a firm basis by allying them with nationalism. This point of view is not wholly new;[6] but it is only with the Action française that the national interest is made the sole ground for demanding the return of the king.

By abandoning the religious and metaphysical arguments of his predecessors,[7] and approaching political problems from a purely positive angle, Maurras has given royalist theory, which had become scarcely more than the traditional creed of a few faithful spirits, a new lease of life. His pragmatic arguments appeal to a much wider public than that which could be reached today by men like the theocrats, or

[6] It was foreshadowed by Berryer. See above, p. 126.

[7] He did not deny the validity of these metaphysical arguments, but he said that positivism leads to the same conclusions.

Blanc de St. Bonnet. They furnish a common ground on which Catholics and non-Catholics, royalists by tradition and royalists by reason can meet. This combination of positivism and nationalism as a basis for authoritarian doctrines is Maurras' chief contribution to political theory.

Maurras appeals to patriotism, one of the strongest of human motives, by urging men to prefer the interests of their country to the rights of an abstract man.[8] There is justice in his criticism of the naïve humanitarianism of certain eighteenth-century philosophers, but it is not certain that the nation is really the ultimate type of association. Some people consider that a wider form of human solidarity is already necessary if the nations themselves are not to perish, and to them Maurras' extreme nationalism will seem both narrow and dangerous. It must be remembered, however, that many Frenchmen believe that their country is perpetually menaced, and therefore doctrines which seem to promise her greater strength have a peculiar appeal for them. There can be no doubt that the nationalism of the Action française is, in part at least, a reaction to that of other countries, and particularly of Germany.[9] Its source is not economic ambition, but the feeling that the nation is supremely valuable because it is the creator of a superior civilization. It desires a concentration and epuration, rather

[8] "Patriotism," he said, "can concord with justice and love of humanity," but he did not say what will be the result if they do not so accord. *Romantisme et révolution*, p. 107.

[9] Maurras was much impressed by the attitude of Fichte. He spoke with great contempt of his literary merit, as well as of his philosophy, but Fichte's extreme nationalism, the violence of his attacks on Latin civilization, and his glorification of Germany and German culture, were, Maurras says, supremely useful to his country. Frenchmen should imitate him in these respects, and violently reject every foreign influence. *Quand les Français ne s'aimaient pas*, pp. 27-42.

than an expansion of national life. Maurras and his colleagues are often violent in their abuse of other countries,
but they do not want to extend French influence by force;
their nationalism has not the imperialistic character of pan-
Germanism, as it existed before 1914, and so it is much less
dangerous to the peace of the world. It has, however, certain
disadvantages. In saying that France alone is civilized, and
that her culture contains all that is valuable to humanity
Maurras is only expressing what all ardent nationalists,
French, German, American, or English, feel about their own
country, but such narrowness of outlook makes a good understanding between nations difficult. Moreover it implies a
certain limitation in the thinker which is apt to mar his
power of comprehension. Maurras often shows such a lack of
understanding with regard to other countries, and his in-
comprehension is often equalled only by his contempt. His
works abound in examples of this prejudice. For instance he
says that England, since it is Anglo-Saxon and Protestant,
is "doubly barbarian."[10] He apparently believes that Queen
Victoria fomented the Dreyfus affair, in order to prevent
Marchand from advancing in East Africa. He refuses to
consider Switzerland as a nation, and he calls Geneva a "center of decomposition."[11] He does not want German to be
taught in the schools, for fear a knowledge of it might induce
the next generation to sympathize with Germany. This will
be no loss, he adds, for there is no real German language;
what passes for such is only a crude dialect.[12] It would be
easy to multiply these examples. Such extreme statements re-

[10] *La Démocratie religieuse,* p. 351.

[11] *Romantisme et révolution,* p. 5.

[12] English is no better treated by him. The study of it, he said, merely
gave him a better understanding of what barbarism is.—*Quand les
Français ne s'aimaient pas,* pp. 87, 122.

sult in part from the ruthless consistency of Maurras' mind. Whatever subject he treats, he sees it exclusively from a national and royalist point of view,[13] and everything must be made to fit it with his theory.[14] This ruthless logic is the result of his need of intellectual certainty. He does not believe in metaphysical truth, but he is determined to find absolute truth on earth! He himself is an illustration of his interesting comments on the French tendency to intellectual fanaticism,[15] and passion for ideas. In *Le Chemin de Paradis* he remarks with regret that people today consider ideas as dead things; they are no longer ready to fight or to die for them.[16] This belief in the absolute truth of ideas is hard to reconcile with an inductive method in the study of social phenomena.

When Maurras criticizes the Republic he is often unjust. The foreign policy of France since 1870, far from being weak and vacillating, as he declares, has, on the whole, been consistent and successful. After the Franco-Prussian war France was discredited, powerless, and entirely isolated in

[13] He has been led into some curious prophecies. For instance he wrote in 1900 that "nebulous America seems to be turning definitely towards some imperial dictatorship," *Enquête*, p. 24. The same consistency is to be found in the newspaper *L'Action française*. Everything that occurs is considered from the point of view of royalist doctrines, and it is remarkable how skillful the editors are in finding in all sorts of subjects, artistic, literary or personal, some connection with royalism.

[14] The results of this method are sometimes curious. For instance Maurras says that Jews have a retarded intelligence, and a childish vocabulary! I need only mention Bergson and Benda among modern French writers to show how astonishing this statement is. The same point of view on the Jews as that held by the Action française is developed by Aldous Huxley in an interesting essay called "One and Many." See Aldous Huxley *Do What You Will* (London, 1931), pp. 15-20. .

[15] See above, p. 252.

[16] *Le Chemin de Paradis*, p. XIV.

Europe. The statesmen of the Republic restored her credit, developed her colonial empire, and provided her with valuable allies. It can well be argued that in modifying its institutions in accordance with the necessities of the War the Republic gave proof of adaptability, and vindicated the power of a democracy to defend itself, at need, even against nations possessing authoritarian governments. France, Maurras says, saved herself, through her own patriotic energy.[17] This is true, but the instrument by which she did so was the Republic! Maurras blames the makers of the peace of Versailles for destroying Austria-Hungary, and leaving Germany united, but the fact is that the Austro-Hungarian Empire fell to pieces as a result of internal disruption, and it is at least extremely doubtful whether any French effort in 1919 would have sufficed to dismember Germany. Maurras does not take sufficiently into account the fact that France did not win the war alone, and that in consequence her statesmen were obliged to reckon with the wishes of her allies. Yet, when all this has been said, Maurras' indictment of the Republic cannot wholly be refuted, and many of his criticisms of it have also been made by non-royalist writers.[18]

Maurras' tendency to violent statement and extreme conclusions detracts from the value of his thought, but it must not be forgotten that, like Guizot, he is not primarily a philosopher, but a man engaged in a political struggle. He advocates the use of revolutionary methods to establish a conservative and authoritarian government, as fascism has done

[17] One of Maurras' books, written on the war, is entitled: *La France se sauve elle-même* (Paris, 1916).

[18] Among them may be mentioned the Socialist, Marcel Sembat (*Faites la paix, sinon faites un roi,* Paris, 1916); the radical, Jules Roche; Robert de Jouvenel (*La République des camarades,* Paris, 1914); and Emile Faguet (*Le Culte de l'incompétence,* Paris 1910).

in Italy, and these methods include violence in speech as well as in act. It is probably the bold and aggressive character of Maurras' thought which has made it attractive to French youth.

The Maurrassian theory has other weaknesses. In the first place its anti-individualism is too extreme. In accordance with the human tendency to think in metaphors it is natural for men to personify the Nation; political theorists, however, should not forget that neither society nor the Nation has any material existence, and that they can only prosper or suffer in the persons of the individuals who compose them. Their value even as spiritual entities depends entirely on the degree in which they serve to promote the moral and physical well-being of those individuals. Nationalism tends to subordinate the individual to the group, and this is particularly evident in the Maurrassian theory. The men of the Action française claim that a royal monarchy by decentralizing would give the average man wider liberties and more responsibility than he now possesses. This is quite possible, but the fundamental point of view of the Action française is fiercely antiliberal. Its insistence on authority, on the State as opposed to the individual, and, above all, on the need for unity of thought, are not consistent with freedom. Their system really amounts to a type of collectivism in which the central authority would be hereditary, instead of elective.

The relations between the individual and society are, of course, the fundamental problem of social and political organization. What these relations should be varies according to time and circumstance, but, as in all matters involving human beings, a good arrangement will always be the result of compromise and delicate adjustment. Extreme solutions are necessarily bad. It is true that a society which is too individualistic is apt to disintegrate, but, on the other hand, one which sacrifices the individual too much may cease to give him a balance of benefit over loss, and he will then legitimately refuse to submit to its exactions. Both the individualism of Benjamin Constant and the nationalistic collectivism of Maurras appear to be too extreme, the one because it makes a vigorous State impossible, the other because it leaves too little freedom to the individual.

For Maurras the community is the producer of values, and the contributions of individuals, unless they conform to the accepted rules, are harmful, or at least dangerous.[19] Yet it seems probable that it is largely through the efforts of gifted individuals that civilization has evolved. Certainly many of the men whose labors and ideas have been most useful to society were considered as dangerous eccentrics in their own time.[20]

The ideal of complete unity of thought in the social group which Maurras advocates is not wholly desirable. It makes no doubt for efficiency, but efficiency is only a means; it is not the object of life. Such complete unity of thought is to be found in primitive societies. There the community gives the individual all his ideas, tastes, and standards, he is entirely subordinated to the social group, every detail of his conduct is determined by conventions, and enforced by taboos, tradition is all-powerful, and innovations are usually severely punished. Such communities are built to a large extent in correspondence with Maurras' doctrines, and they are often very efficient. They have had to become so, under

---

[19] Like Bonald, Maurras distrusts great men. He declares, for instance, that Napoleon, though superior to Rousseau, was really inferior to Peyronnet!—*Romantisme et révolution,* p. 48.

[20] Maurras himself appears so to many people today.

penalty of death, and this may be one reason for their rigidity. They do not, however, seem ideal to most people. With the development of civilization life has become more complex, and men have acquired varied capacities and needs. In consequence they demand a wider freedom of choice and activity than under primitive conditions. Gradually, through struggle and effort, unity of thought has given place to variety and tolerance. Today many even of the most socially-minded people would prefer to sacrifice some degree of order and efficiency for the sake of this variety and freedom. It is to be hoped that a rigid organization of society will become less and less necessary for survival, and tolerance between nations, as between individuals, would be the best means of securing this.

Maurras' conception of society, like that of most of the royalists, is static. This is due, in part at least, to a belief in the existence of fixed and unalterable social laws, which can be discovered by the study of history. The truth of this is doubtful. Human history is relatively short, and it contains too many complex factors to allow us to deduce general laws from it with absolute precision. Unlike chemical products, human beings always contain an element of the uncalculable, and with our present limited knowledge of man and his mentality sociology cannot be considered as an exact science. Therefore, Maurras' conclusions, based on what he considers to be irrefutable laws established by experience, are not as absolutely compelling as he assumes. The empirical wisdom of the past is valuable, and it should be respected, but this wisdom is itself the result of experience acquired by the method of trial and error. Man may remain the same, but the economic and material conditions of his life do change, and political and social systems must change with them. Each generation has new problems to face, and it has the right to make its own experiments, even if in doing so it modifies the social structure.

In spite of these defects, Maurras' ideas are stimulating. The chief value of his criticism of the existing political system lies, as he himself says, in the fact that it is not based exclusively on theoretical consideration, but on an examination of the events of the last fifty years. During these years democracy has been in the ascendent; we are reaping its fruits today, and in common with many other people, Maurras finds them bitter.

He has brought forward cogent practical arguments in favor of a permanent authority, independent of popular opinion, and supreme in those matters where foresight and a wide view of the general welfare are most necessary. These arguments also tend to prove that an increase of efficiency and well-being might result from a qualitative and hierarchical organization of society. Any theory which offers an alternative to democracy, equality, and majority rule is of interest today, and the Maurrassian doctrines form a well-thought-out system of this sort. In its present form it is only applicable to France, for it is largely the result of her historic traditions, but it has elements of interest for political theorists of all nations.

CHAPTER XVI

CONCLUSION

It is evident from the preceding chapters that there has been a marked evolution in royalist theory in France since 1815. During that period the doctrines of constitutional monarchy developed and then gradually disappeared, while those of authoritarian monarchy, starting from the theocratic mysticism of Bonald and Maistre, have reached the pragmatic nationalism of Maurras. These changes have resulted from the various efforts made by the royalists to adapt their theory to the needs of the times.

As a reaction against the ideas and events of the Revolution, three definite conceptions of royal monarchy appeared at the Restoration:

(1) The theocrats, Bonald and Maistre, gave a new and vigorous expression to the doctrines of authority. According to them the king possesses an absolute sovereignty, founded on natural and historic right, and sanctioned by God. His power must not be limited by any constitution, though it is tempered by custom, and by traditional institutions, such as the States General. He holds the legislative, executive, and judicial powers in his own hands, but he exercises them through an hereditary nobility. The throne is closely allied to the Catholic Church, which it is its principal duty to support, and to whose guidance it must submit in matters regarding religion or morals. There should be no toleration for other creeds.

(2) The doctrinaire, Royer-Collard, evolved a theory of legitimate monarchy, founded on the provisions of the Char-

ter of 1814. According to him, justice alone possesses absolute sovereignty, and all powers must be limited by the necessity of conforming to it. In France the king exercises the sovereign power by natural and historic right, but, according to the Charte, he can only do so in agreement with two chambers, one hereditary, and one elective. The executive power remains in the king's hands, but he shares the legislative power with the chambers. The Catholic Church is favored and supported by the State, but it is subordinate to it, and other creeds are tolerated.

(3) The liberal, Benjamin Constant, developed the theory of constitutional monarchy. According to him sovereignty belongs in the last analysis to the people, but it is not absolute; it must always be limited by the rights of the individual. In practice, the function of sovereignty in France is divided between the king and two chambers, one hereditary and one elective. Through the renewal of the latter at intervals prescribed by the constitution the people retain their ultimate right of sovereignty. The king does not govern, but serves as a mediator between the other powers, including the electoral body. All creeds and churches alike are to be supported by the State, and all are to be completely free and autonomous.

The struggle between liberalism and reaction led to the Revolution of 1830, and it was the liberals, who, by appealing to the latent forces of democracy succeeded in overthrowing Charles X. The breach between the absolutists and the constitutional monarchists was complete; the former carried their doctrines and traditions into exile with the elder branch of the Bourbons, while the latter made the July Monarchy an expression of their ideas. Louis-Philippe came to the throne not by virtue of inheritance but, in theory at least, as the choice of the people. He openly recognized the principle of popular sovereignty, and was not "King of France" but "King of the French." His reign was the triumph of the middle classes.

With the fall of the Monarchy of the Restoration, the theory of the doctrinaires, which was an interpretation of monarchy as created by the Charte of Louis XVIII, disappeared. Constitutional monarchy had triumphed in reality, and its theory received a further development during the reign of Louis-Philippe, particularly in the writings of Guizot. The supremacy of parliament was established in fact, and Guizot recognized it in theory. He did not, however, admit the sovereignty of the people. Reason, he said, is sovereign, and only those who possess it should exercise the power. An electoral body determined by a property census will choose those who are best fitted to represent the reason of the nation. The exercise of sovereignty will belong to the chambers so chosen, and the king will act as a permanent and regulating authority, and will wield the executive power in collaboration with them. The State must support and encourage religion, but there must be tolerance for all creeds.

Constitutional monarchy is a compromise, and, as usual with compromises, its theoretical basis is weak, and does not bear close scrutiny. That, as a system, it can be successful, is shown by the history of England, to which French liberals so often pointed, but such a system is probably better adapted to the Anglo-Saxon mind, which considers compromise as the rational method in politics, than to the more logical and doctrinaire French temper. Moreover, liberalism, while it is the product of historic individualism, is not equalitarian, and it was in conflict, in France, with the democratic tendency of the nineteenth century. It was unable to cope with the abuses which accompanied the development of the industrial revolution. The liberal monarchy of which Guizot's doctrines were a justification lasted only eighteen years. It was overthrown in 1848, and a Republic was established, to be succeeded, in 1851, by the authoritarian Empire.

After 1848 the position of the liberal monarchists, the "Orléanists" as they were called, was difficult. They believed in monarchy, but, as they admitted the sovereignty of the nation, a representative government was in accord with their ideas, and they could resign themselves to a conservative republic far better than to a Caesarian dictatorship. Nevertheless, during the short life of the Second Republic, and the reign of Napoléon III, the idea of constitutional monarchy retained a certain vigor. Its supporters (Barante, the two Broglies, Haussonville) developed those of its features which were in contrast with Caesarism or democracy, namely, decentralization and an aristocratic second chamber. They tended, however, to unite with the conservative Republicans in opposition to the Empire, and the theory of constitutional monarchy declined with the declining hopes of the party itself.

During this period (1848-1870) the doctrines of authoritarian royalism, while they remained unaltered in their fundamental tenets (the unlimited sovereignty of the king, his independence of a constitution, or elected bodies, the close alliance of Church and State), showed some signs of change of orientation. Berryer, for many years the leader of the Legitimist party, was less dogmatic and metaphysical in his attitude than Bonald and Maistre. He abandoned the theory of divine right as the basis of monarchy, and declared that it was on history, on his ancestors' record of service to the State, that the king of France could base his claims. The principal reason, he said, for a return to royal monarchy was that it was necessary for the national prosperity. This point of view, which was also that of Balzac, is much like that of the Action française today.

In 1850 La Rochejaquelein and Genoude tried to combine the idea of national sovereignty with royalist theory. They wished the legitimists to demand a plebiscite in order to determine whether the national will was in favor of a republic, or a restoration. This would have given the legitimate monarchy the same democratic and plebiscitary basis as the Empire. The proposal was rejected by the legitimists. They continued to maintain that the king's authority exists independently of any expression of the national will.

After the fall of the Second Empire (1870) it seemed that a royalist restoration might be possible, and in view of this a reconciliation was effected between the two branches of the royal family. Some of the legitimists, like Falloux, were willing to modify their theories, and seek a genuine fusion with the Liberals for the sake of bringing the monarchy back to power. Others, like Veuillot and Blanc de St. Bonnet, considered any compromise with liberalism or the parliamentary system as contrary to the principles of authoritarian royalism. The ideas of these two men marked a return to the religious and metaphysical point of view. They both wished for a restoration because, in their opinion, only the legitimate king could be trusted to bring about a truly Catholic reorganization of society.

After 1830 the social doctrines of authoritarian royalism took on a new importance. Berryer pointed out the weakness of the liberal idea of *laissez faire* in the economic field, and asserted that workers have a right to a corporative existence.

This idea was further developed by Louis Veuillot, and the Comte de Chambord, in a series of letters, adopted it as the official doctrine of the legitimist party.

Thus, between 1830 and 1890 (approximately), the chief features in the evolution of the theory of authoritarian royalism were: (1) a tendency toward a nationalist and positivist point of view, as shown in the ideas of Berryer, Balzac, La Rochejaquelein, and Falloux; (2) a contrary tendency towards a return to the religious and metaphysical point of view, voiced by Veuillot and Blanc de Saint Bonnet; (3) the development of a social theory in character with the royalist traditions and in opposition to liberalism. This theory was developed by Berryer, Veuillot, Blanc de St. Bonnet, and the Comte de Chambord.

After the failure of the attempt at a restoration (1874) the liberal royalists tried to organize a conservative republic under the septennial presidency of MacMahon, hoping in this way to keep the door open for the Orléanist candidate, the Comte de Paris, until the death of the Comte de Chambord. The republican party, however, steadily gained ground, and in 1877 it drove the royalists from power and definitely established the Republic.

The death of the Comte de Chambord in 1883 left the legitimists without a leader, and most of them rallied to the support of the Comte de Paris, head of the Orléanists, in spite of the different doctrines which he represented.

One important point of agreement among the royalists had always been the protection of religion. At the Restoration the Church, bitterly opposed to the revolutionary ideas, was only too willing to support the returning dynasty which, for its part, saw in Catholicism its best ally in the work of restoring the past. Gallicanism had been weakened by the

Concordat and the Bourbons made no attempt to revive it. Although this alliance between the Church and the Throne was greatly modified during the reign of Louis-Philippe, the monarchy continued to respect and protect the Church. As time went on, however, Rome was obliged to reckon more and more with the tendencies of the age. There is much that is democratic in the teachings of Christianity, and liberal ideas made headway among Catholics in France and elsewhere. The Church can accommodate itself as well to a republican régime as to a monarchy, and it has always been its policy to be on good terms, if possible, with *de facto* governments when they are securely established. As the royalists lost ground it was natural that Rome should be disinclined to compromise the Church by identifying it with a lost cause which was not its own. After the failure of the Restoration in 1874, the Pope came to believe that connection with the royalists was injurious to the future of Catholicism in France. Basing himself on the doctrine professed by many of the fathers of the Church, that any form of government is legitimate, provided it assures the general welfare, and protects religion, Leo XIII, in an encyclical published in 1892, urged French Catholics to rally to the Republic, in order better to serve the interests of the Church.

This repudiation by the Vatican of the old alliance between Catholicism and the monarchy was a great blow to the royalists. Many followed the advice of Leo XIII, but others, refusing to concede to the Holy See the right to dictate to Catholics in purely political matters, remained attached to the royalist cause.

The series of reverses suffered by the royalists in 1848, 1874, and 1894 caused the virtual disappearance of the theory of constitutional monarchy which was essentially opportunist and pragmatic. The opinions of Dufeuille (who was at one time an active royalist) are typical of the attitude of the liberal monarchists at the beginning of the new century. He considered constitutional monarchy the best form of government for France, and pointed out its practical and theoretic advantages, but he believed that the chances of a Restoration were so small, that they were scarcely worth the sacrifice of men's energy and influence. The result of the violent overthrow of the existing government would probably be not a return to monarchy, but the creation of some kind of dictatorship, which would be less liberal than the Republic itself. The royal monarchy must be kept in reserve as a last resource for the nation, in case the Republic should fall. These ideas mark an almost complete severance between liberalism and royalism. Thus by the end of the nineteenth century, the theory of constitutional monarchy had almost ceased to exist, except as a matter of personal tradition or preference.

The theory of absolutism derives its strength to a lesser degree from events than that of constitutional monarchy. Being more dogmatic it was better able to survive the successive failures of the royalist parties. Moreover, the authoritarian royalists had developed a different social and economic theory which seemed to promise some remedy for the faults of the existing system. This theory found its most complete expression at the end of the nineteenth and the beginning of the twentieth century in the writings of La Tour du Pin. He combined the doctrines of social Catholicism (a movement which acquired importance in France at this time) with those of traditional and authoritarian monarchy.

Royalist teaching and theory were at their lowest ebb during the last ten years of the nineteenth century. Constitutional monarchy had failed and its practical failure had discredited its doctrine, while the idea of absolutism was abhorrent to the democratic mass of the nation. The Republic seemed to be gradually establishing itself, at least as a *fait accompli,* in the minds and habits of Frenchmen. Yet, at the same time, its glamor was fading as experience revealed some of the weaknesses of parliamentary government. A famous cartoon by Forain represents a rather bedraggled Republic with the caption: "To think she was so beautiful during the Empire!" This probably expressed the feelings of many.

The Dreyfus affair revealed a deep cleavage in thought between conservative and radical Frenchmen, and its results, which were a triumph for democracy and anticlericalism, brought about a vigorous nationalistic reaction. From this reaction sprang the neo-royalist movement of the Action française.

Maurras, the chief theorist of this party, has abandoned the doctrine of divine right as the source of sovereignty, and he ignores most of the metaphysical arguments of his predecessors. He has substituted for them the national interest as the sole basis of royalist convictions. A defense of the Catholic way of life, and of the Church itself is an essential part of his program, but it is no longer its chief reason for being. Maurras' positive and pragmatic point of view had already been foreshadowed by the constitutional monarchists; they wished for a king because they felt that he was useful, but they were liberal individualists and they did not believe in authority. Maurras, on the contrary, points out the faults of democracy, and from them he deduces the necessity of a supreme authority for the welfare of France. This authority, he says, must be the legitimate king.

Maurras and his colleagues have extracted from the writings of the chief French opponents of individualism and democracy, as well as from the royalist philosophers, an indictment of the republican form of government, and a complete political system in opposition to it. The main lines of this system are in accord with the usual ideas of authoritarian royalism.

These may be summarized as follows: (1) The royal power is to be independent of a written constitution and of all expression of popular opinion. (2) Parliament is to be abolished. (3) The king is to be absolute in all matters regarding the national welfare, and particularly in those related to foreign affairs, such as the army, the navy, and the diplomatic service. (4) An *élite* is to be developed which will administer the realm under the king's direction. (5) Individual liberties are to be safeguarded by decentralization, and the creation of local and professional bodies with a large amount of power and responsibility. In this way the king will be the ruler of a series of republics. Among them he will be the coördinating power, and he will represent the unity of the nation. (6) Catholicism is to be the faith of France; other religions are, as far as possible, to be discouraged. (7) The State must support the Church, and at the same time allow it complete autonomy.

It is obvious that the Action française has scarcely altered the fundamental tenets of authoritarian royalist theory, but, by furnishing it with a new basis in nationalism it has given it fresh life. It is, no doubt, to a large extent the triumph of parliamentary democracy which, by bringing to light the faults of the system, has caused a revival of interest in the theory of absolutism. These doctrines, however, have certain features which make them congenial to the French mind. In the first place, they are based on attachment to the past, belief in the value of tradition, and a desire for continuity and order in society. French education early impresses clear-cut standards of taste and modes of thought upon the minds of Frenchmen, so that, although they are individualistic, they are more clearly aware of their own characteristic culture than other peoples. Hence there exists amongst French thinkers an intellectual nationalism which clings to the past, and is unfavorable to dissidence or change.

In the next place, the doctrines of absolutism imply a mistrust of man and of his political virtue which finds ready response in French scepticism.

Finally, France has always been exposed to wars of invasion, so that her need of a strong government with a consistent policy is obvious. She has not had the long experience of political self-discipline which protects a democracy from abuses and disorders. Hence an authoritarian régime, such as unlimited monarchy, has much to recommend it to French thinkers. Here lies the secret of the success of the Empire, which, in theory, was a combination of democracy with authority. Here, too, lies the attraction which led to the Boulangist episode. It is often said that the French have a weakness for a Caesar, and French mentality is in fact not very favorable to liberalism. Ideas are too important to the Frenchman for him readily to feel intellectual tolerance, nor has he the desire for compromise for the sake of immediate achievement which would favor such a system. "Muddling through" is not a French idea. These facts may account both for the disappearance of the idea of constitutional monarchy, and for the survival of the theory of absolutism, even in so democratic a state as modern France.

In the hands of Maurras and his colleagues that theory

has shown a considerable power of adapting itself to the needs of today. Royalism, for the adherents of the Action française, is no longer a matter of personal tradition or of mystical faith, but a practical alternative to parliamentary democracy. Maurras has shown in the monarchy a possible means of escape from the Republic without the complete loss of liberty and tradition which would probably result from the advent of any other form of dictatorship. In this way he appeals both to those Frenchmen who dislike the equalitarian character of democracy, and to those who want a permanent and absolute authority for the sake of the national strength.

Before closing this exposition of royalist theory during the past century it seems appropriate to consider the advantages of the organization which it proposes, in comparison with the existing system. Unlike the preceding summary, however, such a discussion must be largely matter of personal opinion.

It appears to the author that the royalist doctrines do have several points of superiority. In the first place they stress the duties and obligations of men, rather than their rights, and this point of view particularly needs to be emphasized in a day when so many people think that society owes them not only protection, education, and opportunity, but a living.

In the next place the royalists do not share the eighteenth century belief, which is still widely held today, that man is naturally virtuous, and that it is always bad social conditions which corrupt him. Experience seems to prove that this belief, at least in its naïve form, is not well founded; men are not wholly evil, as the theocrats maintained, but they are not perfectly adapted by nature to live together peacefully, and their virtue, even under the most favorable circumstances, has never been sufficient to create a society in

which the use of force was unnecessary. It is interesting to no-
tice that democracy has shown itself particularly unwilling
to trust those who have benefited by the best social conditions!

In the third place, the royalist idea that political rights
are not inherent in men, but should depend on capacity, is
more reasonable than the equalitarian theory of democracy.
Political power is not an object, but an instrument; it exists
to secure the safety and well-being of men living in society,
and to do so it must be efficient. Men may be equal in the
sense that the happiness of one is as valuable as that of another, but they are certainly not equal in wisdom, intelligence, public spirit, or any of the qualities which fit them to
share, even in a small degree, in political power.

In the fourth place, the need of a permanent and independent authority, which the royalists so emphasize, is, to
some extent, a real one. A comprehension of the interest of
society as a whole is essential for good government. Foresight, and the courage to sacrifice today in order to secure
tomorrow are as necessary to nations as to individuals. The
average man cannot usually see farther than his own immediate interests, and therefore public opinion does not always
understand the real needs of society, and as a rule, it takes
small account of the future. It is true that kings have not
always promoted the welfare of their people, but selfish or
unwise political assemblies have also committed many errors
and a good monarch might accomplish more than a good
assembly because he would be freer. It is difficult for the
representatives of democracy to be wiser than public opinion,
because their tenure of power is short, and its renewal depends on the favor of their constituents, who are themselves
average men. A king might be more capable of considering

the public welfare as a whole, for the future as well as for the present, and of acting on this consideration, because he would not be directly dependent on public opinion.

The monarchy as the French royalists conceive it would retain some of the advantages of democracy. A valuable feature of self-government is that it educates the individual in public spirit, and in a sense of responsibility. This has been particularly true, however, in small communities, such as the Greek cities, the primitive Swiss cantons, or the early American townships, where men knew each other personally, and where the administration of affairs, as well as the choice of representatives was divided to some extent among all the citizens. The educative value of democracy is greatly diminished in the vast centralized States of today. To vote once or twice a year for a candidate, whom one may not even know, does not necessarily develop a sense of responsibility.[1] The royalists propose to allow men a much larger measure of local self-government than they now enjoy in France[2] and it is quite possible that this would be of more value in developing public spirit, and a sense of responsibility than the present system. Democracy was destined to protect the individual from exploitation by the State. It is possible that a large measure of local and professional self-government and independence of the central State might accomplish this as effectively as does the parliamentary régime, for an occasional election, while it keeps the representatives of the people in perpetual suspense, does not actually give the voters

[1] The system of Initiative and Referendum, as it is practiced in some of the Swiss Cantons, and also in some States of the Union, may have a certain educational value, if it is well organized.

[2] It must be remembered that France is more highly centralized than the United States. For instance, all education in France is in the hands of the Central State; there is no local militia, and the prefects, unlike our governors, are not elected, but appointed by the central Government.

much power of controlling their activities, once they are elected.

As has already been said, the fundamental problem of government lies in the relation of the individual to the State, and this involves the question of liberty versus authority. Both liberalism and democracy were predicated on the harmony of class interests, and in the belief that in a free and rational society men would work together for the common good. Both liberalism and democracy, however, have, as a rule, actually resulted in the government of a single class. Liberalism was the dominance of the *bourgeoise,* and democracy is that of the masses, and in both cases the result has been the exploitation of one class by another. It may be that a genuinely liberal organization of society is impracticable, or that, at best, it can exist only for a time, under particularly favorable circumstances. If so, men will have to choose between the dictatorship of one, or of a few, and the equally absolute power of majorities in democratic assemblies as they exist in France, and in many of the Western nations today. An authority placed above class interests may be desirable, and today such an authority would inevitably be responsible not to God, but to society.

As a matter of fact, in most of the countries where the existing form of government has broken down for one reason or another, dictatorships of this type have been set up.[3] The principal weaknesses of such dictatorships are: first that, having neither tradition nor custom to restrain them, they are apt to be very arbitrary; second, that if they become intolerable they can only be overthrown by violence;[4]

[3] Among others, Italy, Poland, Hungary and Spain have all made experiments of this kind. Russia is an exception, for there a proletarian "aristocracy" exercises the power.

[4] Political assassination is obviously a natural weapon against a dicta-

and third, that as the succession is not regulated, the disappearance of the dictator is almost sure to bring about disorder, and even civil war. In this respect the old hereditary monarchies had a great advantage.

The royalist program is open to many objections, some of which have been pointed out in the preceding chapters: its dogmatism, its too great insistence on the submission of the individual, its conception of unity rather than variety as the ideal of society, the static character of its political and social views. Its insuperable defect, however, is that it is impossible of realization! The king's authority, as the royalists conceive it, and as it really existed in the past, was based on the assent, tacit but general, of the people. Had this not been the case the monarchy could scarcely have lasted so long. This tacit assent was the result of many factors. Probably the most important were, first, the immense difference in knowledge and education between the classes, a difference which created and maintained a respect for superiority among the people; and, second, an age-long habit and tradition of loyalty. These conditions have ceased to exist. For many years the system of universal education has been spreading the ideas of equality and democracy among the peoples of the Western world. These ideas have too immediate an appeal to the vanity and the self-interest of the average man to be readily abandoned. Only disasters worse than we have yet had could wean men from them. Power may still be seized by violence, but any permanent government, whether it be parliament, dictatorship, or monarchy, must eventually reckon with public opinion, the only king men recognize today.

---

tor. It is curious to note that certain of the royalist philosophers, among them Maistre and Maurras, speak of regicide without marked horror, as a frequent by-product of absolutism.

BIBLIOGRAPHY

ANCIEN RÉGIME

Dunning, W. A., Political Theory from Luther to Montesquieu. New York, 1905.
Franck, Adolphe, Réformateurs et publicistes de l'Europe; dix-septième siècle. Paris, 1907.
Picot, E., Histoire des États généraux. Paris, 1881.
Viollet, Paul, Histoire des institutions françaises. Paris, 1903.
——— Le Roi et ses ministres. Paris, 1912.

BAINVILLE, JACQUES

Bainville, Jacques, Les Conséquences politiques de la paix. Paris, 1920.
——— Histoire de deux peuples. Paris, 1915.
——— Histoire de trois générations. Paris, 1918.
——— L'Allemagne romantique et réaliste. Paris, 1927.

BALZAC, HONORÉ DE

Balzac, Honoré de, De la politique des deux ministres. Paris, 1832.
——— Du droit d'ainesse. Paris, 1824.
——— Étude sur Catherine de Médicis. Paris, 1857.
——— Oeuvres complètes. Paris, 1865.
Carrère, Jean, Les Mauvais Maîtres. Paris, 1922.
Dimier, Louis, Les Maîtres de la contre-révolution en France. Paris, 1906.
Faguet, Émile, Balzac. Paris, 1913.

BARANTE, PROSPER AMABLE DE

Barante, Prosper Amable de, Des communes et de l'aristocratie. Paris, 1816.
——— Discours. Paris, 1835.
——— Questions constitutionnelles. Paris, 1849.
——— Souvenirs. Paris, 1890-99.

Broglie, Victor, duc de, Barante. *Revue des deux mondes,* Paris, 1849 (Vol. I), p. 976.

France, Anatole, La Vie littéraire. Paris, 1892.

Guizot, François, Mélanges biographiques et littéraires. Paris, 1868.

Lanzac de Laborie, Léon de, Barante. *Correspondant,* CLXXI (Paris, 1893), 132.

Sainte-Beuve, C. A. de, Portraits contemporains. Vol. IV, Paris, 1866.

BARRÈS, MAURICE

Barrès, Maurice, L'Appel au soldat. Paris, 1926.
—— Assainissement et féderalisme. Paris, 1895.
—— Les Déracines. Paris, 1920.
—— Scénes et doctrines du nationalisme. Paris, 1925.
—— Un Homme libre. Paris, 1912.

Blanc-Péridier, A., La Route ascendante de Maurice Barrès. Préface de Charles Maurras. Paris, 1925.

BENOIST, CHARLES

Benoist, Charles, La Crise de l'état moderne. Paris, 1894.

BERRYER, ANTOINE

Berryer, Antoine, Discours parlementaires. Paris, 1872-74.
—— Plaidoyers. Paris, 1872-74.
Boullay, Charles, Berryer. Grenoble, n. d.
Dupanloup, Monseigneur, Paroles aux funérailles de Berryer. Paris, 1868.

Lacombe, Charles de, La Vie de Berryer. Paris, 1886-90.

Lecanuet, E., La Vie de Berryer. Paris, 1893.

Mazade, Charles de, L'Opposition royaliste. Paris, 1894.

Nourrisson, Paul, Trois précurseurs. Bar-le-Duc, 1922.

Pascal, F., La Vie de Berryer. *La Quinzaine,* Vol. I (August 15, 1895).

BLANC DE SAINT-BONNET, ANTOINE

Barbey d'Aurévilly, J. A., De Maistre, Blanc de St. Bonnet, Lacordaire. Paris, 1910.

Blanc de Saint-Bonnet, Antoine, De la Restauration française. Paris, 1851.
—— De l'unité spirituelle. Paris, 1841.
—— La Légitimité. Paris, 1873.
—— La Loi électorale. Paris, 1875.
—— Politique réelle. Paris, 1858.
—— Le Socialisme et la société. Lyons, 1880.
Buche, Joseph, Blanc de St. Bonnet. Trevoux, 1904.
Rambaud, Camille, Blanc de Saint-Bonnet. Lyons, 1898.

BLANCS D'ESPAGNE

Bourbon-Parme, Prince Sixte de, Le Traité d'Utrecht. Paris, 1914.
Bourg, Joseph de, Le Droit monarchique. Paris, 1883.
—— La Vérite et le légende. Les Entrevues des princes á Frohsdorf. Paris, 1910.
Cugnac, Pourquoi Monsieur le Comte de Chambord n'a pas regné. Amiens, 1889.
Curé, Monseigneur Amédée, Le Comte de Chambord et Sa Sainteté Léon XIII. Paris, 1905.
Curzon, Hilaire de, La Vérite sur la réconciliation. Poitiers, 1911.
Damien, Charles de, La Loi salique. Cahors, 1922.
Faucigny-Lucinge, A. de, Les Dernières Fleurs de Lys. Paris, 1913.
Friedrichs, Otto, Les Démentis. Paris, 1906.
Henri V et le Comte de Paris. Paris, 1895.
Robinet de Clery, Les Prétentions dynastiques de la branche d'Orléans. Paris, 1910.
Rocher, Philippe, Les Obsèques du Comte de Chambord. Paris, 1921.
Roi légitime, Le. Paris, 1884.

BONALD, LOUIS GABRIEL, VICOMTE DE

Barbey d'Aurévilly, J. A., Prophètes du passé. Paris, 1851.
Bonald, Louis Gabriel, vicomte de, Oeuvres complètes. Paris, 1864.
Bonald, P. H. de, Bonald. Paris, 1841.
Bourget, Paul, et Michel Salomon, Bonald. Paris, 1905.
Esmein, A., Le Droit constitutionnel. Paris, 1894.

308 BIBLIOGRAPHY

Faguet, Émile, Politiques et moralistes du dix-neuvième siècle. Première série. Paris, 1894.
Merriam, C. E., History of the Theory of Sovereignty since Rousseau. New York, 1900.
Montesquiou, Léon de, Le Réalisme de Bonald. Paris, n. d.
Moulinié, Henry, De Bonald. Paris, 1915.
Mauduit, Roger, La Politique de Bonald. Paris, 1913.
Sainte-Beuve, S. A. de, Causeries du Lundi. Vol. IV, Paris, 1864.
Saint-Giron, La Separation des pouvoirs. Paris, 1864.
Vareilles-Sommières, comte de, Les Principes fondamentaux du droit. Paris, 1889.
Veuillot, Louis, Bonald. L'Univers, August 24, 1851.

BROGLIE, ALBERT, DUC DE

Broglie, Albert, duc de, Études morales et littéraires. Paris, 1853.
——— Histoire et diplomatie. Paris, 1889.
——— Histoire et politique. Paris, 1897.
——— La Constitution nouvelle. Paris, 1848.
——— Nouvelles études de littérature et de morale. Paris, 1863.
——— Questions de religion et d'histoire. Paris, 1860.
Désjoyeaux, Claude Noël, Le Projet de chambre haute du Duc de Broglie. Saint-Étienne, 1908.
Fagniez, G., Le Duc de Broglie. Paris, 1902.
Lavergne, Léonce de, Le Duc de Broglie. Paris, 1900.
Maurras, Charles, Le Duc de Broglie. Revue hebdomadaire, February 2, 1901.

BROGLIE, VICTOR, DUC DE

Broglie, Victor, duc de, Decrets et discours. Paris, 1863.
——— Souvenirs. Paris, 1886.
——— Vues sur le gouvernement de la France. Paris, 1870.
Guizot, François, Le Duc de Broglie. Paris, 1860.

CHAMBORD, HENRI DIEUDONNÉ, COMTE DE

Arsac, Henri, Goritz, Frohsdorf. Nancy, 1884.
Bouillé, comte de, Correspondance de la famille royale. Bordeaux, 1884.

Chambord, Henri Dieudonné, comte de, Correspondance. 1841-59. Bordeaux, 1859.

—— Correspondance, 1841-71. Geneva, 1871.

—— Correspondance, 1841-79. Paris, 1880.

—— Lettre á Rodez-Bénavent. Paris, 1873.

—— Lettre en réponse á Monseigneur Dupanloup. Montpellier, 1873.

—— Mes idées. Paris, 1872.

Chesnelong, Charles, La Campagne monarchique d'octobre, 1873. Paris, 1895.

Damas, baron de, Mémoires. Paris, 1923.

Daudet, Ernest, Trois mois d'histoire. Paris, 1923.

Désjoyeaux, Claude Noël, La Fusion monarchique. Paris, 1913.

Dreux-Brézé, marquis de, Notes et souvenirs. Paris, 1902.

Ferronays, Madame de la, Mémoires. Paris, 1874.

Hanotaux, Gabriel, Histoire de la troisième République; l'échec de la monarchie. Paris, 1926.

Jollivet, Gaston, Souvenirs d'un parisien. Paris, 1928.

Laurentie, François, Le Comte de Chambord. Paris, 1912.

Loth, Arthur, L'Échec de la Restauration monarchique. Paris, 1912.

Lucien-Brun, L'Échec de la Monarchie. *Revue catholique,* September-October, 1905.

Luz, Pierre, Henri V. Paris, 1931.

Margerie, A. de, Henri V. *Almanach catholique,* Lille, 1884.

—— L'Urgence. Paris, 1874.

Mayol de Lúpé, comte, Le Comte de Chambord. Paris, 1904.

Merveilleux du Vignaux, Un Peu d'histoire autour d'un nom: Ernoul. La Chappelle-Montligeon, 1900.

Monti de Rezé, Réne de, Souvenirs sur le Comte de Chambord. Paris, 1931.

Muret, Theodore, Vie populaire de Henri de France. Paris, 1846.

Nettement, Alfred, Henri de France. Paris, 1872.

Pesquidoux, Dubosc de, Le Comte de Chambord d'après lui-même. Paris, 1887.

Pène, Henri de, Henri de France. Paris, 1884.

Robinet de Cléry, Les Deux Fusions. Paris, 1908.

Saint-Albin, Alex. de, Histoire d'Henri V. Paris, 1874.

CHATEAUBRIAND, FRANÇOIS RENÉ

Barbey d'Aurévilly, J. A., Les Oeuvres et les hommes. Paris, 1898.

Bourget, Paul, Études et portraits. Paris, 1888.

Cassagne, Albert, Vie politique de Chateaubriand. Paris, 1911.

Chateaubriand, François René de, Œuvres complètes. 18 vols., Paris, 1904-10.

Clergeau, et Vacquerie, Chateaubriand, sa vie politique. Paris, 1860.

Faguet, Émile, Études sur le dix-neuvième siècle. Paris, 1887.

Lemaître, Jules, Chateaubriand. Paris, 1912.

Lionnet, J., L'Évolution des idées. Paris, 1904.

Lomenie, Emmanuel Beau de, La Carrière politique de Chateaubriand. Paris, 1920.

Sainte-Beuve, C. A. de, Chateaubriand et son groupe littéraire sous l'Empire. Paris, 1864.

Villemain, A. F., La Tribune moderne: Chateaubriand. Paris, n. d.

COMTE, AUGUSTE

Comte, Auguste, Appel au conservateurs. Paris, 1855.

—— Principes de philosophie positive. Paris, 1851-54.

—— Système de politique positive. Paris, 1879-83.

Dimier, Louis, Les Maîtres de la contre-révolution. Paris, 1906.

Maurras, Charles, Enquête sur la monarchie. Paris, 1900-1909.

—— La Démocratie religieuse. Paris, 1921.

—— Quand les Français ne s'aimaient pas. Paris, 1916.

—— Romantisme et révolution. Paris, 1922.

Montesquiou, Léon de, Les Consécrations positives de la vie humaine. Paris, 1908.

—— Les Origines et la doctrine de l'Action française. Paris, 1918.

—— La Système politique d'Auguste Comte. Paris, 1904.

CONSTANT DE REBECQUE, BENJAMIN

Bouglé, C., La Philosophie politique de Benjamin Constant. *Revue de Paris*, Vol. II (1914).

Chaumeix, André, Benjamin Constant. *Journal des débats*, August 29, 1907.

Constant de Rebecque, Benjamin, Cours de politique constitutionnelle. Paris, 1818.

—— De l'ésprit de conquête. Paris, 1814.

—— Discours. *Archives parlementaires.*

—— Mélanges littéraires et politiques. Paris, 1829.

—— Les Principes politiques. Paris, 1815.

—— Mémoire sur les cent jours. Paris, 1822.

Daudet, Léon, Benjamin Constant, *Nouvelle revue,* XCII (January, 1895), 152.

Dumont-Wilden, L., Vie de Benjamin Constant. Paris, 1930.

Faguet, Émile, Politiques et moralistes du dix-neuvième siècle. Première série. Paris, 1894.

Guizot, François, Le Temps passé. Paris, 1867.

Hiéstand, Jean, Benjamin Constant et la doctrine parlementaire. Geneva, 1928.

Lauris, G. de, Benjamin Constant et les droits individuels. Paris, 1904.

Redslob, Robert, Le Régime parlementaire. Paris, 1924.

Rod, Édouard, Benjamin Constant. *Bibliothèque universelle et revue suisse,* XXXIV (1904), 449.

Schermerhorn, Elizabeth, Life of Benjamin Constant. London, 1924.

DAUDET, LÉON

Daudet, Léon, L'Agonie du régime. Paris, 1925.

—— La Chambre nationale du seize novembre. Paris, 1925.

—— Le Stupide Dix-neuvième Siècle. Paris, 1922.

—— Vers le roi; souvenirs. Paris, 1921.

DOCTRINAIRES

Barthélémy, Joseph L., Introduction du régime parlementaire en France. Paris, 1904.

Broglie, Victor, duc de, Souvenirs. Paris, 1871.

Guizot, François, Mémoires pour servir a l'histoire de mon temps. Paris, 1858-67.

Thureau-Dangin, Paul, Mémoires. Paris, 1860.

DUFEUILLE, EUGÈNE

Dufeuille, Eugène, Du souverain dans notre République. Paris, 1907.

—— Les Lois et les mœurs. Paris, 1908.
—— Réflexions d'un monarchiste. Paris, 1901.
—— Sur la pente. Paris, 1909.

FALLOUX, COMTE A. P. F. DE

Castellane, A., Essai de psychologie politique. Paris, 1888.
Falloux, Comte A. P. F. de, Antécédents et conséquences de la situation actuelle. Paris, 1860.
—— De la contre-révolution. Paris, 1878.
—— Discours et mélanges politiques. Paris, 1882.
—— De l'unité nationale. Paris, 1880.
—— Du scepticisme politique. Paris, 1872.
—— Études et souvenirs. Paris, 1885.
—— Le Parti catholique. Paris, 1856.
—— Les Républicans et les monarchistes. Toulouse, 1851.
—— Mémoires d'un royaliste. Paris, 1888.
—— Politique nationale. Paris, 1851.
—— Questions monarchiques. Paris, 1873.
Mazade, Charles de, L'Opposition royaliste. Paris, 1894.
Morel, Abbé, Monsieur de Mun et Monsieur de Falloux. Paris, 1879.
Toulguet, A. de, Le Comte de Falloux. Paris, 1869.
Veuillot, Eugène, Le Comte de Falloux et ses mémoires. Geneva, 1888.

FUSTEL DE COULANGES, NUMA DENIS

Dimier, Louis, Les Maîtres de la contre-révolution. Paris, 1906.
—— Les Préjugés ennemies de l'histoire de France. Paris, 1908.
Fustel de Coulanges, Numa Denis, La Cité antique. Paris, 1880.
—— Histoire des institutions de l'ancienne France. Paris, 1889-92.
Maurras, Charles, La Bagarre de Fustel. Paris, 1928.
—— Quand les Français ne s'aimaient pas. Paris, 1916.

GENERAL WORKS

Bardoux, A., Les Légistes et leur influence sur la societé française. Paris, 1877.

Baudrillart, H. J. H., Études de philosophie morale. Paris, 1858.

Block, M., Dictionnaire générale de la politique. Paris, n. d.

Coker, F. W., Political Theory of Recent Times. New York, 1924.

Duguit, L., et H. Monnier, Les Constitutions et les principales lois politiques de la France. Évreux, 1925.

Dunning, H. A., History of Political Theory, Rousseau to Spencer. New York.

Faguet, Émile, Politiques et moralistes du dix-neuvième siècle. Trois séries. Paris, 1894.

Grasserie, Raoul de la, L'Évolution de l'idée de souveraineté. Paris, 1898. Annales de l'institut international de sociologie, Vol. IV.

Gurian, Waldemar, Die politischen und sozialen Idéen des französischen Katholizismus, 1789-1914. Leipzig, 1929.

Hitier, La Théorie de l'absolutisme. Grenoble, 1903. Annales de l'université de Grenoble, Vol. XV.

Merriam, C. E., History of the Theory of Sovereignty since Rousseau. New York, 1900.

Michel, Henry, L'Idée de l'État. Paris, 1895.

Pierre, E., Histoire des assemblées politiques de la France. Paris, n. d.

Vareilles-Sommières, comte de, Principes fondamentaux du droit constitutionnel. Paris, 1889.

GUIZOT, FRANÇOIS

Bardoux, A., Guizot. Paris, 1894.

Faguet, Émile, Politiques et moralistes du dix-neuvième siècle. Paris, 1894.

Guizot, François, De la démocratie en France. Brussels, 1849.

—— Discours. Archives parlementaires.

—— Du gouvernement de la France. Paris, 1820.

—— Du gouvernement représentif. Paris, 1816.

—— Histoire des origines du gouvernement représentif en Europe. Vol. I, chaps. vii, viii; Vol. II, chaps. x, xv, xvi, xviii, xxii. Paris, 1851.

—— Histoire de trois générations. Paris, 1863.

—— Histoire parlementaire. Paris, 1863.

—— "Le Gouvernement représentatif." Encyclopaedie progressive. Paris, n. d.

——— Mélanges politiques et historiques. Paris, 1869.

——— Mémoires pour servir á l'histoire de mon temps. Paris, 1863.

——— Nos méscomptes et nos espérances. *Revue contemporaine,* 1855.

——— Philosophie politique. Unpublished manuscript. Val Richer, Dossiers spéciaux, No. 11. 91 pages, n. d.

Pouthas, Charles H., Guizot pendant le Réstauration. Paris, 1923.

Rémusat, Charles de, Critiques et études. Paris, 1885.

Renouvier, C. B., et F. Pillon, "Guizot." *La Critique philosophique.* Vols. I, II, 1872.

Simon, Julés, Thièrs, Guizot et Rémusat. Paris, 1885.

Woodward, Ernest L., Three Studies in European Conservatism. London, 1929.

D'HAUSSONVILLE, COMTE J. O. B.

D'Haussonville, Comte J. O. B., Du programme de gouvernement. Paris, 1882.

——— Souvenirs. Paris, 1878.

D'HAUSSONVILLE, COMTE OTHENIN

D'Haussonville, Comte Othenin, Discours, *Archives parlementaires.*

——— Études sociales. Paris, 1886.

——— Le Comte de Paris. Paris, 1895.

——— Varia. Paris, 1904.

LA ROCHEJAQUELEIN, HENRI, MARQUIS DE

La Rochejaquelein, Henri, marquis de, A mon pays. Paris, 1850.

——— La Révision de la constitution. Paris, 1851.

——— [Letter.] *Gazette de France,* September 20, 1850.

——— [Letter.] *Journal des débats,* September 22, 1850.

——— Lettre á Monsieur de Lammenais. Paris, 1848.

——— Trois questions. Paris, 1850.

LA TOUR DU PIN CHAMBLY DE LA CHARCE, RENÉ, MARQUIS DE

Boussan, Charles, La Tour du Pin. Paris, 1931.

Chenevers, Raymond, Galerie sociale. Rheims, 1907.

La Tour du Pin Chambly de la Charce, René, marquis de, Vers un ordre social chrétien. Paris, 1907.

Moon, Parker T., The Labor Problem and the Social Catholic Movement in France. New York, 1921.

Mun, Albert de, Combats d'hier. Paris, 1917.

—— Discours. Paris, 1919.

Penty, H. J., A Guildsman's Interpretation of History. London, 1918.

Rivian, Charles, La Tour du Pin précurseur. Paris, 1907.

LE PLAY, FRÉDÉRIC

Le Play, Frédéric, La Constitution de l'Angleterre considerée dans ses rapports avec la loi de Dieu et les coutumes de la paix sociale. Tours, 1875.

—— L'Organisation de la famille selon le vrai modèle signalé par l'histoire de toutes les races et de tous les temps. Paris, 1874.

—— L'Organisation du travail selon la coutume des ateliers et la loi du décalogue. Tours, 1893.

—— Les Ouvriers européens. Paris, 1855.

—— La Réforme sociale en France. Tours, 1874.

LIBERAL MONARCHISTS

Halévy, Daniel, La Fin des notables. Paris, 1930.

Hanotaux, Gabriel, Histoire de la France contemporaine. Paris, 1903-5.

Teste, Louis, Les Monarchistes sous la troisième République. Paris, 1891.

MAISTRE, COMTE JOSEPH DE

Baudrillart, H., Publicistes modernes. Paris, 1884.

Cagordeau, E., et François Descartes, Joseph de Maistre inconnu. Venice, 1904.

Faguet, Émile, Politiques et moralistes du dix-neuvième siècle. Paris, 1894.

Gourmont, Rémi de, Promenades philosophiques. Paris, 1915.

Grasset, Eugène, Joseph de Maistre; sa vie et son œuvre. Chambery, 1901.

Laski, Harold, Studies in the Problem of Sovereignty. London, 1917.
Maistre, Comte Joseph de, Oeuvres complètes. Paris, 1928.
Margerie, Amédée de, La Comte Joseph de Maistre. Paris, 1896.
Morley, John, Miscellanies. Vol. I, London, 1886.
Paulhan, E., Joseph de Maistre et sa philosophie. Paris, 1893.
Rocheblave, S., Joseph de Maistre, *Revue d'histoire et de philosophie religieuse.* Strassbourg, 1902.
Sainte-Beuve, C. A. de, Portraits littéraires. Vol. II, Paris, 1862.
Veuillot, Louis, Mélanges religieux. Vols. V, VI, Paris, 1856.

MAURRAS, CHARLES

Daudet, Léon, Charles Maurras et son temps. Paris, 1930.
Descoqs, Pedro, Á travers l'œuvre de Ch. Maurras. Paris, 1913.
Gilloin, René, Trois crises. Lille, 1929.
Kessel, Joseph, De la rue de Rome au Chemin de Paradis. Paris, 1927.
Maurras, Charles, Les Amants de Venise. Paris, 1902.
—— Anthinéa. Paris, 1901.
—— La Blessure intérieure. Paris, 1918.
—— Le Chemin de Paradis. Paris, 1895.
—— Les Conditions de la victoire. Paris, 1916.
—— Un Débat nouveau sur la République et la décentralisation. Toulouse, 1905.
—— La Démocratie religieuse. Paris, 1921.
—— De Démos á Cesar. Paris, 1930.
—— Enquête sur la monarchie. Paris, 1900-1909.
—— L'Étang de Berre. Paris, 1915.
—— La France se sauve elle-même. Paris, 1916.
—— Gaulois, Germains, Latins. Paris, 1926.
—— L'Idée de la décentralisation. Paris, 1898.
—— Idées royalistes. Paris, 1910.
—— Kiel et Tangier. Paris, 1913.
—— Lettre de Charles Maurras á Sa Sainteté le Pope Pie XI. Versailles, 1927.
—— Libéralisme et libertés. Paris, 1905.
—— La Musique intérieure. Paris, 1925.
—— Napoléon avec la France ou contre la France. Paris, 1929.

—— Le Pape, la guerre et la paix. Paris, 1917.
—— Le Parlement se réunit. Paris, 1917.
—— Pour en sortir. Paris, 1924.
—— Quand les Français ne s'aimaient pas. Paris, 1916.
—— Réflexions sur l'ordre en France. Paris, 1927.
—— Romantisme et révolution. Paris, 1922.
—— Sous le Signe de Flore. Paris, 1931.
—— Tombeaux. Paris, 1921.
—— Le Tombeau du Prince. Versailles, 1927.
—— Les Trois Aspects du President Wilson. Paris, 1920.
—— La Violence et la mesure. Paris, 1924.
L'Oeuvre de Charles Maurras; essai de bibliographie. Paris, 1930.
Roux, M. de, Charles Maurras et le nationalisme de l'Action française. Paris, 1927.
Segard, Achille, Charles Maurras et les royalistes. Paris, 1919.
Thibaudet, Albert, Trente ans de vie française; les idées de Charles Mauras. Paris, 1920.
Truc, Gonzague, Charles Maurras et son temps. Paris, 1917.
Vaugeois, Henri, Notre pays. Paris, 1916.

MONTESQUIOU, LÉON DE

Condekerque-Lambrecht, Madame de, Léon de Montesquiou. Paris, 1925.
Montesquiou, Léon de, De l'anarchie á la monarchie. Paris, 1911.
—— L'Antipatriotisme. Paris, 1904.
—— La Noblesse. Paris, 1919.
—— Les Origines de l'Action française. Paris, 1905.
—— Le Raison d'état. Paris, 1906.
—— Les Raisons du nationalisme. Paris, 1905.
—— Le Salût publique. Paris, 1901.
—— Nos traditions. Bourges, 1904.

PHILIPPE D'ORLÉANS, COMTE DE PARIS

Flers, Robert, marquis de, Le Comte de Paris. Paris, 1898.
D'Haussonville, Comte Othenin, Le Comte de Paris. Paris, 1895.
Monarchie française, lettres et documents, La: 1844-1907. Paris, 1907.

Paris, Philippe d'Orléans, Comte de, Les Associations ouvrières. Paris, 1869.
———— Une Liberté nécessaire. Paris, 1894.

PROUDHON, PIERRE JOSEPH

Proudhon, Pierre Joseph, Œuvres complètes. Paris, 1866-83.

RALLIEMENT, LE

Barthelme, G., Le Ralliement. Le Havre, 1897.
Cheyssac, Léon de, Une Page d'histoire politique. Paris, 1906.
Corvilleau, Robert, Le Ralliement. Paris, 1927.
Gilloin, René, Trois crises. Lille, 1929.
Goyau, Georges, Du toast á l'encyclique. Paris, n. d. Published anonymously.
D'Haussonville, Comte Othenin, Discours. Paris, 1904.
Lecomte, Maxime, Les Ralliés. Paris, 1897.
Leo XIII, Encycliques et correspondance. Paris, 1910.
Mermeix, Le Ralliement et l'Action française. Paris, 1927.
Montagne, Havard de la, Le Ralliement. Lille, 1913.
———— Á propos d'un centenaire. Paris, 1926.
Moon, Parker T., The Labor Problem and the Social Catholic Movement in France. New York, 1921.
Mun, Albert de, L'Action libérale catholique. Paris, 1902.
———— Combats d'hier. Paris, 1917.
Piou, Jacques, Le Comte de Mun. Paris, 1925.
———— Le Ralliement. Paris, 1928.

RENAN, ERNEST

Renan, Ernest, Dialogues et fragments philosophiques. Paris, 1886.
———— L'Ávenir de la sciènce; penseés de 1848. Paris, 1890.
———— Drames philosophiques. Paris, 1888.
———— Questions contemporaines. Paris, 1868.
———— La Réforme intellectuelle et morale de la France. Paris, 1872.

RESTORATION

Barthélémy, Joseph, L'Introduction du régime parlementaire er. France. Paris, 1904.

Charléty, S., La Restauration. Paris, 1921.

Hauranne, Duvergier de, Histoire du gouvernement parlementaire. Paris, 1857-71.

Simon, Pierre, L'Établissement de la charte de 1814. Paris, 1903.

Thureau-Dangin, Paul, Le Parti libéral sous la Restauration. Paris, 1876.

——— Royalistes et républicains. Paris, 1874.

ROYER-COLLARD, PIERRE PAUL

Barante, Prosper Amable de, Vie politique de Royer-Collard. Paris, 1857.

Baudrillart, H., Publicistes modernes. Paris, 1863.

Faguet, Émile, Politiques et moralistes du dix-neuvième siècle. Paris, 1894.

Gilardoni, C., Vie de Royer-Collard. Vitry-le-François, 1894.

Laski, Harold, Authority in the Modern State. New York, 1919.

Nesmes-Desmarets, Robert, Doctrines politiques de Royer-Collard. Montpelier, 1906.

Philippe, A., Royer-Collard. Paris, 1857.

Rémusat, Charles de, Royer-Collard, *Revue des deux mondes,* October 15, 1865.

Royer-Collard, P. P., Discours. *Archives parlementaires.*

Scherer, Edmond, Études critiques sur la littérature contemporaine Paris, 1863.

Spuller, Eugène, Royer-Collard. Paris, 1895.

Vingtain, Louis, Vie politique de Royer-Collard. Paris, 1857.

TAINE, HYPPOLYTE ADOLPHE

Taine, Hyppolyte Adolphe, Les Origines de la France contemporaine. Paris, 1877-85.

TOCQUEVILLE, ALEXIS DE

Barbey d'Aurévilly, J. A., Les Oeuvres et les hommes. Paris, 1892.

Darien, E., La Philosophie politique d'Alexis de Tocqueville. *Revue contemporaine.* 1860.

Eichthal, Eugène d', Tocqueville et la démocratie libérale. Paris, 1897.

Faguet, Émile, Politiques et moralistes du dix-neuvième siècle. Paris, 1899.

Janet, P. A., De Tocqueville. *Revue des deux mondes,* 1861.

Laboulaye, E. R. de, L'État et ses limites. Paris, 1863.

Lanzac-de-Laborie, Léon de, Tocqueville. *Correspondant,* CLXXI (1893), 152.

Rémusat, Charles de, Royer-Collard et Tocqueville. *Revue des deux mondes,* 1861.

Sainte-Beuve, C. A. de, Causeries du Lundi. Vol. XV, Paris, 1862.

—— Nouveaux Lundis. Vol. X, Paris, 1863.

Tocqueville, Alexis de, Correspondance avec Gobineau. Paris, 1908.

—— Oeuvres complètes. Paris, 1864-68.

VEUILLOT, LOUIS

Bartoux, G., Louis Veuillot. Paris, 1919.

Cerceau, G., Table générale des mélanges de Louis Veuillot. Paris, 1913.

Dimier, Louis, Les Maîtres de la contre-révolution. Paris, 1906.

Laurentie, François, Louis Veuillot. Paris, 1898.

Lemaître, Jules, Les Contemporains. Paris, 1890.

Lecque, C., Louis Veuillot. Paris, 1914.

Leroy-Beaulieu, A., Les Catholiques libéraux. Paris, 1885.

Ségur, N., et Belléssort, André, Louis Veuillot. Paris, 1911.

Talbot, Hector, Louis Veuillot et la Monarchie. Paris, n. d.

Veuillot, Eugène, et Veuillot, François, Vie de Louis Veuillot. Paris, 1864-1914.

Veuillot, Louis, Derniers mélanges. Paris, 1875.

—— Le Droit du seigneur. Paris, 1856.

—— L'Esclave Vindex. Paris, 1849.

—— Le Fond de Giboyer. Paris, 1863.

—— La Légalité. Paris, 1852.

—— L'Illusion libérale. Paris, 1866.

—— Le Parti catholique. Paris, 1856.

—— Mélanges. Trois séries. Paris, 1856-75.

—— Oeuvres complètes. Paris, 1920- . In course of publication.

—— Paris pendant deux sièges. Paris, 1871.

INDEX

Absolutism, in France, 217 ff., Bonald and Maistre on, 21-25; tyranny of, 55; and constitutional monarchy, 77, 87; and popular sovereignty, 48, 90; and freedom, 140; not despotic, 162; versus authoritarian monarchy, 260; theory of 296; theory revived, 298, 299

Action française, 8,183, 200, 217 ff., 219

Aguesseau, d', 4

Ancien régime, La Tour du Pin on, 205, 208

Andrieu, 271

Angoulême, duc d', 166

Angoulême, duchesse d', 167

Anjou, duc d', 271

Aquinas, Thomas, Saint. See Thomas Aquinas, Saint

Aristocracies, theocrats on, 26-28; Chateaubriand on, 42-43; Constant on, 80; Guizot on, 97; Tocqueville on, 110; Blanc de St. Bonnet on, 151-52; La Tour du Pin on, 207-8; Maurras on, 261

Association, right of, 85, 130, 163, 174

Audiffret-Pasquier, duc d', 114, 117

Augustine, Saint, 183

Austria-Hungary, 257, 284

Authority, 18, 29, 32, 48, 121; nature of, 51; should persuade, 72, 74; source of, 74, 121; is sacred, 124; Church as supreme, 164; Saint Thomas Aquinas on, 182; Maurras on, 252-53, 255, 260, 288;

theocrats on, 289; need of a permanent, 30; King's 304

Bainville, Jacques, 220, 233, 244, 277-78

Ballanche, 12, 145

Balzac, Honoré de, 142-44, 224, 293, 294

Barante, Prosper Amable de, 49, 104, 105, 107, 115, 292

Barbey d'Aurevilly, 31

Barrès, Maurice, 69, 71, 219, 221, 240-41, 261

Barthélémy, Joseph, 54

Bayle, 4

Becquet, 49

Bellarmin, 183

Benoist, Charles, 39, 275

Bergson, 283

Berry, duc de, 167

Berry, duchesse de, 88, 132, 166

Berryer, Antoine, 123 ff., 139, 165, 174, 175, 194, 200, 231, 280, 292, 293, 294

Beugnot, 49

Blacas, comte de, 185

Blanc de St. Bonnet, 144-59, 164, 194, 202, 215, 224, 231, 281, 293, 294

Bonald, Louis Gabriel, vicomte de, 12 ff., 49, 52, 55, 91, 123, 127, 137, 145, 154, 155, 157, 194, 224, 235, 280, 286, 292. See also Theocrats

Bonapartists, 68, 184, 198, 243

Bordeaux, duc de. See Chambord, comte de

Bossuet, 4, 123, 148, 162